Essentials of Mathematics 11

Essentials of Mathematics 11

Celia Baron
Don Bradford
Angela Kaisser
David Sufrin
Dave Tambellini
Rick Wunderlich

British Columbia Ministry of Education
Victoria Canada

Copyright 2002 British Columbia Ministry of Education

ISBN 0-7726-4823-9

This textbook was developed for the British Columbia Ministry of Education by Pacific Educational Press, Faculty of Education, University of British Columbia, 6365 Biological Sciences Rd., Vancouver, Canada V6T 1Z4.

National Library of Canada Cataloguing in Publication Data
Main entry under title:
    Essentials of mathematics 11

"Developed for the British Columbia Ministry of Education by Pacific Educational Press, Faculty of Education, University of British Columbia"--t.p. verso.
    ISBN 0-7726-4823-9

    1. Business mathematics–Textbooks. 2. Finance, Personal–Mathematics–Textbooks. I. Baron, Celia. II. British Columbia. Ministry of Education.

QA107.E87 2002   513.1   C2002-960173-8

Editing: Catherine Edwards
Photo Research: Barbara Kuhne
Answer Key: Martin Balcaen
Design: Warren Clark

Printed and bound in Canada

03 04 5 4 3 2

Acknowledgements
Funding for this student resource was provided by the British Columbia Ministry of Education; Manitoba Education, Training and Youth; the Yukon Department of Education; the Northwest Territories Department of Education; and the Nunavut Territory Department of Education. Original materials developed by Manitoba Education, Training and Youth have been adapted for this publication.

This resource was made possible through the support and contributions of the following: Bruce McAskill, British Columbia Ministry of Education; Richard V. DeMerchant, British Columbia Ministry of Education; Wayne Watt, Manitoba Education, Training and Youth; Carole Bilyk, Manitoba Education, Training and Youth; Marcel Druwé, Manitoba Education, Training and Youth; Lee Kubica, Yukon Department of Education; Steven Daniel, Northwest Territories Department of Education; Brian Yamamura, Nunavut Department of Education.

Contents

Chapter 4 Measurement Technology

Chapter 5 Relations and Formulas

How To Use This Book

Essentials of Mathematics 11 demonstrates how to use mathematics in everyday life. The skills that are taught are those that informed citizens need. The textbook has eight chapters and each focusses on a particular topic. Topics include income and debt; data analysis; owning and operating a vehicle; measurement technology; relations and formulas; applications of probability; personal income tax; and preparing a business plan.

Chapter Introduction

Each chapter begins with an introduction that describes what the chapter will teach and lists the goals of that chapter. The introduction also starts you thinking about the chapter project.

Chapter Project

Each chapter contains a project related to the mathematical theme of the chapter. The project is ongoing and you will accumulate materials in your project file as you work through the chapter. At the end of the chapter, you will organize the materials in your file into a presentation.

Explorations

Chapters are divided into explorations. Each exploration is a lesson on a particular mathematical topic. A short introduction describes the topic and lists the goals of the lesson. Examples and solutions are provided that show you how to use the mathematical ideas to solve problems. Many explorations contain activities to complete in small groups or with the rest of your class. Explorations may also contain activities connected to the chapter project. Each exploration concludes with a notebook assignment that allows you to practise the skills you have learned.

Chapter Review

The chapter review helps you revisit the mathematical ideas and skills explored in the chapter and solve problems using these skills.

Project Presentation

The final step in the chapter project is to organize the materials you have researched or created into a presentation.

Case Study

Each chapter concludes with a case study that allows you to apply the mathematics of the chapter in a new context.

Other Features of the Text

Career Connection

Each Career Connection contains a profile of a fictitious individual. The description of the job, current wages, educational requirements, career goal, and keyword search are based on real possibilities. The keyword search invites you to do an internet search on the career and will provide links to colleges and other institutions that have specific career or educational information.

New Terms

Mathematical terms that may be new or unfamiliar are defined or explained in the New Terms box.

Hints

Hints suggest ways to deal with the mathematics and provide useful reminders, abbreviations, conversion factors, and other techniques helpful in solving the problems.

Technology

This section shows how technology such as computers can be used to help solve problems or do research.

Mental Math

Mental Math invites you to practise solving mathematical exercises in your head.

Problem Analysis

Each chapter contains a problem activity that allows you to use a variety of problem-solving strategies. Some activities were chosen to illustrate consumer applications of mathematics. Others challenge you to analyze mathematical thinking.

 Each chapter contains a challenging mathematical game. Some of these games have been played since ancient times and in different cultures around the world. You are required to play each game and to analyze it in order to increase your chances of winning.

Answer Keys

The answer key at the back of the book lists the answers to each Notebook Assignment.

Chapter 1

Income & Debt

Earning and Spending Money

Have you thought about your future? What career path will you take? Have you considered how employees in different occupations are paid? Most people think of an annual salary or an hourly wage, but there are many different ways to calculate someone's income. This chapter will introduce you to some of the other ways to do this.

You will also investigate how to make the most of the money you earn. You will consider various investments that earn interest and learn to calculate the cost of buying goods and services with a credit card or by borrowing money from a financial institution. You will explore the true costs to the buyer of in-store promotions so you can judge whether an advertised "deal" is really such a great deal.

You will discover the value of Canadian currency compared to the currencies of other countries. The money skills you will learn will help you become a wiser consumer and get the most for your money.

Goals

In this chapter, you will learn to calculate income when you are paid according to on-the-job performance. You will also learn to calculate the total amount you pay for purchases made with a credit card, a personal loan, by taking advantage of an in-store promotion, or when you travel to or purchase products from another country.

Career Connection

Name: Nuria Dhaliwal

Job: bank teller in Mission, BC

Current wages: $22,000/year

Education: grade 12

Career goal: bank manager

Keyword search: Canada courses bank teller

Chapter Project

In the project for this chapter you will plan and research a two-week trip outside Canada. You will investigate some of your pre-trip expenses and decisions about how to finance your trip. You will estimate your budget and look at the cost of borrowing money and converting Canadian dollars to foreign currency.

As you complete the project activities, you will add the following items to your project file:

1. information on in-store promotions on luggage
2. applications for credit card, a line of credit, and a personal loan
3. a description of your destination and an estimated budget for your trip
4. an estimate of the currency you will need and how much it will cost in Canadian dollars.

Exploration 1

Performance-Based Income: Commission

Many people earn an income based on their on-the-job performance. Performance can be measured in a variety of ways. The number of items you make, the value of the products or services you sell, your ability to keep expenses within a certain budget, or your ability to sell more than an expected quota are some of the bases on which income can be calculated.

Some employees' income is based on commission. A commission is a percent amount paid to the employee. It is often a percentage of the value of goods or services sold. For people paid a commission, there is an incentive to sell as much as possible in order to earn the maximum amount of money. As a result, the company also benefits with greater sales.

A person's earnings can be based on straight commission, a salary plus commission, an hourly wage plus commission, or a graduated commission. A graduated commission rate increases as sales increase, according to a set schedule.

Goals

In this exploration, you will be introduced to performance-based income. You will learn how to calculate income for a person who earns a commission on sales.

New Terms

commission: an amount paid as income based on a percentage of sales.

performance-based income: income based on the amount of work completed or goods and services sold.

quota: a set amount; could be a set amount of sales or a set amount of items manufactured.

Straight Commission

Earning a straight commission means that a person will not receive an hourly wage or salary. Instead, his or her salary will be calculated as a percent of sales or a specific amount for each item sold.

Example 1

Myra is an insurance salesperson. She receives a 30% commission on the first year's premium of each life insurance policy she sells. One week, Myra sells three life insurance policies. If the premiums for the first year are $850.00, $400.00, and $340.00, what is Myra's gross pay for this week?

Solution

Total sales: $850.00 + $400.00 + $340.00 = $1,590.00
Commission: $1,590.00 × 0.3 = $477.00

Myra's gross pay for the week is $477.00.

Salary Plus Commission

A person who earns a salary plus commission earns a salary paid by the hour, week, or year, plus a commission. The commission may be calculated on the value of each sale, or as a percent of the sales above a certain quota. Merchandise that is difficult to sell may have a higher commission rate than goods that are sold frequently.

Example 2

Joe works for a farm equipment company that pays him a weekly salary of $350.00 and a commission of 6% on sales. One week he sells goods worth $5,688. What is his gross pay?

Solution

Amount of commission: $5,688.00 × 0.06 = $341.28
Joe's gross pay: $350.00 + $341.28 = $691.28

Joe's gross pay for the week is $691.28.

Graduated Commission

When a person is paid on a graduated commission basis, he or she is paid increasing commission rates depending upon the amount of goods or services sold.

Example 3

Johann is a produce broker. He earns 2% on the first $10,000 he sells, 4% on the next $10,000, and 6% on anything above $20,000. What would his gross pay be if he sold $40,000 of goods?

Solution

Calculate the commission earned on the first $10,000 sold:
$10,000 × 0.02 = $200.00

Calculate the commission earned on the next $10,000 sold:
$10,000 × 0.04 = $400.00

Find the amount of commissionable earnings over $20,000 in sales:
$40,000 − $10,000 − $10,000 = $20,000

Commission earned on the amount over the first $20,000:
$20,000 × 0.06 = $1,200.00

Add the commission amounts to find Johann's gross pay:
$200.00 + $400.00 + $1,200.00 = $1,800.00

Johann's gross pay on $40,000 of sales is $1,800.00.

Small Group Discussion

Brainstorm and list as many careers as you can that may be paid on a commission basis. Then consider the following three job offers for sales associate positions. The way the income for each job is calculated is described below.

Offer 1

Pays a base weekly salary of $300 plus 5% commission on sales.

Offer 2

Pays 8% straight commission.

Offer 3

Pays 2% commission on the first $2,000 worth of goods sold, 5% commission on the next $7,000 sold, and 10% commission on any sales over $9,000.

    a) Which of the three job offers would you accept if sales were $10,000?

    b) Explain your choice.

    c) Demonstrate mathematically why you made your choice.

    d) Would you make a different choice if sales were $30,000?

Technology

Many businesses post job opportunities on their web sites.

Career Connection

Name: Jessica Lambert

Job: car sales associate in Victoria, BC

Current wages: $35,000 – $60,000 based on commission on sales

Education: grade 12; business management and entrepreneurship certificate

Career goal: to own her own car dealership

Keyword search: Canada courses business management

Mental Math

Express the following percentages as decimals.

a) 12%

b) 5%

c) 3.6%

d) 100%

Hints

To write a percent as a decimal, move the decimal place two places to the left.

14% = 0.14

9% = 0.09

6.8% = 0.068

Notebook Assignment

1. Patti is a sales representative for a cosmetics company. She is paid a commission on each item she sells. The commission varies from product to product. If she sells the following quantities of the products listed below, what is her commission?

Item	Qty	Price	Rate of Commission	Total Price	Commission
shampoo	3	$7.28	39%	3 x $7.28 = $21.84	$21.84 x 0.39 = $8.52
hair spray	4	$8.24	41%		
razor blades	5	$6.21	54%		
shaving foam	2	$4.99	42%		
shower gel	3	$4.09	39%		

2. Seppa works for a northern construction contractor. He receives a 3% commission on all sales. If he sells $32,000 worth of pipes, what is his gross pay?

3. Keaton sold $8,500 worth of goods. He receives a 2% commission on the sales he makes. What is his gross pay? What is his net pay if his deductions are approximately 30% of his gross pay?

4. April sells wicker furniture. She earns $150 a week plus a 3% commission on her sales. Complete a table like the one below to find out how much money April earns for the month of August.

Week	Total Sales	Commission (3%)	Regular Salary	Total Weekly Earnings
Week 1	$10,400.95	$312.03	$150	$462.03
Week 2	$12,500.00		$150	
Week 3	$16,500.00		$150	
Week 4	$9,789.00		$150	
Total Earnings for August: $				

5. Complete the following table calculating each employee's weekly gross income. If you have access to a computer, create a spreadsheet to complete the table using formulas.

Employee #	Total Sales	Rate of Commission	Commission	Weekly Base Salary	Total Gross Income
89432	$13,400.15	3.5%	$469.01	$100	$569.01
89551	$19,220.99	2%		$200	
89553	$15,555.15	4%		$130	
89554	$4,950.65	3.75%		$150	
89556	$7,350.00	2.5%		$200	

6. Janessa works for a furniture company. She is paid a salary of $250 a week plus a commission of 2% on sales. If she sells a living-room suite for $1,399.99 and a kitchen suite for $849.99 one week, what is her gross pay?

7. Art works in a department store. He earns weekly commissions based on a graduated scale. Complete the chart to calculate his monthly salary.

Weekly Sales	≤ $2,500	$2,501 – $4,000	>$4,000	Weekly Commission
	15%	17½%	20%	
Week 1: $3,750				
Week 2: $2,880				
Week 3: $4,400				
Week 4: $3,900				
Total Commission				

8. Savannah, a real estate agent, sold one house this week for $120,000. A fee of 6% of the selling price is paid to the company that sells the house. The 6% fee is broken down among several parties. One percent is paid to the multiple listing group, 2.5% goes to the company that lists the house, and 2.5% goes to the company that sells the house. Savannah is paid 60% of the money that her company retains for selling the house. What is her gross pay if another agency listed the house?

9. Gigantor Construction Equipment pays its salespeople on the following commission rate schedule: 1% on all sales up to $50,000; 3% on all sales from $50,000 to $80,000; and 5% on all sales over $80,000. Find the commission rate and the net pay of the following salespeople.

   a) Kelly's sales totalled $45,000 and his deductions are approximately 33% of his gross pay.

   b) Arielle's sales totalled $60,000 and her deductions are approximately 35% of her gross pay.

   c) Gerry's sales totalled $90,000 and his deductions are approximately 42% of his gross pay.

10. Rhoda's company is letting her choose how she is paid. She can choose either a 6% commission on any sales she makes or a base salary of $300.00 a week plus a 2% commission on sales. Assume that her deductions are approximately 33% of her gross earnings.

    a) If Rhoda's sales total $5,000, what will her net pay be for both methods?

    b) If her sales total $10,000, what will her net pay be for both methods?

    c) Which way is the better way to be paid? Explain your choice.

11. Enookie is a car sales associate. He earns 5% of his gross sales. If it happens to be a slow selling month the company will top up his earnings so they equal what he would make working at minimum wage for that month. Last month Enookie worked 40 hours a week for 4 weeks. The minimum wage is $10.35 an hour, and Enookie's total gross vehicle sales were $38,000.

    a) What were his earnings based on sales?

    b) Did Enookie's employer have to top up his earnings to reach the minimum wage amount? If yes, by how much?

Extension

12. Chef Minèka earns $55,000 a year running the kitchen of the five-star restaurant Belvedere's. She earns a bonus each month if she is able to keep her kitchen expenses below $22,000. Her bonus is calculated on a graduated scale. If her expenses are:

- up to $1,000 less than $22,000, she receives 1.5% of her monthly salary as a bonus.
- from $1,000 – $2,000 less than $22,000, she receives 2.5% of her monthly salary as a bonus.
- from $2,000 – $3,000 less than $22,000, she receives 4% of her monthly salary as a bonus.

The owner feels that anything more than $3,000 less than $22,000 would jeopardize the quality of the food served at Belvedere's.

Calculate Chef Minèka's annual earnings last year if her kitchen expenses were:

January	$21,500
February	$20,200
March	$22,300
April	$19,700
May	$22,000
June	$23,500
July	$21,775
August	$19,100
September	$21,800
October	$21,100
November	$22,200
December	$23,000

Exploration 2

Performance-Based Income: Piecework

Another performance-based method to calculate income is on a piecework basis. An employee is paid based on the number of items they make or repair. For example, in the garment industry, a person may get paid by the number of jackets that he or she completes in a day. In the construction industry, a bricklayer could be paid by the number of bricks he or she lays down in a day or may get paid by the job. A roofer might be paid according to the number of rafters he or she installs. If you are paid by the piece, you make a better wage if you are quick and accurate. The slower you are, the less you earn, and you will not be paid for items that are not properly made or completed.

A highly skilled bricklayer may earn more if he is paid by the brick than by the job.

Goals

In this exploration, you will learn how someone earns a living at a job paid by the piece.

Technology

Canada Employment Offices and web sites offer a host of places to search for job opportunities. Check them out at http://workplace.hrdc-drhc.gc.ca.

Example 1

Raja is a commercial fisherman. He is paid by the pound for the fish that he catches. The price varies according to market demand. Assume that he is paid $5.25 a pound on average and catches 14 000 lbs. of fish annually. What is his gross income?

Solution

14 000 lb × $5.25/lb. = $73,500.00

Raja's annual gross income is $73,500.00.

Example 2

The Jeans R Us factory pays $20.00 for every 100 zippers that are sewn into pairs of jeans. If Louisa can sew in 400 zippers in one day, how much does she make in a five-day week?

Solution

400 zippers ÷ 100 × $20.00 = $80 gross pay per day
$80.00/day × 5 days = $400.00

Louisa earns $400.00 gross pay in one week.

Example 3

Penny picks strawberries at a large strawberry farm. She is paid 35 cents for each quart basket of strawberries she picks. On average, she picks 40 quart baskets an hour. If she works 40 hours a week for four weeks, what is her gross pay?

Solution

$0.35/qt. × 40 qt./h × 40 hours = $560 a week
4 × $560/wk = $2,240

Penny's gross pay for 4 weeks is $2,240.00

Mental Math

a) 6 + 84

b) 105 + 236

c) 550 + 320 + 8

d) 2000 + 456 + 321 + 7

e) 10 987 + 432 + 9087

Research Activity

1. Use the internet to find two jobs, one paid on commission and the other paid on a piecework basis. Investigate how employees' income is calculated. Write a paragraph explaining your findings for each job.

2. Create a help wanted ad for each of the two jobs. Try to write an ad that will attract hard-working and skilled employees. Design the ad so it could be used in one of the following media: the internet, newspaper, television, or radio.

Notebook Assignment

1. In your opinion, is it better to be paid an hourly wage or by the piece? Why?

2. Why might a company choose to pay their employees by the piece instead of an hourly wage?

3. Thomas works part-time packaging condiments for the fast-food industry. He earns 8¢ for each package he assembles. Calculate his earnings for one week.

Day	# of Packages	Daily Earnings
Monday	760	760 x $0.08 = $60.80
Tuesday	690	
Wednesday	792	
Thursday	420	
Friday	608	
Saturday	201	
Weekly Earnings		

4. The Forestt Manufacturing Co. assembles boxes for transportation. They pay $16 for every 12 boxes assembled. If a worker can assemble 115 boxes in one day, what is his or her gross pay for a five-day week? Payment is made only for completed sets of 12 calculated on a weekly basis.

5. Kay's Industrial Sewing Co. makes sandbags. Sandy gets paid $0.25 a bag. She makes 224 bags a day, six days a week. What is her gross pay?

6. David works part-time in a department store that pays him $3.00 to assemble one bicycle. On average, he assembles 25 bikes every week. How much does he make bi-weekly?

7. Reed sews pockets for jackets. He is paid $6.07 for each 100. He can sew a dozen sets of 100 a day. What will be his gross pay in a six-day week?

8. One summer, Lynda is contracted to paint the town's lamp posts at $15 a pole. If there are 250 poles in the town, how much is her gross pay?

9. Acme Enterprises offers a bonus for pieces completed above a minimum quota per day. In one department, the rate is 50¢ a piece up to a quota of 110 items and 53¢ a piece thereafter. Jaime produced the following in one week:

Monday	101
Tuesday	108
Wednesday	121
Thursday	148
Friday	161

Find Jaime's weekly gross earnings.

10. Larry works for a plastics company that pays him for the units he completes. He receives 80¢ a unit for the first 60 units he produces each day, 87¢ a unit for the next 40, and 90¢ a unit for all units over 100. Find his weekly earnings if his daily production is the following:

Monday	85
Tuesday	90
Wednesday	100
Thursday	108
Friday	115
Saturday	101

11. Cedar Sawmill pays a bonus to their sawyers of $0.01 a board foot if they saw over 5000 board feet a day. Charlie sawed the following amounts:

Monday	25 500
Tuesday	18 500
Wednesday	32 000
Thursday	28 000
Friday	21 500

Calculate his bonus for the week.

Extension

12. Katya works as a seamstress for an international clothing manufacturer in Winnipeg. She earns $3.00 for a blouse, $0.25 for a pair of pockets, $4.00 for a pair of pants, $3.00 for a skirt, and $6.00 for a jacket. In one hour, Katya can complete 5 blouses or 100 pairs of pockets or 6 pairs of pants or 10 skirts or 4 jackets.

a) If she sews 45 blouses, 975 pairs of pockets, 30 pairs of pants, 70 skirts, and 13 jackets in one week, what is her gross pay?

b) What should Katya sew most to earn the most money? Justify your answer.

Sewing in a crafts factory in Arviat, NU, provides employment for local women.

c) If Katya had to sew a minimum number of each item, as shown below, what should she sew for the rest of her 40-hour work week to maximize her gross earnings?

blouses	10
pockets	200 pairs
pants	20
skirts	30
jackets	10

Exploration 3

Simple Interest

Money, money, money. What do people do with the money they have earned? They shop, pay bills, travel, and save. When people invest and save, it is usually done through a financial institution or investment firm. When you deposit or invest your money in a financial institution, you are lending it your money. In return for the loan of your money, the financial institution pays you interest.

What does the financial institution do with the money you have lent it? They in turn lend the money to their customers at a higher interest rate. The difference between the interest rate it pays you and the interest rate the clients pay to the financial institution is the financial institution's profit.

Interest can be calculated in several ways. Simple interest is calculated as a percentage of the principal amount invested or borrowed. The formula to calculate simple interest is:

I = Prt, where
I = interest
P = principal, the amount invested or borrowed
r = annual percent rate of interest expressed as a decimal
t = length of time in years

Goals

In this exploration, you will learn to calculate simple interest.

New Terms

financial institution: bank, credit union, trust company, caisse populaire, or other institution that handles the lending, borrowing, and investing of money.

interest: a fee paid for borrowing money or earned for lending money.

per annum: per year, once a year.

principal: amount invested or borrowed.

simple interest: interest calculated as a percentage of the principal using the formula $I = Prt$.

Example 1

Randy deposits $2,000.00 into a savings account earning 3% simple interest per annum. Calculate the interest his money will have earned at the end of one year.

Solution

$I = Prt$ $P = \$2,000$ $r = 0.03$ $t = 1$ year
$I = \$2,000 \times 0.03 \times 1$ year
$I = \$60.00$

Randy will earn $60.00 interest in one year.

Example 2

How much interest would Randy earn in 5 months?

Solution

Remember that t (time) must be expressed in the form of years. To convert 5 months to years, divide 5 by 12.

$I = Prt$ $P = \$2,000$ $r = 0.03$ $t = \dfrac{5}{12}$ years

$I = \$2,000 \times 0.03 \times \dfrac{5}{12}$ years
$I = \$25.00$

Randy would earn $25.00 in 5 months.

Technology

You can use spreadsheet software to set up spreadsheets that calculate interest.

Mental Math

a) $8.00 x 20

b) $1.5 \times 8.00 \times 3$

Example 3

Robyn invested a certain sum of money in a financial institution. She earned $300.00 interest after four years. If the annual interest rate was 6%, how much money did Robyn invest?

Solution

$I = Prt$

$I = \$300 \qquad P = ? \qquad r = 0.06 \qquad t = 4$ years

$\$300 = P(.06)(4)$

$\$300 = 0.24P$

$\dfrac{\$300}{0.24} = P$

$\$1{,}250 = P$

Robyn invested $1,250.00.

Example 4

Wael has $15,000 to invest in a financial institution. Calculate the annual rate of interest if he plans to earn $3,500 at the end of two years.

Solution

$I = Prt$

$I = \$3{,}500 \qquad P = \$15{,}000 \qquad r = ? \qquad t = 2$

$\$3{,}500 = \$15{,}000(r)(2)$

$r = \dfrac{\$3{,}500}{\$30{,}000}$

$r = 0.116666$

$0.116666 \times 100\% = 11.7\%$

$r = 11.7\%$ (rounded)

Wael would need to earn an annual interest rate of approximately 11.7% to earn $3,500 interest in two years.

Pairs Discussion

Discuss with a partner why Wael needs a rate of about 11.7%. How much interest would he earn if the rate was 11.6%? Write your discussion results and recalculation in your notebook.

Technology

On-line trading over the internet allows people to buy and sell investments for a flat-rate.

Example 5

Miranda invests $1,500 in an account earning simple interest at a rate of 7.25%.

a) Calculate the number of months she left her money in the account if it earned $300 interest.

b) Calculate the number of days she must keep the money in her account to earn $250 in interest.

Solution

$I = Prt$

a) $I = \$300$ $P = \$1,500$ $r = 7.25\%$ or 0.0725 $t = ?$

$$\$300 = \$1,500(0.0725)t$$

$$\frac{300}{108.75} = t$$

$$t = 2.7586207 \text{ years}$$
$$t = 2.7586207 \times 12 \text{ months}$$
$$t = 33.103448 \text{ months}$$

It would take about 34 months for Miranda's money to earn $300 at a rate of 7.25%.

b) $I = \$250$ $P = \$1,500$ $r = 7.25\%$ or 0.0725 $t = ?$

$$\$250 = \$1,500(0.0725)t$$
$$\$250 = 108.75t$$

$$\frac{250}{108.75} = t$$

$$t = 2.2988506 \text{ years}$$
$$t = 2.2988506 \times 365 \text{ days}$$
$$t = 839.0804 \text{ days}$$

Miranda must keep her money in the account for approximately 840 days.

Hints

The formula $I = Prt$ expresses time in years, so you need to multiply the answer in years by 12 to calculate the number of months. To calculate the number of days, multiply the answer in years by 365.

Notebook Assignment

In this assignment, interest is simple interest and all interest rates are annual. Round your answers to two decimal places.

1. Find the simple interest for each of the following cases and complete the chart.

Principal Paid	Rate of Interest	Term	Interest
$530	4%	2 years	
$1600	5.2%	3 years	
$1200	3.6%	8 months	
$840	2.5%	80 days	
$1860	3.8%	10 months	
$4000	6.6%	7 years	
$3600	4.8%	200 days	

2. Find the following:

   a) If the interest is $22.00 and the rate is 6% for two years, what is the principal?

   b) Find the time in days if the interest is $180, the principal is $5,000, and the interest rate is 8%.

   c) Find the annual rate if the interest is $410 on a principal of $4,040 for three years.

   d) Find the amount of a loan if the interest is $385 and the rate is 12% for seven months.

   e) Find the time in days if a deposit is $3,580, the rate is 4.5%, and the interest is $155.

3. Claude borrowed $550 from a business associate. Four months later he repaid the loan and interest with a cheque of $562.83. What was the interest rate?

4. Andrew loaned $5,000 to his brother at 6%. If his brother gave him $5,750 cash, how long in years did Andrew have to wait to get paid?

5. Tanya borrows money from a bank to buy a used car. Her bank charges 9% on this personal loan. If Tanya repays the loan in ten months, including interest of $225, how much did she borrow?

6. Julie took out a personal loan of $5,000 for ten months. If the amount of interest was $455, what was the annual interest rate?

7. Andy wants to save for a trip to Mexico in two years. What amount will he have to put away in a fund if he is able to earn simple interest of $425.00 at a rate of 9.75%?

Exploration 4

Compound Interest

"Work smarter, not harder for your money."
"Let your money work for you, not you for your money."
"Time is on your side."

Have you ever heard such sayings? Each one reflects what earning compound interest is all about.

In the last exploration you learned how to calculate simple interest. If you keep the interest earned invested, new interest will be paid on the principal amount plus the first year's interest. You will earn interest on the interest.

Compound interest is great when you are investing because the interest your investments earn is also earning interest. Compound interest is not so great when you borrow money because it costs more than simple interest.

The longer your investment is compounding, the greater the amount of interest you earn. If you invest for a long term, it is in the last years of the term that you see the biggest impact of compounding. The earlier you start saving, the more time there is for an investment to grow.

Goals

In this exploration, you will see how compounding can help make your investments grow.

Interest is not always compounded annually. Some financial institutions add interest to the principal every six months. In that case, the interest is compounded semi-annually. There are also daily savings accounts, where interest is compounded on a daily basis.

Example 1

Genevieve invests $5,000 in a financial institution at 6%, compounded annually. Calculate the interest her money will have earned at the end of 3 years.

Solution

Interest period	Interest ($I = Prt$)	Amount of investment	Initial investment $5,000.00
1	$I = \$5,000 \times .06 \times 1 = \$300.00$	$5,300.00	
2	$I = \$5,300 \times .06 \times 1 = \$318.00$	$5,618.00	
3	$I = \$5,618 \times .06 \times 1 = \$337.08$	$5,955.08	

The total interest is:
$300.00 + $318.00 + $337.08 = $955.08
She earned $955.08 interest over the 3 years.

New Terms

compounded annually: the interest is added to the principal once a year.

compounded daily: the interest is added to the principal each day.

compounded semi-annually: the interest is added to the principal twice a year.

Example 2

Genevieve invests $5,000 in a financial institution at 6%, compounded annually. Calculate the interest her money will have earned at the end of 3 years. Calculate compound interest using the formula:

$A = P(1+ r/n)^{nt}$, where
A = final amount (principal + interest)
P = principal, or the amount invested or borrowed
r = annual percent rate of interest expressed as a decimal
n = number of interest periods in a year
t = length of time in years

Solution

$A = P(1+ r/n)^{nt}$
$P = \$5,000 \qquad r = 0.06 \qquad n = 1 \qquad t = 3$
$A = \$5,000(1 + 0.06/1)^{1 \times 3}$
$A = \$5,000(1 + 0.06)^3$
$A = \$5,000(1.06)^3$
$A = \$5,000(1.191016)$
$A = \$5,955.08$

After 3 years, the investment is worth $5,955.08.

The interest earned is:
$5,955.08 − $5,000 = $955.08

Technology

To evaluate a power such as $(1.06)^3$, on your calculator, press:

Hints

Remember the order of operations:

brackets

exponents

multiplication and division from left to right

addition and subtraction from left to right

Example 3

Viola invests $1,000 at 10%, compounded annually. Calculate the interest she will have earned at the end of 7 years and 8 years. Approximately how many years did it take for the initial investment of $1,000 to double?

Solution

Year	Investment Value Beginning of Year	Interest Rate	Interest Earned	Year-end Value of Investment
1	$1,000.00	0.10	$100.00	$1,100.00
2	$1,100.00	0.10	$110.00	$1,210.00
3	$1,210.00	0.10	$121.00	$1,331.00
4	$1,331.00	0.10	$133.10	$1,464.10
5	$1,464.10	0.10	$146.41	$1,610.51
6	$1,610.51	0.10	$161.05	$1,771.56
7	$1,771.56	0.10	$177.16	$1,948.72
8	$1,948.72	0.10	$194.87	$2,143.59

After 7 years she will have earned $1,948.72 − $1,000 = $948.72.

After 8 years she will have earned $2,143.59 − $1,000 = $1,143.59.
It took approximately 7 years for the investment to double.

The Rule of 72

To quickly estimate the length of time it takes for an investment to double, use the Rule of 72. All you need is the interest rate and the number 72.

Divide 72 by the interest rate (as a number, not a percentage) to find the time in years.

If the interest rate is 10%, divide 72 by 10 to find the time in years:
72 ÷ 10 = 7.2 years

Note that 7.2 years is not 7 years and 2 months. It is 7 years plus 0.2 times 12 months. 7.2 years is therefore 7 years plus 2.4 months.

Hints

1. Interest earned = interest rate × investment amount.

2. Year-end value = investment value at beginning + interest earned.

Notebook Assignment

1. Complete the chart to calculate the balance after six years compounded annually. The interest rate is 5% per annum.

Year	Principal (P)	Interest Rate (r)/year	Time (t)	Interest Earned (I = Prt)
1	$5,000	5%	1	$5,000 × 0.05 × 1 = $250
2	$5,250	5%	1	
3				
4				
5				
6				

2. Calculate these compounded amounts:

   a) $1,000 for 2 years at 7.25%, compounded annually

   b) $1,000 for 2 years at 7.25%, compounded semi-annually

3. Find these compounded amounts:

   a) $400 for two years at 3%, compounded daily

   b) $650 for three years at 4.75%, compounded monthly

   c) $1,600 for four years at 5.5%, compounded quarterly

4. Barb invests $2,000 into an account that pays interest at a rate of 8% compounded quarterly. How much interest will she get at the end of three years?

5. Which gives more interest when compounded: annually, semi-annually, or quarterly? Explain why.

6. What are some important rules of investing?

7. State the Rule of 72.

8. Using the rule of 72, how many years would it take your investment to double at the following rates, which are compounded annually?

   a) 10%   **e)** 8%

   b) $\frac{3}{4}$%   **f)** $2\frac{7}{8}$%

   c) 4.25%   **g)** 12%

   d) 6%   **h)** 3%

9. Explain two ways to calculate the percent rate of interest earned.

10. Set up a spreadsheet template that calculates the interest earned on an investment of $1,000 for 10 years and its value after 30 years with an estimated annual interest rate of 10%.

    One suggestion for the spreadsheet columns is:

Year Invested	Amt Invested	Amt Earning Interest	Interest Rate	Interest Earned	Year-End Value
1	$1,000	$1,000	10%	$100	$1,100
2	$1,000	$2,100	10%	$210	$2,310

    Print two copies of your spreadsheet, one showing the data, and the second showing the formulas.

Mental Math

Estimate the length of time it would take investments to double with the following interest rates

a) 10%   **d)** 15%

b) 2%   **e)** 8%

c) 5%

Exploration 5

● ● ● ● ● ● ● ● ● ● ● ● ● ● ● ● ● ● ●

Shopping with a Credit Card

Have you ever been in a store and found something that you really liked, but you couldn't buy it because you didn't get paid for a week? Do you prefer not to carry cash on you? Do you buy items on the internet, over the telephone, or by mail order? Have you had an unexpected financial emergency arise? If you answered yes to any of these questions, chances are that you have been in a situation where you could have used a credit card.

Credit cards are convenient because they allow you to make purchases without carrying cash. Many businesses will only accept cash, debit cards, or credit cards. Personal cheques are less often accepted.

There are many types of credit cards. Some are issued by banks under the Visa or MasterCard logo, some by department stores or oil companies. The terms of cards vary. Some have annual fees or transaction fees; some provide you with insurance coverage for your purchases or offer other options. It is important to be aware of the terms and conditions of your credit cards. Shop around for a credit card that suits your needs.

To obtain a credit card, you must apply for it once you are 18 or older. You will have to fill out a credit application and be approved. The credit card company is agreeing to loan you the money for your purchase(s) with your promise to repay them under the terms of the agreement. The credit card company will apply a limit to your credit card, which is based on your income and credit rating.

Goals

In this exploration, you will learn how to use a credit card and to calculate the costs of using one.

New Terms

credit rating: a rating used by financial institutions to indicate a person's ability to repay their credit debt.

credit application: a form to request credit.

Each month the credit card company will issue you a statement listing all of your purchases, returns, payments, interest charges, total balance due, minimum payment required and the payment due date. If you pay the balance by the due date you will not have to pay any interest charges. If you do not pay the entire balance, you will be charged interest daily from the date of each purchase. The rate of interest will vary but typically ranges between 15% and 25%. The amount of interest owing can add up very quickly and that bargain you got at the time of purchase is no longer such a great deal.

If you took a cash advance on your credit card, you will be charged interest from the day that the cash advance was taken and the interest rate is usually higher than purchase interest.

Example 1

Credit card interest rates are stated per annum. When the balance is not paid in full the interest on purchases is calculated daily. What is the daily rate if the annual interest rate is 19%?

Solution

$19 \div 365 = .0520548\%$

Note that there are 365 days in a year.

Technology

More and more people are shopping over the internet. You can pay your credit card and other monthly bills on-line. When you use a credit card on the internet it is important that you deal with a reputable company and that the site is secure. Secure sites have a padlock or key in the bottom right-hand corner of the screen and the URL has an address beginning with http.

Example 2

What is the yearly rate if the daily interest rate is 0.049315%?

Solution

Multiply the daily interest rate by 365.

0.049315% × 365 days = 17.999975 = 18%

The yearly rate is 18%.

Example 3

On January 5, Monica makes a purchase of $400 on her credit card. The purchase appears on her monthly statement issued January 20. Monica does not pay for the purchase by the due date indicated on the January statement. Her next monthly statement is issued February 20. Calculate the interest she is charged for the January 5th purchase on her February statement, assuming the bank charges 21% annual interest.

Solution

Count the number of days from January 5 to February 20:
27 days left in January
20 days in February
27 + 20 = 47 days

Since the interest rate quoted by the company is per annum (year), you must calculate the percentage of interest it will charge a day and multiply it by the number of days that interest is being charged.

0.21 ÷ 365 × 47 = 0.027041095

0.027041095 is the interest that will be charged for those 47 days.

0.027041095 × 400 = 10.81643836 = $10.82

$10.82 is the interest amount that will be charged.

Or use the formula $I = Prt$, where
$$P = \$400 \qquad r = 0.21 \qquad t = \frac{47}{365}$$
$I = Prt$
$I = \$400 × 0.21 × (47 ÷ 365)$
$I = \$10.82$ (rounded)

Example 4

Alex's monthly statement shows a previous balance of $963.45. During the month Alex made a payment of $500 and purchased goods totalling $626.95. Assume his interest charges for the month are $17.50. Calculate his new balance.

Solution

New balance = old balance − payments + purchases + interest
New balance = $963.45 − $500.00 + $626.95 + $17.50
New balance = $1,107.90

Example 5

Alex's minimum monthly payment will be 5% of the closing balance or $10, whichever is greater. Calculate Alex's minimum payment.

Solution

Calculate 5% of the closing balance.
$0.05 \times \$1,107.90 = \$55.40$ (rounded)
The minimum payment is $55.40.

Mental Math

a) $100 \div 5$

b) $80 \div 4$

c) $60 \div 2$

d) $44 \div 4$

e) $30 \div 6$

f) $126 \div 3$

g) $120 \div 12$

h) $1696 \div 8$

i) $450 \div 30$

Notebook Assignment

1. Bill Friesen has a credit card from a department store. He makes purchases and payments against the card on a regular basis. Complete the chart below. He makes regular payments of $95.00 or 5%, whichever is greater. Interest is shown on the chart.

Month	Previous Balance	Payment	Unpaid Balance	Interest on Unpaid Balance	Purchases	New Balance	Payment Due
Jan.	$1,000.00	$95.00	$905.00	$18.10	$900.00	$1,823.10	$91.16
Feb.	$1,823.00			$34.56	$400.00		
Mar.				$41.09	$0.00		
Apr.				$39.82	$200.00		

2. Use the statement below to answer the questions that follow:

Last Statement 05/03/97			Card Number 5222 2322 1422 0222	This Statement 05/04/97	Payment Due 28/04/97

Trans date	Post date	Ref #	Description	Amount	Previous Bal
					1556.58
03/01	03/06	1	Cana Air Wpg Can	1676.19	Purchases
03/07	03/10	2	Count HTL. Wpg Can	62.34	3958.46
03/07	03/10	3	Count HTL. Wpg Can	32.55	Interest
03/08	03/10	4	Cerabin HTL. Tor Can	109.35	Fees
03/08	03/10	5	The DragonRest NAS BHS	62.50	Payment
03/10	03/12	6	Lantis HTL NAS BHS	74.50	1556.58 CR
03/11	03/14	7	US120@1.408100 Bahm Divers NAS BHS	168.97	Credit Adj
03/12	03/14	8	The Cave NAS BHS	72.36	New Balance
03/13	03/15	9	The Plasa NAS BHS	86.45	3958.46
03/14	03/16	10	US120@1.408100 Bahm Divers NAS BHS	168.97	Amt Past Due
03/15	03/17	11	Pirate's Cove NAS BHS	1444.28	Min. Payment (5%) 197.92

Credit Limit 5800.00

Current Statement	Last Month Statement	Previous Statements	Total Interest	Interest Rate Next Period Annual % Daily	Credit Available
				18.400 0.05041	1841.54

a) How many purchases were made in Winnipeg?

b) How much was charged at the Dragon Restaurant?

c) On what day was the charge made at the Cerabin Hotel?

d) What was the total amount charged in March?

e) What was the previous balance?

f) What is the minimum payment?

g) Did the card-holder have to pay any interest? Why or why not?

h) What is the payment due date?

3. What is the daily interest rate if the yearly rate is:

a) 14%

b) 17%

c) 22%

4. What is the yearly interest rate if the daily rate is:

a) 0.0275%

b) 0.012%

c) 0.0035%

5. If you received a credit card statement in October and paid nothing by the first due date, calculate the daily interest charge for each of the following unpaid items if the annual rate is 20.805%.

a) $375.85 bought on Oct. 1 (50 days)

b) $635.90 bought on Oct. 5 (46 days)

c) $1,444.99 bought on Oct. 10 (41 days)

6. Use the following credit card statement to calculate each of the following.

   a) the unpaid balance

   b) the interest to be paid

   c) the purchases made

   d) the new balance

   e) the minimum payment if it is 5% or $10.00, whichever is greater

   f) the credit available

Last Statement 05/02/97			Card Number 5222 2322 1422 0222	This Statement 05/03/97	Payment Due 28/03/97	
Trans date	Post date	Ref #	Description		Amount	Previous Bal 556.58
02/06	02/06	1	Safeway Wpg Can		75.85	Purchases
02/07	02/10	2	Tu's Electric Wpg Can		62.34	Interest
02/07	02/10	3	First for Food Wpg Can		32.55	Fees
02/08	02/10	4	Safeway Wpg Can		19.35	
02/08	02/10	5	Right's Clothing Wpg Can		62.50	Payment
02/10	02/12	6	The Pancake Hut Wpg Can		24.50	556.58 CR
02/11	02/14	7	Sports Inc. Wpg Can		68.97	Credit Adj
02/12	02/14	8	Wally World Wpg Can		72.36	Other
02/13	02/15	9	Plaza Gas Bar Wpg Can		26.45	New Balance
02/14	02/16	10	Safeway Wpg Can		168.97	Amt Past Due
02/15	02/17	11	Angela's Hut Wpg Can		44.28	Min Payment
					Credit Limit 5800.00	
Current Statement	Last Month Statement	Previous Statements	Total Interest	Interest Rate Next Period Annual % Daily 21.00 0.057534	Credit Available	

7. Andrea had a previous balance of $296.97 on her credit card statement. She was charged $4.85 in interest. During the last month she made purchases totalling $205.93 with interest of $4.12. Find her minimum payment if it must be at least $10 or 5% of the balance.

Extension

8. Barney has decided to only pay the minimum balance on his statement, shown below, by the due date. Calculate how much interest he will owe on his next statement.

Royal Credit Wise Credit Card
8765 Westshore
Vancouver, BC
Barney McAskill

Statement Date April 30, 2002	Due Date May 15, 2002			Interest Rate 21.3% annually	
Trans. Date	Action	Debit	Credit		Balance
Apr. 8	Grease & Shine Auto Repair	$278.00			$278.00
Apr. 10	Gweyn's Coiffure	$45.00			$323.00
Apr. 20	Love Your Pet	$18.00			$341.00
Apr. 25	Babette's Limousine Service	$250.00			$591.00

Previous Balance	Payments	Purchases	Interest	Minimum Payment	Balance
$0.00	$0.00	$591.00	$0.00	$29.55	$591.00

9. You bought a DVD player for $499.99 on Jan. 2. The interest rate is 18% per year and the minimum payment is 5% or $10, whichever is greater. The first bill is due on Jan. 20 and you only pay the minimum payment. The next bill is due on February 20. You must pay interest from the day you bought the item. You pay only the minimum payment. The third bill is due on March 20. From now on you pay interest on the balance. You only pay the minimum payment for the next 6 months.

   a) Create a spreadsheet that shows the daily interest, minimum payment, and the new balance for nine months.

   b) What happens if the interest changes to 21% per year?

   c) What happens if the minimum payment changes to 6%?

   d) Do you think you should only pay the minimum payment? Why or why not?

Problem Analysis

Painting a Cube

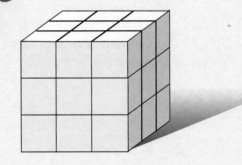

The cube is 3 cm in each dimension. It is made up of 27 1-centimetre cubes.

The large cube is to be painted. Some of the individual cubes will have paint on three faces, others will have paint on two faces, and others paint on just one face. There may be cubes which have paint on no faces. As the size of the cube increases, the numbers above will change. Complete the chart below.

Size of Large Cube	Total Number of Small Cubes	Number of Cubes Painted On			
		3 Faces	2 Faces	1 Face	0 Faces
3 x 3 x 3	27				1
4 x 4 x 4					
5 x 5 x 5					
6 x 6 x 6					
10 x 10 x 10					

1. Describe any patterns you see in the sets of numbers above.

2. If you were told that a cube had a side measure of 1374 cm, could you describe how you could calculate the numbers to fit the chart above?

3. How would the above change if, instead of a cube, you had a rectangular solid? Remember, a rectangular solid built of cubes would have rectangular faces, some of which are not square.

Games

The Game of Kalah

There are a variety of games that have been played since ancient times and in many different cultures around the world. One of those games is described below. One of the features that these games have in common is that the rules are fairly simple and the games can be played by children yet at the same time are a challenge to adults. All these games have winning strategies. After you have a chance to play the game with a partner a few times, try to determine the winning strategy.

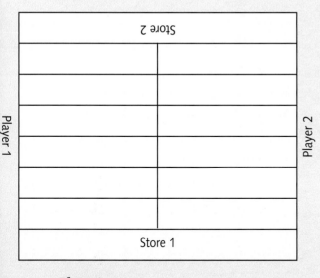

Players: two
Game pieces: The game board and seventy-two markers or beans
Objective: To have the most markers in your "store" or kalah.

Rules

- The board (or use an empty egg carton) has six holes for each player as well as a store for each person.
- Place six markers in each hole.
- A player takes all the markers from any one of his or her holes. Moving counter-clockwise from that hole, he or she places them one at a time into each hole on the board, including his or her own store, but excluding his or her opponent's store.
- If the last marker lands in the player's own store, the player may take an extra turn.
- If the last marker lands in an empty hole on the player's side, the player captures the markers in the opponent's opposite hole. Captured markers are placed in the player's store.
- The game ends when one player has no markers left on his or her side.
- The player with the most markers in the store wins.

1. What is your stategy for winning this game? Describe it in writing.
2. Describe your strategy to a classmate other than your playing partner. See if he or she can use the stategy to win.

Exploration 6

In-Store Promotions

Whenever you walk into a store, read an advertisement, or shop on the internet, it seems that special deals are offered. Have you ever stopped to think what such in-store promotions may actually cost consumers? Why do companies offer these incentives?

There are many incentives that stores use to attract customers. Examples include offers such as:

"Buy one, get one free"
"Buy one and receive a free gift"

These promotions are a means of getting customers into stores. Remember that you still should compare prices with other stores; sometimes you will find the same items at a lower price without a "deal" being offered. Always read the fine print on "Don't pay for a year" promotions. Even though the ad says you do not have to pay interest for a year, you may have to pay administration fees. A cash price may be lower than a time-payment price. You will need to assess the final cost of the item(s) and your financial situation to enable you to make the best decision for yourself.

In this exploration you will look at the costs of these incentives including installment buying and buy-now, pay-later promotions. Companies that offer installment buying or buy-now, pay-later promotions are providing credit to customers so they can purchase their products. Such promotions are usually offered on large purchases such as furniture and appliances.

Goals

In this exploration, you will discover the real costs of in-store promotions.

New Terms

administration fees: the fee a company charges for handling the paperwork of items purchased through an installment or buy-now, pay-later promotion.

installment buying: making a down payment on an item and paying the remaining balance in equal payments.

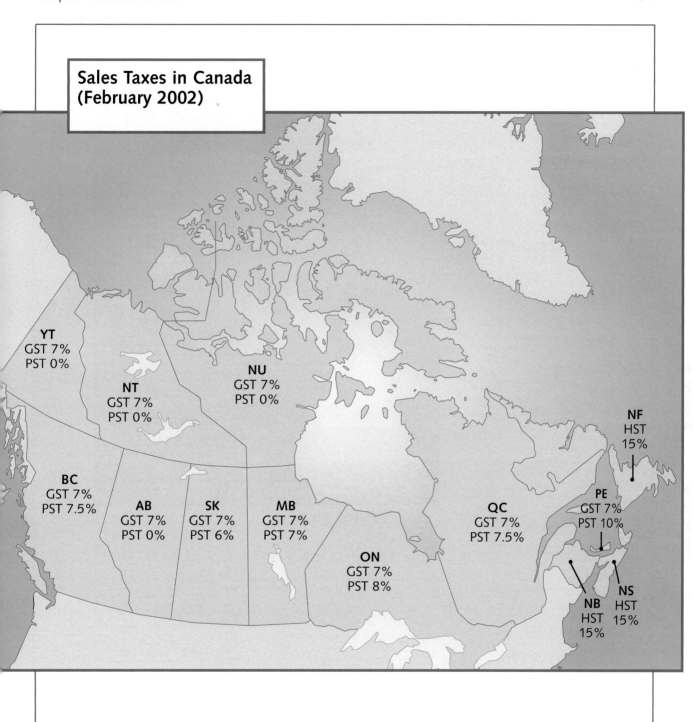

Sales Taxes in Canada
(February 2002)

YT
GST 7%
PST 0%

NT
GST 7%
PST 0%

NU
GST 7%
PST 0%

NF
HST
15%

BC
GST 7%
PST 7.5%

AB
GST 7%
PST 0%

SK
GST 7%
PST 6%

MB
GST 7%
PST 7%

QC
GST 7%
PST 7.5%

PE
GST 7%
PST 10%

ON
GST 7%
PST 8%

NB
HST
15%

NS
HST
15%

Career Connection

Name: Lydia Chong

Job: music store sales associate

Current wages: $22,400

Education: grade 12; continuing education courses in retailing

Career goal: store manager

Keyword search: Canada courses retail management

Installment Buying

Installment buying allows consumers to pay for a portion of the purchase immediately and have the remaining balance owing divided into equal payments.

Example 1

Jacqueline's washing machine broke. She goes shopping and finds a washing machine for $889.45 plus taxes at Wilkinson's Hardware in Abbotsford, BC. The store offers an installment plan for $150.00 down and $90.00 a month for 12 months. Calculate the cash selling price of the washing machine. Calculate the installment price of the washing machine. In your opinion, should she purchase the washing machine in installments?

Solution

GST: $889.45 × 0.07 = 62.2615 = $62.26
PST: $889.45 × 0.075 = 66.70875 = $66.71
$889.45 + $62.26 + $66.71 = $1,018.42

$1,018.42 is the cash selling price of the washing machine, including taxes. Multiply the monthly installment fee by the term:
$90.00 × 12 months = $1,080.00

Add the down payment and the total installment costs:
$150 + $1,080 = $1,230.00
$1,230.00 is the total cost of the washing machine if it is purchased on the installment plan.

If Jacqueline can afford to pay for the washing machine now, it is to her advantage to pay cash since it will cost her $211.58 less than it would if she buys it on the installment plan. However, if Jacqueline is unable to pay for it in full, and needs the washer right away, then she may need to use the installment plan.

Deferred Payment

The buy-now, pay-later promotion is a deferred payment plan in which the customer enjoys their purchase now and pays for it at a later date. At the time of purchase the customer will be required to pay certain costs, including taxes, administration fees, and delivery charges (if applicable). There are no interest charges, but if the customer does not pay for the purchase by the specified date, interest will be charged.

New Terms

installment price: the sum of the down payment plus all the installment payments.

deferred payment: a plan whereby consumers do not pay for a purchase until a later date while enjoying their purchase immediately.

finance or carrying charges: the difference between the installment price and the cash price of an item.

Example 2

René purchases a sofa from Fluff 'N Stuff in Flin Flon, MB. He can either pay for the sofa at the time of purchase or purchase it on the Fluff 'N Stuff buy-now, pay-later plan. The cash price for the sofa is $924.95 (plus taxes) and the delivery charge is $25.00. The buy-now, pay-later cost of the sofa is $999.95 plus taxes and René must pay the taxes, a $25.00 delivery charge, and a $49.95 administration fee at the time of sale. He has one year to pay for his purchase without any interest charges.

Calculate Rene's pay-now price. Calculate how much René has to pay at the time of purchase if he chooses the buy-now, pay-later option.

Calculate Rene's pay-later price. How much more does René pay if he chooses the pay-later option? Compare the pay-later price to the pay-now price as a percentage.

Solution

Multiply the pay-now price by the GST and PST:
$924.95 × .07 = $64.75 GST
$924.95 × .07 = $64.75 PST
Add the pay-now price, the taxes, and the delivery charge:
$924.95 + $64.75 + $64.75 + $25.00 = $1,079.45
The total pay-now price is $1,079.45.

Taxes on pay–later price: $999.95 × 0.07 = $ 70.00 (rounded) for both GST and PST
Add the taxes, delivery charge, and the administration fee:
$70.00 + $70.00 + $25.00 + $49.95 = $214.95
René has to pay $214.95 at the time of purchase.

Add the pay-later price and the fees at the time of purchase:
$999.95 + $214.95 = $1,214.90

René would pay $1,214.90 total for the pay-later price.
Subtract the pay-now price from the pay-later price.
$1,214.90 − $1,079.45 = $135.45

The difference between the pay-now price and the pay-later price is $135.45.

Divide the difference in the pay-now and pay-later prices by the pay-now price and multiply by 100 to turn it into a percentage.

$\frac{\$135.45}{\$1,079.45} \times 100 = 12.54805$ or 12.5% (rounded)

The pay-later price is 12.5% higher than the pay-now price.

Project Activity

1. You are planning a trip to a destination of your choice. One of your expenses will be a good set of luggage. Check prices in newspapers, flyers, and on the internet.

2. Because you are anticipating numerous trip expenses, you are considering buying your luggage on a buy-now, pay-later plan. You find a suitcase with a matching carry-on bag offered for $300 at a travel store. You see the same suitcase and carry-on bag at a discount department store on a buy-now, pay-later plan. In this plan, you would pay $50.00 down and $25.00 a month for a year.

   Which option is the least expensive? Which option would you select? Prepare a mini-report in which you include your reasoning and explain your choice of luggage.

Technology

Did you know that when you purchase an item over the internet that you will pay shipping charges? If it is purchased from another country you may have to pay brokerage fees to have the item brought into Canada.

Notebook Assignment

1. Charlie's Save-A-Lot in Yellowknife, NT is offering a chance to "save money." If you buy a bedroom suite consisting of a bed, a dresser, and two night tables you do not have to pay for one full year. You will have to pay an administration fee of $45 per item, plus GST. The suite costs $1,500 plus tax.

   a) What is the total administration fee?

   b) What is the ratio of this fee to the total cash price?

2. Jake went shopping at Trix, Vernon, BC's best skateboarding and snowboarding store. He found the ultimate snowboard for $400. He does not have $400. Trix offers an installment plan to its customers, $120 down and $65 per month for six months.

   a) Calculate the cash selling price of the snowboard.

   b) Calculate the installment price of the snowboard.

   c) Calculate the finance charge.

3. Nixes Furniture Store in Steinbach, MB is having a sale. There will be no down payment and no interest for six months. Monthly interest of 9% per annum is billed from the date of purchase unless you pay in full within the first six months. The minimum purchase is $399.99.

   a) If you buy a kitchen set for $749 plus taxes and pay the entire bill in five months, how much will you pay?

   b) If you buy this kitchen set for $749 plus taxes and pay the full price at the end of the year, how much will you pay:

   i) using simple interest?
   ii) compounded monthly?
   iii) compounded daily?

4. Carr's House in Summerside, PE has announced that if you buy any television set in stock, you will not have to pay for six months. If you take them up on this deal, the cost to you will only be $789 plus applicable taxes. If you decide to pay immediately you will pay $729 plus applicable taxes.

   a) What is the difference in price?

   b) What is the rate of this difference compared to the cash price?

Exploration 7

• • • • • • • • • • • • • • • • •

Personal Loans

In addition to credit cards, another way to finance a trip or the purchase of an item if you do not have enough cash is with a personal loan. A personal loan allows you to borrow a specified sum of money from a financial institution and to repay it over a period of time, usually one to five years. Loans can be used to buy investments, home improvements, major appliances, computer equipment, or vacations.

Before a financial institution will agree to loan you money, you must be 18 or older and you must fill out an application. You will be asked for personal information about your financial background, assets, credit/debt obligations, work history, marital status, and the purpose of the loan. The financial institution will look at your debt ratio, net worth, job stability, and credit history to make a decision.

Goals

In this exploration, you will look into the world of personal loans and learn how to calculate the interest you would have to pay on a loan.

Technology

You can apply for a personal loan on-line or over the telephone. Financial institutions have loan calculators to help you calculate the monthly payments on a loan.

In addition to repaying the principal portion of the loan, you will have to pay interest to the financial institution. Interest is the fee the financial institution charges for loaning you the money. It is the cost of borrowing. The interest rate on a loan can be a variable or a fixed rate. Variable rates fluctuate with the prime lending rate and are lower than fixed rates. A fixed rate remains the same for the term of the loan. Fixed interest rates are higher than variable rates.

Why would anyone choose the fixed interest rate? One can never predict whether interest rates will rise or fall, and there is always a possibility that the rate could increase so it is higher than a fixed rate.

The fixed interest rate for a loan depends on the financial institution you choose, the amount of the loan, and the term of the loan. The amount of time it will take to repay a loan is called the amortization period.

Remember to shop around at the different financial institutions for the best interest rates. Compare their on-line and telephone rates too. Rates and terms vary from institution to institution, as does the procedure you follow to apply for a loan. Financial institutions compete with each other for your business. Once you have established a credit history and a relationship with a financial institution, you may be able to negotiate the terms of a loan for personal use.

New Terms

amortization period: the number of months/years it will take to repay a loan.

cost of borrowing: the dollar amount of interest you will pay over the term of the loan.

fixed rate: fixed interest rate for the term of the loan.

prime lending rate: the lending interest rate set by the Bank of Canada.

term: the period of the loan where the conditions remain unchanged.

variable rate: fluctuating interest rate that is a set amount above the prime-lending rate.

This table is a Personal Loan Payment Calculator. To use it, look up the interest rate of a loan in the left-hand column, then find the term in years on the same line. The amount under the term is the payment for each $1,000 you borrow.

Personal Loan Payment Calculator
Monthly Payment per $1,000

Interest Rate %	Term in Years				
	1	2	3	4	5
3.00	84.69	42.98	29.08	22.13	17.97
3.25	84.81	43.09	29.19	22.24	18.08
3.50	84.92	43.20	29.30	22.36	18.19
3.75	85.04	43.31	29.41	22.47	18.30
4.00	85.23	43.47	29.58	22.66	18.52
4.25	85.34	43.58	29.69	22.77	18.63
4.50	85.45	43.69	29.80	22.88	18.74
4.75	85.56	43.80	29.91	22.99	18.85
5.00	85.67	43.91	30.02	23.10	18.96
5.25	85.78	44.02	30.13	23.21	19.07
5.50	85.89	44.13	30.24	23.32	19.18
5.75	86.00	44.24	30.35	23.43	19.29
6.00	86.07	44.33	30.43	23.49	19.34
6.25	86.18	44.44	30.54	23.61	19.46
6.50	86.30	44.56	30.66	23.72	19.57
6.75	86.41	44.67	30.77	23.84	19.69
7.00	86.53	44.78	30.88	23.95	19.81
7.25	86.64	44.89	31.00	24.07	19.93
7.50	86.76	45.01	31.11	24.19	20.05
7.75	86.87	45.12	31.23	24.30	20.16
8.00	86.99	45.24	31.34	24.42	20.28
8.25	87.10	45.34	31.46	24.53	20.40
8.50	87.22	45.46	31.57	24.65	20.52
8.75	87.34	45.57	31.68	24.71	20.64
9.00	87.45	45.68	31.80	24.89	20.76
9.25	87.57	45.80	31.92	25.00	20.88
9.50	87.68	45.91	32.03	25.12	21.00
9.75	87.80	46.03	32.15	25.24	21.12
10.00	87.92	46.14	32.27	25.36	21.25
10.25	88.03	46.26	32.38	25.48	21.37
10.50	88.15	46.38	32.50	25.60	21.49
10.75	88.27	46.49	32.62	25.72	21.62
11.00	88.38	46.61	32.74	25.85	21.74
11.25	88.50	46.72	32.86	25.97	21.87
11.50	88.62	46.84	32.98	26.09	21.99
11.75	88.73	46.96	33.10	26.21	22.12
12.00	88.85	47.07	33.21	26.33	22.24

Example 1

Jesse requires a personal loan of $10,000 for home renovations. His financial institution offers him a three-year loan at a fixed rate of 10.25%.

   How much must Jesse pay the financial institution each month? How much will he pay for the loan? How much interest will Jesse have paid at the end of three years?

Solution

Find the rate of 10.25% on the Personal Loan Repayment Calculator. Then look across to the column for the term of the loan, 3 years. The amount in that column is the amount to be paid each month for each thousand dollars of the loan.

$32.38 is to be paid each month for each thousand dollars of the loan.

Divide the amount of the loan by 1000, then multiply by $32.38 to calculate the monthly payment:

$$\frac{\$10,000}{1000} \times \$32.38 = \$323.80$$

$323.80 is the amount Jesse will pay each month to borrow $10,000 at a rate of 10.25%.

How many months will it take Jesse to repay the loan?
3 years × 12 = 36
It will take 36 months to repay the loan.

Multiply the number of monthly payments by the monthly payment:
36 × $323.80 = $11,656.80
$11,656.80 is the total amount paid over the three years.

Subtract the principal amount from the total paid for the loan:
$11,656.80 − $10,000 = $1,656.80
$1,656.80 is the total cost of borrowing the money, meaning the total amount of interest paid.

Example 2

Amy would like to buy a computer. She lives in North Bay, ON. She has found one that she likes for $2,400 plus taxes. She does not have enough money right now so she decides to take out a personal fixed rate loan. How much will she need to borrow? How much will she pay each month if the loan has a term of two years and an interest rate of 11.75%? How much interest will she pay?

Solution

Calculate the total cost of the computer. Multiply the price by the GST and PST rates:

$2,400 × .07 = $168.00 GST
$2,400 × .08 = $192.00 PST

Add the price and taxes to find the total cost:

$2,400 + $168 + $192 = $2,760

Amy needs to borrow $2,760. To calculate her monthly payment, look up the interest rate and term on the Personal Loan Payment Calculator and multiply the amount per $1,000 by the amount of her loan divided by 1000:

$$\frac{\$2,760}{1000} \times \$46.96 = \$129.61 \text{ (rounded)}$$

Amy's monthly payment would be $129.61.

To calculate the total paid, multiply the number of months by the payment amount:
2 years × 12 months = 24 months
24 × $129.61 = $3,110.64

To find the total interest she will pay, subtract the principal from the total paid:

$3,110.64 − $2,760 = $350.64
The total amount of interest is $350.64.

Project Activity

1. In preparation for the trip you are planning you will probably want to have a credit card. Do some research by telephone or internet to find out the terms that various credit card companies offer. Be sure to get the application forms and read all the conditions that apply. Select the card you wish to apply for, complete the application, and add it to your project file.

2. For the purposes of this project, assume that you have a job and a work history, and choose an approximate salary for yourself. Contact a bank or credit union to find out what steps are involved in applying for a line of credit or a personal loan. What is the maximum loan you qualify for to pay for your trip? Complete the loan and line of credit application forms and add them to your project file.

Notebook Assignment

1. Alan lives in Atlin, BC and wants to buy a customized mountain bike. He finds one that he likes for $3,500 plus taxes. He takes out a personal fixed rate loan for two years at 8.25%.

   a) How much will it cost him each month?

   b) How much will he pay in interest?

2. Cindy lives in Churchill, MB. Cindy has found a snowmobile that she would like to purchase. It will cost her $7,500 plus taxes plus $450 shipping. She takes out a personal fixed rate loan at 10.5% for four years.

   a) How much will she pay each month?

   b) How much will she have paid in interest over four years?

3. Harvey has just moved into an apartment in Golden, BC, and he needs some new furniture. He takes out a personal fixed rate loan at 7% to cover purchases of $6,600 plus taxes to be paid over the next three years.

   a) How much will he pay each month?

   b) How much will he have paid in interest over three years?

4. Bart has found the motorcycle of his dreams in Lunenburg, NS. The cost will be $16,435 plus taxes. He takes out a personal fixed rate loan at 9.75% and would like to be able to pay this off in five years.

   a) What will he pay each month?

   b) What will he pay in interest over five years?

5. Trina has decided to buy a sewing machine for her summer business in Dawson City, YT. The one she has picked out will cost $1,675 plus taxes. She takes out a personal fixed rate loan at 6.5% and wants to pay this off in two years.

   a) What will she pay each month?

   b) How much will she have paid in interest at the end of two years?

Exploration 8

Exchange Rates

Buying items over the internet or through mail order is a terrific time-saver, but often the prices you pay will be in a foreign currency. It is important to take into consideration the cost of converting Canadian funds into the foreign currency as part of the over-all price of any purchase. This is also done when travelling to another country.

If you are taking a trip to Hawaii you need American currency. A financial institution will sell you the foreign currency using their selling rate to calculate how much American currency you will receive for your Canadian money.

After your fabulous vacation in Hawaii, if you still have American money, you will want to convert it back to Canadian funds. The financial institution will buy the foreign currency from you using their buying rate. The buying rate is lower than the selling rate, because of service charges.

When you are exchanging money, it is a good idea to shop around. Different institutions may have different rates, and stores and other retail outlets may accept foreign currency at a buying rate set by the store.

You can use a credit card to make a purchase valued in a foreign currency. The exchange rate the credit card company uses will be the rate on the day that the company you made the purchase from submits their statements to the credit card company. This is not necessarily the same day you made the purchase.

Did you know that not all banks have every foreign currency in stock? If the currency that you need is not often requested, the bank may have to order it for you. Since banks charge a fee for this service, it is important to comparison shop to find the best rates of exchange.

Goals

In this exploration, you will convert Canadian money into a foreign currency and foreign currency into Canadian dollars.

New Terms

exchange rate: the value of different currencies compared as a decimal or percent.

bank buying rate: the rate at which the bank buys foreign currency.

bank selling rate: the rate at which the bank sells foreign currency.

Canadian Dollar–Based Rates

Bank Buying Rate	Country	Currency	Bank Selling Rate
.7933	Australia	dollar	.8766
1.43765	Austria	euro	1.4748
1.43765	Belgium	euro	1.4748
0.5168	Brazil	real	0.6906
.1842	Denmark	krone	.1999
2.2580	England	pound	2.3616
1.43765	European Economic Community (EEC)	euro	1.4748
0.6252	Fiji	dollar	0.8174
1.43765	Finland	euro	1.4748
1.43765	France	euro	1.4748
1.43765	Germany	euro	1.4748
1.43765	Greece	euro	1.4748
.1919	Hong Kong	dollar	.2173
1.43765	Italy	euro	1.4748
.011805	Japan	yen	.012554
.1646	Mexico	peso	.1912
1.43765	Netherlands	euro	1.4748
.6486	New Zealand	dollar	.7262
2.2436	N. Ireland	pound	2.3714
.1715	Norway	krone	.1864
1.43765	Portugal	euro	1.4748
2.2436	Scotland	pound	2.3714
.8177	Singapore	dollar	.9141
1.43765	S. Ireland	euro	1.4748
1.43765	Spain	euro	1.4748
.1483	Sweden	krone	.1611
.9353	Switzerland	franc	.9970
0.2365	Tobago	dollar	0.2749
1.5752	*United States Dollar	dollar	1.613

January 5, 2002

*Different rates may be applied to the US dollar, depending on the amount of money exchanged. The greater the amount, the better the rate will be.

Example 1

You are taking a trip to Mexico. You have $800 Canadian to spend. How many Mexican pesos can you buy?

Solution

Look up the bank selling rate on the chart. It is 0.1912. Divide the number of Canadian dollars by the bank selling rate:

$800 ÷ 0.1912 = 4,184.1004184 or 4,184.10 pesos

You will have 4,184.10 pesos to spend in Mexico.

Technology

Currency exchange calculators are available on financial institution web sites. You can search for such a site with the terms: currency exchange calculator.

Hints

If you do not know the foreign currency symbol, do not use a $ sign. Instead, write out the name of the currency, for example, 100 Norwegian krone.

Example 2

You had to cancel your trip to Mexico. You go to the bank to convert your money back to Canadian funds. How much will you receive back?

Solution

Look up the bank buying rate for the foreign currency. It is 0.1646.
Multiply the foreign currency by the bank buying rate:

$4,184.10 \times 0.1646 = 688.70286$ or $688.70

You will receive $688.70 back in Canadian funds.
The difference between the amount you gave the bank and the amount you received back is the bank's earnings for providing this service.

Example 3

You are travelling to England and wish to buy 500 pounds sterling. How many Canadian dollars will you pay?

Solution

Look up the bank selling rate: 2.3616.
Multiply the foreign currency by the bank selling rate:

$500 \times 2.3616 = \$1,180.80$

It will cost $1,180.80 Canadian to purchase 500 pounds sterling.

Example 4

What would 6,500 Northern Ireland pounds be valued at in Canadian currency?

Solution

Look up the bank selling rate.

6,500 × 2.3714 = $15,414.10

6,500 Northern Ireland pounds is worth $15,414.10 Canadian.

Project Activity

1. Start to plan and research the specifics of your trip. What is your destination? What will it cost to get there?

2. Prepare a budget that estimates the cost of accommodation and meals. Use newspapers, the internet, travel magazines, the Canadian Automobile Association, or travel agents as sources of information. Determine what the cost of the foreign currency would be in Canadian funds.

3. Assume that your local transportation and sightseeing costs will be the equivalent of $500 Canadian dollars. Convert this to the currency of the country you are visiting.

Add all of this information to your project file.

Notebook Assignment

Use the table on p. 65 to answer the following questions.

1. What exchange rates would you use to convert your Canadian money to the following currencies?

   a) euro

   b) Hong Kong dollar

   c) Swiss franc

2. If you had the following foreign currencies, what rate would you use when the bank is buying the currency from you?

   a) Mexican peso

   b) British pound

   c) United States dollar

The Swiss franc currently sells for about $1 Cdn.

3. Calculate what the following foreign currencies are worth in Canadian dollars.

   a) 4,000 Danish krone

   b) 25,000 Australian dollars

   c) 2,200 euro

   d) 8,545 Swiss francs

4. Megan is planning a trip to Germany. She has saved $1,200 Cdn. How much money will she have to spend in Germany?

5. Opal is planning a trip to Europe. She wishes to buy $650 Canadian dollars' worth of each of the following currencies. How much of each currency will she have?

   a) euro

   b) British pounds

   c) Swedish krone

6. Kevin has planned a trip to Mexico. He goes to his bank and purchases Mexican pesos with $400 Canadian. Due to an emergency, he must cancel his trip. Kevin returns to the bank to exchange the pesos for Canadian dollars.

a) How much did Kevin receive in pesos?

b) How much did Kevin receive in Canadian dollars after he cancelled his trip?

c) Why did Kevin receive a lower amount back in Canadian dollars?

7. Pedro is planning an around-the-world golfing trip. He plans on golfing at some of the world's finest golf courses. He estimates how much money he will need in each of the different currencies. For each of the different countries that he will visit, calculate how much in Canadian dollars he will need. What is the amount of Canadian money he needs?

Country	Golf Course	Estimated Funds Needed
United States	Pebble Beach	$5,000 US
Scotland	Royal Troon	£8,500
Canada	Glen Abbey	$3,000 Cdn
Singapore	SAFRA Resort & CC	$15,000 Singapore
Austria	Lake Karrinyup	4,000 euro

Chapter Review

• •

1. Heidi earns a straight commission of 30%. One week she had sales of $1,560. Find her gross pay for the week.

2. Doris receives a salary of $150 per week plus a commission of 2.5% on all sales. Last week her sales totalled $6,660.

    a) Find her gross pay for the week.

    b) Find her net pay, if her deductions are 36% of her gross earnings.

3. Dale is paid $550 per month plus a commission of 4% on the first $2,000 of sales, and 5.5% on sales over $2,000. He sold $10,600 worth of lumber last month. Find his gross pay for the month.

4. Pokok receives a salary of $625 per week plus a commission of 4% on the first $2,000, 5% on sales between $2,000 and $3,500, and 6% on sales over $3,500.

    a) Find her gross pay for the week if her sales were $11,400.

    b) Find her net pay if her deductions total 39% of her gross earnings.

5. Rosie has a part-time job at Christmas, working for a courier company. She receives $3.00 for each package that she delivers. She delivers 20 packages on average in an evening. What will her gross pay be if she works six nights a week?

6. Find the simple interest on the following:

    a) $200 for one year at 5%

    b) $350 for five months at 5.5%

    c) $900 at 8.6% for 200 days

7. Solve the following simple interest problems:

   a) Find the principal if $45 of interest is earned in three years at a rate of 6.245%.

   b) Find the rate of interest if the principal of $5,400 earns $117.45 in three months.

   c) A principal of $2,000 earns $145 interest when invested at a rate of 9.5%. How many months was it invested?

8. Find the amount of interest earned for each of the following investments.

   a) $500 at 6% compounded annually for five years.

   b) $400 at 5% compounded quarterly for four years.

   c) $600 at 7% compounded semi-annually for three years.

9. The previous balance on Dharma's credit statement for April was $200. During the month of May, she charged purchases of $12.00, $16.49, and $49.40 and made a payment of $85. If the monthly interest is $13.75, what is the new balance for the month of May?

10. Clare has an unpaid balance of $345 on her credit card. During the month she paid $290 and made purchases of $456. The interest charge for the month is $15.75. What would be her minimum monthly payment if it must correspond to 5% of the ending balance or $10, whichever is greater?

11. Brandee is shopping for a leather jacket. She has found the perfect jacket at Leather Hideaway in Winnipeg, MB. It costs $390. The manager of Leather Hideaway has told her that today they are offering their customers the option to buy using the installment plan. The price of this jacket on the installment plan is $200 with $80 a month for 6 months.

    a) What is the cash price?

    b) What is the installment price?

12. Andrea buys a dishwasher at Almay's Appliances in Kelowna, BC. The cost is $519 plus taxes if she pays at the time of purchase. Since she is unable to pay for it at that time, she decides to use their buy-now, pay-later plan. The buy-now, pay-later price is $610, plus she must pay an administration fee of $49.95, and taxes.

a) How much would she have had to pay if she paid cash?

b) How much will she pay on the buy-now, pay-later plan?

c) How much interest will she have paid by the end of the year?

d) What is the percent rate of interest?

13. Joe takes out a personal fixed rate loan for $7,800 at 9% interest. He plans to repay this loan in three years.

   a) What will his monthly payment be?

   b) How much interest will he have paid at the end of the three years?

14. Justin wishes to purchase 400 euro. How much in Canadian dollars will it cost him to purchase them?

15. You have $500 Canadian to buy Scottish pounds. How many Scottish pounds will you buy?

16. Ernie spent a year teaching in Japan. He saved 150,000 yen while he was there. How much has he saved in Canadian dollars?

17. Jake travels to the United States and makes the following purchases while he is there. He buys a pair of jeans for $19.95 and a sweater for $34.95. What is the total cost of these purchases in Canadian dollars? (Assume that Jake was in the US long enough not to have to pay duty.)

18. Leanne has planned a trip to Nevada. At her bank she purchases American dollars worth $700 Canadian. However, she is unable to go on her trip and decides to convert the American dollars back to Canadian dollars at the bank.

   a) How many American dollars did she buy?

   b) How many Canadian dollars did she receive back from the bank?

   c) Explain why the amount she receives back is different from the amount she gave the bank.

Project Presentation

From the information on trip planning that you have assembled in your project file, present your project as a report, a presentation to the class, or a multimedia presentation (for example, in PowerPoint).

1. Report on your choice of luggage:

    a) Describe the luggage you chose.

    b) List the in-store promotions you researched.

    c) How much did the luggage cost on a delayed payment plan? How much did it cost if you paid cash? What percentage more would you pay on the payment plan?

    d) Did you decide to buy on a delayed payment plan? Explain your reasons.

2. Report on your applications for a credit card, a line of credit, and a personal loan.

    a) Present your completed application forms for each.

    b) Do you intend to take out a personal loan, charge your expenses to a credit card or save your money before going on the trip? Explain the choice you make about financing your trip.

3. Describe the trip you are planning and present a budget. Include:

    a) the destination

    b) estimated travel costs

    c) the currency of the country you are visiting

    d) estimated costs of your accommodation and meal costs; list the costs both in the foreign currency and in Canadian dollars

    e) in the foreign currency, how much will you be spending for sightseeing and local travel?

    f) estimate your pre-trip costs, including luggage

    g) estimate the total cost of your trip in Canadian dollars

Case Study

· · · · · · · · · · · · · ·

In this case study you will help Jang make some career and financial decisions. Here is some background information on Jang.

Jang lives in Vancouver, BC and works for a publishing company that pays him $9.75 an hour and time and a half if he works more than 8 hours a day. He is not paid for his lunch hour.

Jang is an excellent worker and has been offered positions with two other companies. Jang has also been considering a career change, and is thinking of becoming a salesperson because he enjoys dealing with people. However, he also feels very confident with the quality of work that he produces where he works now. Jang has the skills and qualifications needed for each of the different job options he is considering.

Assume that Jang's payroll deductions would be 20% of his gross earnings.

Current Job

Jang works with a great group of people. He works 40 hours a week and averages 3–5 hours of overtime every two weeks.

Offer #1

Design It, a web site design company has offered Jang a position as a web site designer. He would be paid $800 for each site that he designs, and $30 an hour for any modifications he makes to each site thereafter. Jang has designed a few sites for friends of his. Jang would be able to work at home, choosing the hours that he works. He would have to ensure that the work would be completed by the deadline.

Offer #2

Fancy Cars, the top-selling used car dealership in western Canada, has offered Jang a position selling vehicles. He would earn 25% of the gross sale on the first 10 vehicles sold each month. Upon selling the 11th vehicle, Jang would earn 30% of the gross sale on that vehicle and all previously sold vehicles as well as on any others he sells that month. On average the number of vehicles sold each month by the salespeople ranges from 8–30. The average gross sale of a vehicle sold is approximately $1,000 (gross sales means the company's gross profit).

1. Should Jang change careers? Justify your answer. Be sure to include mathematical calculations to support your choice.

2. Ping, Jang's brother, asks to borrow $3,000. He says that he will repay Jang over 2 years with an interest rate of 4.5%.

   a) If Jang should accept Ping's offer, how much would Jang earn in interest?

   b) Should Jang accept Ping's offer? Justify your answer mathematically.

3. Jang just won $10,000 on a lottery ticket. He wants to invest his money. Approximately how long will it take his money to double if he could earn the following interest rates:

   a) 4%

   b) 6.4%

   c) 18%

   d) 11.25%

4. Jang decides to start investing 10% of his gross income from this current job.

   a) Approximately what amount would Jang be investing?

   b) Would it be better for Jang to invest in something that earns compound or simple interest? Explain your choice.

   c) If Jang were to invest $2,400 per year in a compound interest investment, how much money would he have at the end of 30 years with an average interest rate of 10.5%? Assume interest is compounded annually.

5. Jang took a trip across Canada. He drove to Jasper, Saskatoon, and Winnipeg, and then flew to Rankin Inlet. Because he did not want to carry cash, Jang put all of his meals, accommodations, and purchases on his credit card. Look at the credit card statement on p.77 and answer the questions that follow it.

Royal Credit Wise Credit Card
8765 Westshore
Vancouver, BC

Jang Detweiler	Statement Date	Due Date
5211 Parkhill Drive	November 28, 2002	December 12, 2002
Vancouver, BC		

Trans. Date	Transaction	Debit	Credit	Balance
Nov. 12	K-Town (gas)	$50.54		$50.54
Nov. 12	Olive's Seafood	$42.55		$93.09
Nov. 12	Toys For Tots	$19.11		$112.20
Nov. 13	Paradise Hotel	$125.72		$237.92
Nov. 13	Riverside Restaurant	$63.54		$301.46
Nov. 14	Keatons Dept. Store	$75.00		$376.46
Nov. 14	Special Gifts 'N More	$62.25		$438.71
Nov. 14	Cash Advance	$150.00		$588.71
Nov. 15	Highway Hotel	$45.00		$633.71
Nov. 16	Jasper Jazz Club	$48.56		$682.27
Nov. 16	Gas Pump	$35.00		$717.27
Nov. 17	Jasper Inn	$189.00		$906.27
Nov. 17	Nik Nak Shak	$68.33		$974.60
Nov. 18	Galant Hair Salon	$32.75		$1,007.35
Nov. 18	Highwayside Full Serve	$48.00		$1,055.35
Nov. 18	Flaxcombe Museum	$15.49		$1,070.84
Nov. 19	Winnipeg Mall	$126.88		$1,197.72
Nov. 19	Pump'N Fill Gas	$39.00		$1,236.72
Nov. 19	Winnipeg Five Star Hotel	$138.41		$1,375.13
Nov. 20	Western Star Restaurant	$72.65		$1,447.78
Nov. 20	Airfare	$350.00		$1,797.78
Nov. 20	You Drive It Car Rental	$532.12		$2,329.90
Nov. 21	Nunavut Inn	$110.00		$2,439.90
Nov. 21	Polarbear Cruise	$212.50		$2,652.40
Nov. 21	Restaurant	$60.78		$2,713.18
Nov. 22	Airfare	$872.00		$3,585.18

Previous Balance	Purchases & Interest	Payments	Current Balance	Minimum Payment
$0.00	$3,585.18	$0.00	$3,585.18	$252.00

a) What was Jang's previous balance?

b) What date is the payment due on Jang's credit card?

c) Will all transactions on Jang's credit card be interest free if Jang pays the full amount by the payment due date?

d) If the interest is 18.7% for a purchase and 19.2% for cash advances per annum, how much interest will Jang pay on the cash advance?

6. Jang wishes to buy a car. He has found a used SUV for $14,800. Jang has to pay PST and has a cash down payment of $4,000. His credit union has approved Jang's application for a loan with a fixed interest rate of 7.25% for 4 years.

a) How much does Jang have to finance in a personal loan?

b) How much would Jang pay each month for this loan?

c) How much interest in total would Jang pay for borrowing the money?

7. Jang's boss just notified him that the company would pay for him to attend a conference in San Francisco. The company would pay for all accommodations and meals; he would only have to bring spending money. Jang accepts the offer and packs his bags. On his way to the airport, Jang stops at his financial institution to exchange some Canadian funds for US funds.

a) If Jang converts $500 Canadian, how much US spending money will he have?

b) When he returns from his fabulous trip, Jang has $125 US left over. He returns to the financial institution to exchange it for Canadian funds. How much will he receive?

Chapter 2
Data Analysis

Using Statistics Wisely

Statistics is the branch of mathematics that focusses on collecting, organizing, analyzing, and interpreting data. TV ratings, sports statistics, popularity polls, and election predictions all analyze and interpret data.

Over a hundred years ago, science fiction writer H.G. Wells made the following prediction: "Statistical thinking will one day be as necessary for efficient citizenship as the ability to read and write." That day has certainly arrived.

For instance, when people try to sell a product or to promote a point of view, they may try to influence us through the way they present data. They may even mislead us by misusing statistics. Understanding data can help us make informed decisions.

It is equally important to know how to display data accurately. In this age of information overload, it is vital to analyze correctly to obtain accurate information.

Goals

In this chapter, you will learn how to represent data effectively using averages, tables, charts, plots, and graphs. You will make predictions and inferences based on averages and graphs and recognize how data can be manipulated to stress a particular point of view.

Chapter Project

In this project, you will locate a table of data that interests you and conduct a statistical analysis of that data. You will also locate a bar graph that represents data accurately and manipulate the graph to examine the effects of data representation. As you work on the project, you will add the following items to your project file:

1. A table of data.

2. A bar graph representing data and variations you will create.

3. A circle graph representing your data.

4. Examples of graphs that present biased and unbiased representation of data.

Career Connection

Name: Jan de Haan

Job: part–time sports statistician with the Simon Fraser University women's basketball team

Current wages: $20.00 a game

Education: grade 12 graduation; extensive volunteer work on statistics with school sports teams.

Career goal: sports journalist

Keyword search: Canada college journalism course

Exploration 1

Line Plots

The ancient proverb "A picture is worth a thousand words" is as true for numbers as it is for words. A visual representation of numerical data can allow you to extract most of the important statistical information contained in a set of data.

A line plot is one way to represent data graphically. It is a horizontal line on which numerical data is arranged. A line plot is a tool that you can use to organize and study data because it displays information about how data is distributed over a range of values. A line plot is usually used to display a data set with fewer than 50 numbers.

Goals

In this exploration, you will learn to construct line plots and use them to display and analyze data.

Example 1

The following table contains test results for the students in Mr. Abrams' mathematics class. The test has a maximum of 30 marks and a passing grade is 50%. Construct a line plot that represents this set of data and analyze the information that becomes apparent in the line plot.

Student	Mark	Student	Mark	Student	Mark
Sarah Bartlett	19	Si Lun Gao	22	Peter Moore	21
Larry Hayton	10	Michelle Garneau	15	Karl Nagy	19
Gloria Chan	16	Joanne Beestra	21	Shane O'Reilly	21
Dave Dutoff	22	Ruby Hill	25	Maria Pacheco	22
Manjit Dhesi	20	Fatima Iqbal	30	Baljit Prasad	22
Eduardo Diaz	25	Benjamin Kane	19	Michael Proudfoot	26
Slava Elasov	21	In Kim	22	Sophie St. Pierre	20
John Buchanan	19	Miwa Kishi	26	Hans Weber	25
Dana Fornelli	26	Dan MacGauley	22	Jana Williams	26

Solution

To draw a line plot of the students' marks, follow these steps:

1. First, draw a horizontal line with a ruler.

2. Next, construct a scale below the line using a ruler. To do this, take the smallest and largest marks, in this case 10 and 30, and choose a suitable scale. A suitable scale could run from 10 to 30.

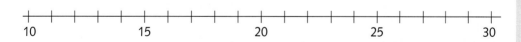

continued on the next page

Hints

Graph paper is helpful in constructing line plots.

3. Next, plot each mark by placing an X (or some other symbol) above the line at the appropriate location. For example, Dana Fornelli earned a mark of 26. Therefore, an X goes above the number 26.

4. Continue until you have plotted each mark. For values with more than one entry, place the Xs directly above each other to avoid crowding.

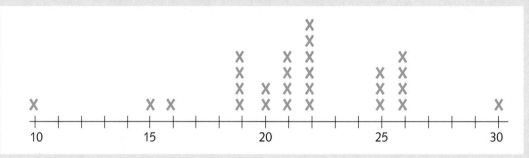

Once the data is plotted, you can see the following features that are not apparent when you examine the table.
- The range is 20:
  $30 - 10 = 20$
- The values 10 and 30 are the only outliers.
- There are 3 clusters of data: one large cluster between 19 and 22, and two smaller ones at 15 and 16 and 25 and 26.
- The two largest gaps in the data are between 10 and 15 and between 26 and 30.

Based on the line plot, the following can be said about the test:
- The test appears to be fair, since only one person failed.
- Most of the class (16 out of 27 students) scored between 19 and 22 out of 30.
- The test was not too easy. Only one student out of 27 scored a perfect 30 out of 30.

New Terms

cluster: a place where values are grouped or clustered together.

gap: a large space between values.

outlier: value that is widely separated from the rest of the data.

range: the difference between the smallest and largest values in the data.

Small Group Activity

Consider the following table. Construct a line plot of this data, then discuss the questions that follow.

Twelve Top-Grossing Movies

Movie	Gross Earnings Since Opening	Year Released
Star Wars: New Hope	$720,211,976	1977
Star Wars: The Empire Strikes Back	$453,373,048	1980
ET: The Extraterrestrial	$624,694,592	1982
Star Wars: Return of the Jedi	$483,008,451	1983
Jurassic Park	$557,562,070	1993
Forrest Gump	$515,142,147	1994
The Lion King	$488,836,814	1994
Independence Day	$478,207,747	1996
Titanic	$938,729,768	1997
Star Wars: The Phantom Menace	$657,539,756	1999
The Sixth Sense	$458,557,675	1999
Harry Potter & the Philosopher's Stone	$455,615,965	2001

a) What is the range of the gross earnings?

b) List any outliers for the data.

c) Identify any clusters.

d) What is the largest gap between the values on the line plot?

e) Does there appear to be a relationship between the age of a movie and its ranking on the list?

f) What other information can you extract from the line plot?

Project Activity

Search for a table of data that interests you. You might choose statistics from sports, the weather, entertainment, geography, or social data from Statistics Canada. Your data must include at least ten values. If necessary, use your school or local library to search magazines and newspapers for interesting statistical data.

a) Identify the source of your data.

b) Construct an accurate line plot of the data.

c) From the line plot, identify any outliers, clusters, or gaps.

d) State the range of your data.

e) Is a line plot appropriate for graphing the data? Why or why not?

Notebook Assignment

1. The following table lists the top 15 medal–winning countries at the 2002 Winter Olympics held in Salt Lake City. Construct a line plot of this data and answer the questions that follow.

Fifteen Top Medal-Winning Countries, 2002 Winter Olympics

Country	Total Medals	Country	Total Medals
Austria	16	Norway	24
Canada	17	Russia	16
China	8	Sweden	6
Croatia	4	Switzerland	11
Finland	7	United States	34
France	11	Korea	4
Germany	35	Netherlands	8
Italy	12		

a) Identify any outlier(s) for this set of data.

b) Determine the range of medals per country.

c) What clusters are evident from this line plot?

d) Where is the largest gap between the values on this line plot?

e) How many countries won 15 or fewer medals?

f) How many countries won more than 30 medals?

g) How many countries fall into the largest cluster on your line plot?

h) Describe how Canada compares to the other countries in this data.

Canada's women's hockey team at the 2002 Winter Olympics brought home the gold!

2. The following chart lists the 25 top-selling albums of all time. They are ranked according to the number of albums that have been sold worldwide. The numbers in brackets indicate whether the album is a double (2) or a triple (3) record set. Construct a line plot of the total number of albums sold, and then answer the questions that follow.

Top 25 Albums Sold (2002)

Rank	Album	Millions Sold
1	**Eagles:** *Greatest Hits* (1976)	27
2	**Michael Jackson:** *Thriller* (1982)	26
3	**Pink Floyd:** *The Wall* (1979)	23 (2)
4	**Led Zeppelin:** *Untitled (IV)* (1971)	22
5	**Billy Joel:** *Greatest Hits Volume I & II* (1985)	21 (2)
6	**AC/DC:** *Back in Black* (1980)	19
7	**The Beatles:** *The Beatles [White Album]* (1968)	18 (2)
8	**Fleetwood Mac:** *Rumours* (1977)	18
9	**Shania Twain:** *Come on Over* (1997)	18
10	**Whitney Houston:** *The Bodyguard* (1992)	16
11	**Boston:** *Boston* (1976)	16
12	**Alanis Morissette:** *Jagged Little Pill* (1995)	16
13	**Garth Brooks:** *No Fences* (1990)	16
14	**Hootie & the Blowfish:** *Cracked Rear View* (1995)	16
15	**Eagles:** *Hotel California* (1976)	16
16	**The Beatles:** *1967-70* (1973)	15 (2)
17	**Bruce Springsteen:** *Born in the U.S.A.* (1984)	15
18	**Pink Floyd:** *Dark Side of the Moon* (1973)	15
19	**Guns 'N Roses:** *Appetite for Destruction* (1987)	15
20	**Elton John:** *Greatest Hits* (1974)	15
21	**The Bee Gees:** *Saturday Night Fever* (1977)	15
22	**Led Zeppelin:** *Physical Graffiti* (1975)	15 (2)
23	**The Beatles:** *1962-66* (1973)	15 (2)
24	**Garth Brooks:** *Ropin' the Wind* (1991)	14
25	**Santana:** *Supernatural* (1999)	14

a) List any outlier(s) for the data.

b) What is the most obvious gap between the values of the line plot?

c) What clusters are evident from the line plot?

d) Determine the range of values for the data.

e) At the time the data was gathered, how many albums were more than 25 years old?

f) How many albums were 10 years old or less?

g) Does there appear to be a relationship between the number of albums sold, and the age of the album?

h) Which artist or band has the greatest number of albums sold?

i) How many albums did this artist or band sell?

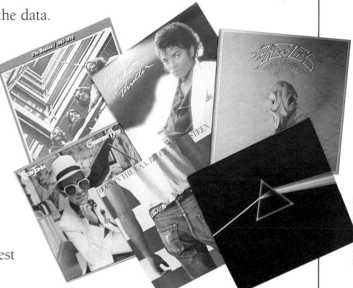

Extension

3. Refer to the table of the Twelve Top-Grossing Movies on p. 85 and answer the following questions:

a) *Star Wars: New Hope* grossed a sizeable portion of its income in the late 1970s. How might this fact be important when you compare the gross income of movies?

b) What ways can be used to compare the popularity of movies other than money earned?

Hints

When an album sells a million copies, it is said to go "platinum."

Exploration 2

Determining Measures of Central Tendency

Although line plots can help you organize and study data, they do not always provide enough information about a set of values. You can also determine measures of central tendency that will help you understand a set of data in more depth.

There are three ways to measure the central tendencies—often referred to as "averages"—of a set of numbers. The three measures are the mean, the median, and the mode. Although all three tend to be located near the centre of a data set, each represents a different quantity.

Each measure identifies a different feature of the data set, and you need to be able to select the measure of central tendency that meets your purpose. Each measure has advantages and disadvantages in its ability to describe data. Together, these three different measures of central tendency help describe the data more completely.

Goals

In this exploration, you will calculate the mean, median, and mode of a set of data. You will also learn about the appropriate use of each of these statistical measures.

New Terms

measure of central tendency: a central measure that best represents a distribution of data.

Example 1

Assume that Marcelo received the following scores on five mathematics tests: 70, 92, 84, 91, and 70. Each test has a possible total of 100 marks. Compute the mean, median, and mode of Marcelo's scores.

Solution

a) Mean

Use this formula to find the mean:

$$\bar{x} = \frac{\Sigma x}{n}$$

$$\bar{x} = \frac{70 + 92 + 84 + 91 + 70}{5}$$

$$= \frac{407}{5}$$

$$= 81.4$$

The mean of Marcelo's test scores is 81.4.

b) Median

To find the median of Marcelo's five test scores, arrange his scores in order from smallest to largest:

70, 70, 84, 91, 92

The test score in the middle, 84, is the median.
Therefore, the median of Marcelo's test scores is 84. Note that half his test scores are lower than 84, and half are higher.

c) Mode

In this set of data, the value 70 occurs twice. Therefore, 70 is the mode. If all values occur only once, there would be no mode.

Class Discussion

Which of the three measures of central tendency would the teacher likely use to determine Marcelo's grade? Which of the three measures of central tendency would Marcelo prefer his teacher use to calculate his grade? Discuss which of the three is the most appropriate measure of Marcelo's test performance.

Hints

The formula for mean is:
$$\bar{x} = \frac{\Sigma x}{n}$$
where

$\bar{x}$ = mean

Σx = sum of all the values

n = number of values

New Terms

arithmetic mean: the measure of central tendency found by adding the values in a set of data and then dividing by the number of values in the set. This is commonly called the mean.

Example 2

Suppose that following a prolonged illness, Marcelo wrote a sixth test and received a mark of 22. What are the mean, median, and mode of his marks?

Solution

a) Mean

$$\bar{x} = \frac{\Sigma x}{n}$$

$$= \frac{429}{6}$$

$$= 71.5$$

The new mean is 71.5

b) Median

Arranging the marks in order, we have 22, 70, 70, 84, 91, 92 . Whenever we have an even number of values, the median is the mean of the two middle values. The two middle values are 70 and 84. Halfway between is 77.

c) Mode

The mark that occurs most often is still 70.

Class Discussion

Which of the three measures of central tendency was most affected by the outlier 22? Based on the mean of his first five tests, Marcelo feels that he should be allowed to rewrite his sixth test. Do you agree?

Small Group Activity

Words in English vary greatly in length. The shortest consist of one letter, for example, the words "a" and "I." The longest word in the *Oxford English Dictionary* has 45 letters: it is "pneumonoultramicroscopicsilicovolcanoconiosis," and means a lung disease caused by inhaling fine dust.

Mental Math

Calculate the mean for the following pairs of numbers:

a) 150 and 170

b) 25 and 35

c) 2000 and 8000

d) 2 and 9

Consider this statement:

"Statistics is one of the most useful branches of mathematics for daily life. It helps us understand the world around us and organize information in ways that make it easier to comprehend."

a) Construct a line plot showing the number of letters per word in the statement quoted above.

b) Calculate the mean, median, and mode of the number of letters per word.

c) Which measure of central tendency is least appropriate to indicate the length of a typical word in this paragraph? Which measure of central tendency is most appropriate to indicate the length of a typical word in this paragraph?

d) What do all three measures of central tendency tell about the data?

 ## Project Activity

Use the set of data you collected in exploration 1.

1. Compute the median, mean, and mode of your data.

2. Determine which of the three measures of central tendency is the most appropriate to interpret the particular data you have chosen. Which is the least appropriate? Explain your answer.

Notebook Assignment

1. Consider the data from the Fifteen Top Medal-Winning Countries, 2002 Winter Olympics table on p. 86.

a) Determine the mean, median, and mode of the number of medals won by the top 15 countries.

b) Which measure of central tendency best represents the "average" number of medals won by the top 15 countries? Explain.

2. Use the data from the Top 25 Albums Sold table on p. 88.

   a) Calculate the mean, median, and mode of the total number of albums sold.

   b) Determine which measure of central tendency best represents the "average" of the number of albums sold. Explain.

3. Why do statisticians use more than one measure of central tendency to describe a set of data?

4. Which of the three measures of central tendency is most suitable to describe the following sets of data? Explain.

   a) the average annual rainfall in Invermere, BC

   b) the average size of T–shirt sold at a fund-raiser

   c) the average number of pages in a daily newspaper

   d) the average mark of a student in a course

   e) the average salary of a company employee

5. For six days, Mr. Chiang recorded the number of tune-ups that he completed at his service station.

Day	Number of Tune-ups
Monday	5
Tuesday	6
Wednesday	6
Thursday	8
Friday	9
Saturday	11

   a) Draw a line plot for these values, and find the mean, median, mode, and range.

   b) Double the value of each number in the set. Draw a line plot of the new data set, and find the mean, median, mode, and range.

   c) How does doubling the number affect the mean, median, mode, and range?

6. Consider the set of data from question 5.

   a) Increase each number in the set by 5. Draw a line plot of the new data set, and find its mean, median, mode, and range.

   b) How does increasing each number by 5 affect the mean, median, mode, and range?

7. Over its first three games of the season, Nick's basketball team scored a mean of 50 points a game. In its fourth game, the team scored 70 points. Since the mean of 50 and 70 is 60, Nick reported that the team's mean over four game was 60 points a game. Is his reasoning correct? Explain.

Extension

8. Using the data in question 7, calculate the team's scoring mean over its first four games.

Exploration 3

Adjusting Measures of Central Tendency

In this exploration, you will explore measures of central tendency in depth.

First, you will compute the mean, median, and mode of data presented in a different tabular form. Then, given particular information about central tendencies, you will create your own data sets. Finally, you will learn a useful skill in computing your own course averages.

Example 1

A computer sales department consists of three levels. At each level, the annual salary for each employee is the same. Salaries are indicated in the table below. Find the mean, median, and mode of the annual salaries.

Level	Number of Employees	Annual Salary of Each Employee
Managers	2	$76,000
Technicians	3	$40,000
Salespeople	5	$28,000

Goals

In this exploration, you will solve problems involving mean, median, and mode.

Solution

The number of employees that earns each wage varies, so you cannot compute the mean by adding the three figures in the third column and dividing by 3. Listed from smallest to largest, the salaries are as follows:

$28,000, $28,000, $28,000, $28,000, $28,000, $40,000, $40,000, $40,000, $76,000, $76,000

Multiply to compute the mean:

$$\text{mean salary} = \frac{(5 \times \$28{,}000) + (3 \times \$40{,}000) + (2 \times \$76{,}000)}{10} = \frac{\$412{,}000}{10}$$

$$= \$41{,}200$$

The mean salary is $41,200.

$$\text{The median salary is } \frac{\$40{,}000 + \$28{,}000}{2} = \$34{,}000.$$

The mode salary is $28,000.

Class Discussion

In example 1, which measure of central tendency could be used to make the salaries appear higher? Which measure could be used to make the salaries appear lower? Which measure best represents the average annual salary of the employees?

Technology

Spreadsheets can be used to find the mean, median, and mode of a set of data.

Example 2

Because he was away from school for several days, Larry Hayton scored only 33% on his first mathematics test. Since then, he has earned marks of 69%, 76%, 72%, and 70%.

   Ms. Van Kirk has agreed to allow Larry to rewrite his first test. What is the lowest mark he can receive in order to obtain a B average (73%)?

Solution

If Larry's mean mark is 73%, it will be calculated in the following way:

$$\text{mean mark} = \frac{\_ + 69 + 76 + 72 + 70}{5} = 73$$

The sum of his marks must be $73 \times 5 = 365$. In other words,

$\_ + 69 + 76 + 72 + 70 = 365$

So his first test mark must be

$\_ = 365 - (69 + 76 + 72 + 70) = 78$

Larry must score 78% on his retest in order to achieve a mean of 73%.

Example 3

Create a list of five numbers from 0 to 10 having the following characteristics:

a) the mean is 6

b) the median is 7

c) the mode is 3

Solution

Write the list from smallest to biggest.
Since the median is 7, choose 7 for the middle number.

___ , ___ , 7, ___ , ___

Since the mode is 3, the lowest two numbers have to be 3.

3, 3, 7, ___ , ___ ,

For the numbers to have a mean of 6, the sum of the numbers must be:

$5 \times 6 = 30$

This is because the mean is calculated as follows.

$$\frac{3 + 3 + 7 +\_ + \_}{5} = 6$$

Thus, $3 + 3 + 7 +\_ + \_ = 30$

Since $3 + 3 + 7 = 13$, the two remaining numbers must total $30 - 13 = 17$.

Two numbers less than 10 that add up to 17 are 8 and 9.

Thus the required list is 3, 3, 7, 8, 9.

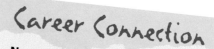

Career Connection

Name: Mimi Beliveau

Job: purchasing agent at a medical laboratory

Current wages: $4,700 a month

Education: grade 12, Certified Professional Purchaser Diploma (through the Purchasing Management Association of Canada)

Keyword search: Canada College purchasing agent course

Notebook Assignment

1. One month, Ian Mead buys two lunches at $2.95 each, five lunches at $3.75 each, and one lunch at $5.25. Find the mean, median, and mode for the amount Ian spends on lunches during the month.

2. Consider the following set of numbers: 12, 34, 30, 16, 23, 18, 23, 28

    a) Calculate the mean, median, and mode.

    b) What do you notice about the mean, median, and mode for this set of numbers?

3. Create a list of seven numbers from 0 to 10 having the following characteristics:
   - the mean is 6
   - the median is 5
   - the mode is 3
   - no number appears more than twice

4. For your answer in question 3, change no more than two numbers so that the following become true:
   - the mean is 5
   - the median is 5
   - the mode is 5
   - no number appears more than twice

5. Varinder Singh receives the following marks on her first four history tests: 85, 75, 84, 54.

   a) What is the lowest mark Varinder can receive on her fifth history test in order to achieve a mean of at least 75%?

   b) Is it realistic for Varinder to expect such a mark?

Extension

6. Mr. Poitras gave five exams for which both Eduardo and Sophie have a mean of 70%. However, Sophie did better on all the exams except one. What could Eduardo's and Sophie's scores be?

7. Complete one of the following scenarios.

Scenario A: Who Wins the Gold?

For some Olympic sports such as gymnastics, a panel of judges rates each athlete's performance. Judges often score a routine out of 10 points.

A gymnast loses 0.10 points for small errors, 0.20 or 0.30 points for medium flaws, and 0.40 for big mistakes. If a gymnast falls, 0.50 points are deducted. Once the deductions are added up, a score is awarded.

Of all the judges' scores, the highest and lowest are thrown out. The eight remaining scores are averaged, making the final score.

Study the scores that ten judges gave to the following three gymnasts.

Olga Pavlova

| 8.8 | 8.7 | 8.6 | 8.8 | 7.5 | 9.2 | 9.0 | 8.9 | 8.6 | 9.1 |

Nadia Ionescu

| 9.4 | 9.6 | 7.5 | 9.0 | 9.2 | 9.2 | 9.5 | 9.1 | 9.4 | 9.4 |

Rita O'Brien

| 9.3 | 9.7 | 8.7 | 8.8 | 9.4 | 9.2 | 9.1 | 9.5 | 9.3 | 9.3 |

a) For each gymnast, make a line plot of the scores.

b) Do any of the sets of data have outliers? If so, state what they are.

c) Without dropping the high and low scores, calculate the mean, median, and mode for each gymnast.

d) Which gymnast would win the gold if the mean was used? The median? The mode?

e) Drop the low and high outliers for each gymnast, and then recalculate the mean, median, and mode.

f) In a real Olympic competition, the mean is used to decide the medal winners. Which gymnast would win the gold medal after the high and low scores are dropped?

g) How is the mean affected by a low outlier? By a high outlier?

h) Explain how dropping a low and high outlier might not affect the mean.

Scenario B: Who Is Right?

Lisa Williams, the president of Greenwood Manufacturing, is negotiating with Andrew Berton, the head of Local 250 of the United Millworkers Union.

Mr. Berton said, "We need a pay increase because of inflation. No person in our union earns more than $50,000 a year."

Technology

For more information on the controversies surrounding scoring in events such as gymnastics or figure skating, search the worldwide web using the keywords "Olympic scoring."

Ms Williams answered, "The cost of doing business has been increasing for our company as well. We have to pay higher prices for our raw materials, so our profits are lower. I don't see how we can afford to give you a raise. Besides, the average salary in our company is over $45,000."

At the next union meeting, a payroll clerk spoke up. "We payroll clerks make only $37,000 a year. Most of the workers in the union make $40,000. We want our pay increased to that level."

Based on the information in the spreadsheet below, who is right, Ms Williams, Mr. Berton, or the sales clerk? Analyze the data and decide.

Payroll Information for Greenwood Manufacturing Ltd.

Type of Job Position	Number of Employees	Salary	Total Salary	Union Member
President	1	$250,000		No
Vice-President	2	$130,000		No
Plant Manager	2	$75,000		No
Supervisor	12	$50,000		Yes
Labourer	30	$40,000		Yes
Payroll Clerk	3	$37,000		Yes
Custodian	5	$35,000		Yes
Sales Clerk	10	$32,000		Yes
Secretary	6	$24,000		Yes
	Total:		Total:	

a) Complete a spreadsheet like the one above to find the total number of employees, and the total amount of salaries paid for the whole company. Then,

    i) determine all three measures of central tendency for all employees; and

    ii) determine all three measures of central tendency for union members only.

b) Why was Ms. Williams able to say that the company's average salary is over $45,000?

c) How many of the company's employees earned more than $45,000? How many earned less?

d) What measure of central tendency did the sales clerk use to justify his statement that most union workers make $40,000?

e) Which measure of central tendency do you think gives the best picture of the salaries of all the company's employees? Of the union members? Explain.

f) Assume that the 24 lowest paid employees had their salaries increased to $40,000.

    i) What would be the new mean, median, and mode for all employees?

    ii) Describe how this salary increase would affect all three measures of central tendency.

    iii) Which measure(s) of central tendency would not change? Explain why.

g) The company wishes to hire more employees. Which "average" is likely to be used in job advertisements?

h) When a company president and a union negotiator each quote a different "average," they are using data for their own reasons. Give an example of a situation where choosing the median would be more accurate than choosing the mode. Explain your answer.

Exploration 4

Using Bar Graphs to Represent Data

You have seen how data can be manipulated by choosing one of the three measures of central tendency to describe it. There are other ways that people can use data to represent a particular point of view.

Here you will learn how to construct an unbiased bar graph that describes a set of data. Then you will create both a bar graph that exaggerates differences among the data and a bar graph that minimizes the differences in data.

Example 1

The table below contains data on criminal code offences committed in Canada between 1996 and 2000. Construct a bar graph that represents this data accurately.

Criminal Code Offences

Year	Number of Offences
1996	2 644 893
1997	2 534 766
1998	2 461 156
1999	2 356 831
2000	2 353 926

Goals

In this exploration, you will learn to construct bar graphs and to analyze misleading bar graphs.

Solution

The first step in creating a bar graph is to identify an appropriate scale. In an unbiased bar graph, the vertical scale usually begins at 0. If you are using ¼ inch graph paper, a good scale might be one tick = 100 000 offenses. This means that the vertical axis will rise to just over 26 ticks. The range of data is 2 644 893 minus 2 353 926, which equals 290 967. The chosen scale will show this range clearly.

By convention, time units are placed horizontally, so the years are distributed along the bottom of the graph.

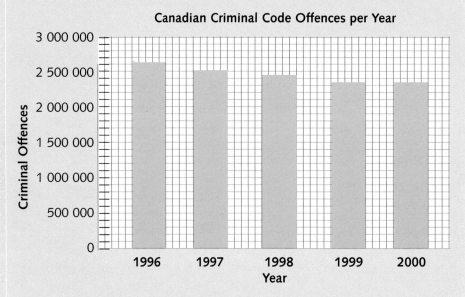

Canadian Criminal Code Offences per Year

This bar graph shows a steady but modest decrease in the Canadian crime rate over the last five years of the twentieth century.

Example 2

The Board of Tourism wishes to demonstrate that the government's policies and practices have caused a dramatic decrease in the crime rate. A statistician has produced this graph for the board. How did the statistician create this impression?

Solution

By starting the vertical scale at 2 200 000 crimes, the difference in criminal offences between years appears much greater than the graph shown in example 1.

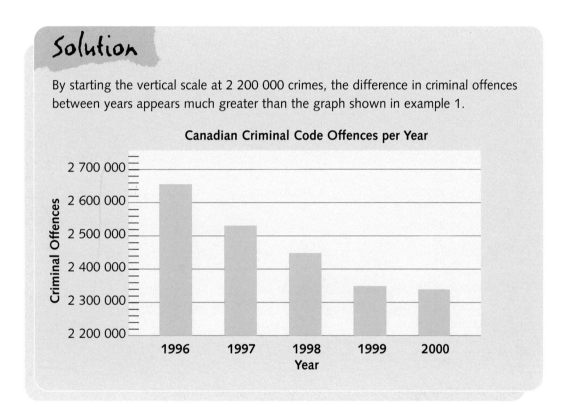

Example 3

A reporter wishes to demonstrate that the decrease in crime from 1996 to 2000 has been small. Accordingly, a newspaper statistician created the following bar graph to display the crime data. How did this statistician create the impression the reporter wished to make?

Solution

By choosing a maximum value of 4 000 000 crimes on the vertical axis, the differences among the years appear much smaller than they do in the graph in example 1.

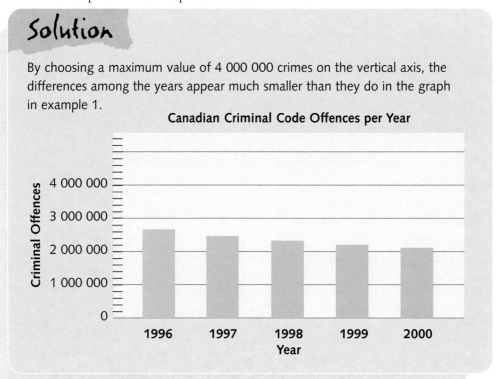

Canadian Criminal Code Offences per Year

Drawing a Bar Graph

To draw an unbiased bar graph, follow these steps:

a) Begin the vertical axis at 0.

b) Make sure the maximum value on the vertical axis is slightly greater than the maximum value of the data.

To draw a bar graph that exaggerates the differences between values, truncate the vertical axis. To do this, follow these steps.

a) Begin the vertical axis at a value just slightly less than the smallest data value.

b) Keep the maximum value close to the maximum value of the data.

To draw a bar graph that downplays the difference between the values, extend the vertical axis. To do this, set up the vertical axis as follows:

a) Begin the vertical axis at 0.

b) Choose a maximum value on the vertical axis that is much greater than the maximum value of the data.

Project Activity

Create an unbiased bar graph that represents the data you have chosen for your project.

1. Briefly summarize the story surrounding the graph you created.

2. Using the same data, construct the following:

a) a bar graph that exaggerates the differences among the data.

b) a bar graph that minimizes the differences among the data.

3. For each bar graph, describe how changes in the vertical scale affect the appearance of the data.

4. Finally, explain why someone might want to intentionally distort the data by

a) dramatizing the differences between the numbers; and

b) downplaying the differences between the numbers.

Technology

There are several computer programs that you can use to construct bar graphs and circle graphs. Most of these programs let you input your data on a spreadsheet first, choose your scale, and label the axes.

Notebook Assignment

1. Using the following table, construct a bar graph that displays this data.

World's Most Widely Spoken Languages

Language	Estimated Number of Speakers
1. Chinese (Mandarin)	1 075 000 000
2. Hindustani	602 000 000
3. English	514 000 000
4. Spanish	425 000 000
5. Russian	275 000 000
6. Arabic	256 000 000
7. Bengali	215 000 000
8. Portuguese	194 000 000
9. Malay–Indonesian	176 000 000
10. French	129 000 000

2. Suppose an IBM executive wishes to downplay the financial differences between his and other companies. Construct a bar graph that appears to minimize these differences.

World's Most Valuable Brands

Brand	Country	Industry	Value (in 000's of Cdn $)
1. Coca-Cola	U.S.	soft drinks	109,000,000
2. Microsoft	U.S.	technology	105,000,000
3. IBM	U.S.	technology	79,800,000
4. Intel	U.S.	technology	58,500,000
5. Nokia	Finland	technology	57,800,000
6. General Electric	U.S.	diverse products	57,200,000
7. Ford	U.S.	autos	54,600,000
8. Disney	U.S.	recreation	50,400,000
9. McDonald's	U.S.	fast food	41,900,000

3. The following is *Forbes Magazine*'s 2001 list of the world's richest people. Construct a bar graph that maximizes the differences between the Walton family's net worth and the wealth of the other billionaires.

World's Richest People

Name	Country	Business	Wealth (in Cdn $)
1. Walton family	U.S.	Wal-Mart	$139,650,000,000
2. Bill Gates	U.S.	Microsoft	$88,050,000,000
3. Warren Buffett	U.S.	Investments	$48,450,000,000
4. Paul Allen	U.S.	Microsoft	$45,600,000,000
5. Lawrence Ellison	U.S.	Oracle	$39,000,000,000
6. T. & K. Albrecht	Germany	Retail	$37,500,000,000
7. Prince Alwaleed	Saudi Arabia	Investments	$30,000,000,000
8. Johanna Quandt	Germany	BMW	$26,700,000,000
9. Steven Ballmer	U.S.	Microsoft	$24,900,000,000
10. Kenneth Thompson	Canada	Publishing	$16,400,000,000

Extension

4. Baljit, Aaron, and Tanya are the leaders in a fund-raising contest. To raise money for the school track team, they are selling bags of compost in their neighbourhoods. Below is a table depicting their sales at the halfway point of the campaign.

Name	Baljit	Tanya	Aaron
Sales	20 bags	30 bags	10 bags

Mr. Magnus, the track coach, produced the following bar graph to depict their progress.

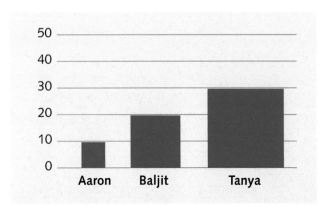

Aaron protested to Mr. Magnus that his bar graph did not fairly describe each student's sales progress. Was he correct? Explain.

Problem Analysis

Timing the Baking

Irene is having a dinner party where she wants to serve two kinds of rolls and one kind of bread. She owns a bread machine and needs to decide when to start preparing everything so the bread and the buns are both done 15 minutes before supper starts.

The bread machine either prepares the rolls to the point where they just need to be formed and then rise the final time, or it prepares bread right through to baking. Preparing the dough takes the bread machine 1 hour and 20 minutes, and baking the bread takes the machine 3 hours and 40 minutes when using fast-rising yeast. Final rising takes at least 1 hour. Baking the rolls in the oven at 375° takes 15 minutes.

How long before the dinner party should Irene start the buns and bread if they are to be ready on time? What other information do you need to solve the problem? What assumptions are you making?

Games

Farm Folly

A farmer looks into a field and she sees a mixture of hens and sheep. She counts the number of the legs of all the animals. There are 100. She counts the heads of the animals; there are 29.

How many sheep and how many hens are in the field?

Note: There are a variety of ways to solve this problem. A spreadsheet might prove useful.

Exploration 5

Using Circle Graphs to Represent Data

You have seen how bar graphs can represent or misrepresent data. Circle graphs can be manipulated in a similar way.

Circle graphs are useful in displaying percentages, or parts of a whole.

Example 1

The following data was collected from a telephone poll of 1000 Canadians. Each person was asked to name his/her favourite spectator sport. Draw a circle graph that represents the data.

Favourite Sport	Number out of 1000
Hockey	450
Football	240
Baseball	120
Basketball	89
Soccer	58
Volleyball	24
Other	19
Total	**1000**

Markus Naslund of the Vancouver Canucks—a favourite of local hockey fans.

Goals

In this exploration, you will learn how to construct an accurate circle graph. You will also investigate how circle graphs might depict data inaccurately.

Solution

A circle graph is like a pie or pizza cut up in pieces. In this example, each piece of the pie will represent one sport. The pieces will vary in size: the most popular sport—hockey—will have the biggest piece. The more popular the sport, the bigger the piece of the pie it will have. The mathematical term for these pieces is "sector."

To construct a circle graph of this data, follow these steps.

a) Express each number as a percent of the total number of people surveyed. For example, 450 out of 1000 people surveyed named hockey. Convert 450 out of 1000 to a percent:

$$\frac{450}{1000} = 0.45 \text{ or } 0.45 \times 100 = 45\%$$

45% of the people surveyed favoured hockey.

The percentages for the other sports are listed in the table below.

Favourite Sport	Number out of 1000	Number as a percent
Hockey	450	45%
Football	240	24%
Baseball	120	12%
Basketball	89	8.9%
Soccer	58	5.8%
Volleyball	24	2.4%
Other	19	1.9%
Total	**1000**	**100%**

continued on the next page

New Terms

sector of a circle: a section of the interior of a circle bounded by 2 radii and the arc between them.

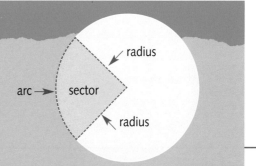

b) Next, express each number as a sector of the circle. Since a complete circle consists of 360°, multiply each percent by 360. For example, the sector devoted to hockey will occupy 45% of the circle. The sector angle will be:

45% × 360°

= 0.45 × 360°

= 162°

You may also use the % key on your calculator.

45 360 162

Likewise, the sector angle for football will be 24 360° = 86°.

Below are the values for the other sector angles.

Favourite Sport	Number out of 1000	Number as a percentage	Sector Angles in Degrees (rounded)
Hockey	450	45%	162°
Football	240	24%	86°
Baseball	120	12%	43°
Basketball	89	8.9%	32°
Soccer	58	5.8%	21°
Volleyball	24	2.4%	9°
Other	19	1.9%	7°
Total	**1000**	**100%**	**360°**

c) Using a protractor, draw an angle of 162° at the centre of the circle. Remember to include a legend for your circle graph.

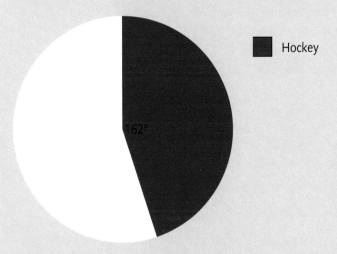

d) Repeat step c) for 86° and each of the other sports in the table. Round off the size of each sector angle to the nearest degree before drawing it with the protractor.

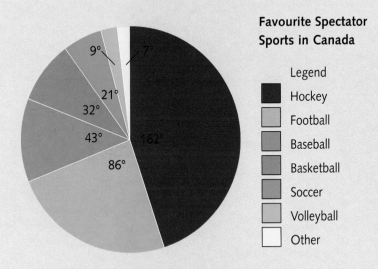

Favourite Spectator Sports in Canada

Legend
- Hockey
- Football
- Baseball
- Basketball
- Soccer
- Volleyball
- Other

e) Finally, include an appropriate title, shading, and a legend.

Classroom Activity

Compare the following circle graphs and discuss the questions that follow.
The graphs represent the top 10 countries of origin for immigrants to
Australia and to Canada.

Immigration to Australia (1999)

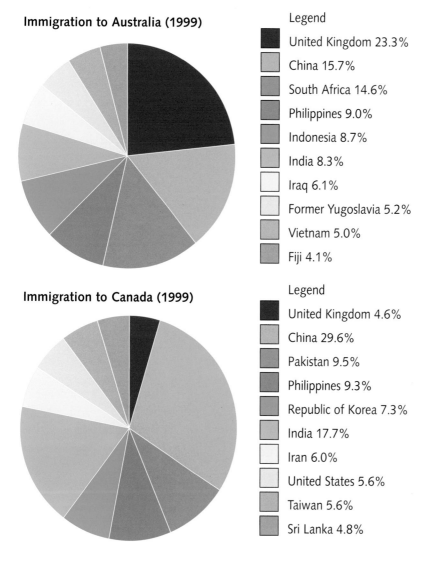

Legend

- United Kingdom 23.3%
- China 15.7%
- South Africa 14.6%
- Philippines 9.0%
- Indonesia 8.7%
- India 8.3%
- Iraq 6.1%
- Former Yugoslavia 5.2%
- Vietnam 5.0%
- Fiji 4.1%

Immigration to Canada (1999)

Legend

- United Kingdom 4.6%
- China 29.6%
- Pakistan 9.5%
- Philippines 9.3%
- Republic of Korea 7.3%
- India 17.7%
- Iran 6.0%
- United States 5.6%
- Taiwan 5.6%
- Sri Lanka 4.8%

*New Canadian
citizens are
welcomed in an
official ceremony.*

1. Which country contributed the most immigrants to Canada in 1999?

2. Which country contributed the most immigrants to Australia in
   1999?

3. Using the circle graphs, compare the percentage of Filipino immigrants to Australia with the percentage of Filipino immigrants to Canada.

4. Using the circle graphs, compare the percentage of Chinese newcomers to Canada with the percentage of Chinese newcomers to Australia.

5. Comment on the percentage of immigrants Canada received from the United Kingdom compared to the percentage of immigrants Australia received from the United Kingdom.

6. The following table contains the actual numbers of immigrants to both countries. Use this data to answer questions 3, 4, and 5 again. How do your answers compare? Explain any differences among them. Why is it sometimes impossible to compare data on circle graphs?

Country of Origin	Immigrants to Australia (1999)	Immigrants to Canada (1999)
United Kingdom	8876	4476
China	5982	29 095
India	3156	17 415
Pakistan	n/a	9285
South Africa	5558	n/a
Philippines	3409	9160
Indonesia	3313	n/a
Iraq	2307	n/a
Iran	n/a	5903
Yugoslavia	1998	n/a
Vietnam	1889	n/a
Republic of Korea	n/a	7212
Sri Lanka	n/a	4719
Taiwan	n/a	5461
United States	n/a	5514
Fiji	1554	n/a
Top 10 Totals	**38 042**	**98 240**

Project Activity

Represent the data from your project as a circle graph. What are the advantages of using a circle graph? What are the disadvantages of using a circle graph? Find examples of circle graphs that present biased and unbiased representation of data, and add them to your project file.

Notebook Assignment

1. The following table lists the population of each Canadian province and the northern territories in 2001. Construct an accurate circle graph to portray this data. Round all percentages to the nearest hundredth, and all angles to the nearest degree. Provide a legend.

Province/Territory	Population
Newfoundland and Labrador	533 800
Prince Edward Island	138 500
Nova Scotia	974 700
New Brunswick	757 100
Québec	7 410 500
Ontario	11 874 400
Manitoba	1 150 000
Saskatchewan	1 015 800
Alberta	3 064 200
British Columbia	4 095 900
Northern Territories	99 000
Total (Canada)	**31 139 900**

2. The following circle graphs represent the sales by all the salespersons of C & D Sound's television department. The graphs display data from 2000 and 2001. Examine the graphs and consider the question that follows.

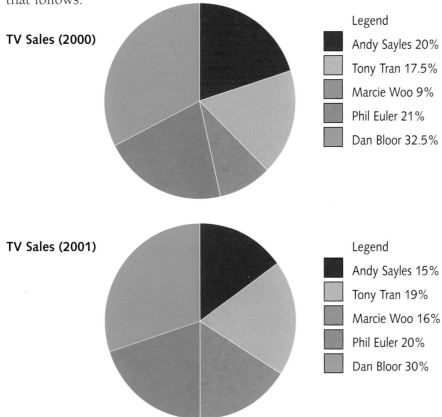

TV Sales (2000)

Legend
- Andy Sayles 20%
- Tony Tran 17.5%
- Marcie Woo 9%
- Phil Euler 21%
- Dan Bloor 32.5%

TV Sales (2001)

Legend
- Andy Sayles 15%
- Tony Tran 19%
- Marcie Woo 16%
- Phil Euler 20%
- Dan Bloor 30%

After studying the graphs, the department manager expressed his disappointment to Andy Sayles about the 5% drop in his sales from 2000 to 2001. Andy found the following actual TV sales figures for the two years.

Year	2000	2001
TV sets sold at C & D	750	1267

Andy thought that his manager could use a course in statistics. What should he tell his manager about his sales record for the two years?

Extension

3. The table below lists the population of Canada's three northern
    territories in 2001. Recall your circle graph from question 1. Should
    you include each of the territories in the same circle graph as the
    provinces? Explain your answer.

Territory	Population in 2001
Yukon	29 900
Northwest Territories	40 900
Nunavut	28 200

Chapter Review

1. The following table lists the Top 10 Point Scorers in an NHL career, up to and including the 2000–2001 season.

Top 10 NHL Point Scorers

Rank	Player	Games	Goals	Assists	Points
1.	Wayne Gretzky	1487	894	1963	2857
2.	Gordie Howe	1767	801	1049	1850
3.	Mark Messier	1561	651	1130	1781
4.	Marcel Dionne	1348	731	1040	1771
5.	Ron Francis	1489	487	1137	1624
6.	Steve Yzerman	1310	645	969	1614
7.	Phil Esposito	1282	717	873	1590
8.	Ray Bourque	1612	410	1169	1579
9.	Mario Lemieux	788	648	922	1570
10.	Paul Coffey	1409	396	1135	1531

a) Construct a line plot of each player's total points.

b) Which clusters are evident from the line plot?

c) Determine the range of values for the total points.

d) Identify any outlier(s) for the data.

e) Identify any noticeable gap(s) in the data.

f) Calculate the mean number of points scored per game for each player. (Round your answers to the nearest tenth.) Does there appear to be a relationship between each player's per game mean and his standing on the Top 10 list?

g) Does there appear to be a relationship between the number of games a player plays and his standing on the Top 10 list?

h) Explain your answers to the last two questions.

2. The following table lists the 10 most expensive paintings ever sold at an auction. Examine the table and answer the questions below.

10 Most Expensive Paintings Ever Sold

Print	Painting/Artist	Date Sold	Price (Cdn $)
1.	*Portrait of Dr. Gachet* Vincent van Gogh (Dutch: 1853–1890)	1990	112,500,000
2.	*Au Moulin de la Galette* Pierre-Auguste Renoir (French: 1841–1919)	1990	106,000,000
3.	*Portrait de l'Artiste sans Barbe* Vincent van Gogh	1998	97,500,000
4.	*Curtain, Pitcher, and Bowl of Fruit* Paul Cézanne (French:1839–1906)	1999	82,500,000
5.	*The Marriage of Pierrette* Pablo Picasso (Spanish: 1881–1973)	1989	77,500,000
6.	*Woman with Crossed Arms* Pablo Picasso	2000	75,000,000
7.	*Irises* Vincent van Gogh	1987	73,500,000
8.	*Woman Sitting in a Garden* Pablo Picasso	1999	67,500,000
9.	*The Dream* Pablo Picasso	1997	66,000,000
10.	*Self Portrait: Yo Picasso* Pablo Picasso	1989	65,500,000

a) Construct a line plot that displays the selling prices.

b) Identify any outlier(s) for the data.

c) What are the most obvious gaps in the data?

d) What clusters are evident?

e) What is the range of the data?

f) Which artist's paintings sold for the most money? How much was paid for all his paintings?

g) Does there appear to be a relationship between the year in which a painting sold and its price? Explain your answer.

3. The heights of six members of a basketball team are as follows:
174 cm, 183 cm, 185 cm, 190 cm, 170 cm, and 174 cm

   a) Calculate the mean, median, and mode of the heights.

   b) A player who is 225 cm tall joins the team. Calculate the new median, mean, and mode.

   c) Which measure of central tendency is most affected by the new data? Explain.

4. Mark Van Rijn receives the following marks on five biology tests: 55, 72, 55, 75, 78. Mark's teacher, Ms. Wise, gives him an average final mark of 67. Mark complains to Ms. Wise and argues that his average final mark should be 72. Ms. Wise tells Mark that if he insists, she will recalculate his final mark. However, the average final mark will be 55.

   a) Can all of these final marks be considered as "averages?" Explain what each mark represents.

   b) Which average do you think best represents Mark's achievement in biology? Explain.

5. Mr. Tzima's class obtained the following scores on a math quiz. Find the mean, median, and mode of the marks. The quiz was out of 10 marks. Explain why the median and mode are so close in value.

Mark	Number of Students	Mark	Number of Students
10	2	5	3
9	4	4	0
8	6	3	1
7	4	2	0
6	7	1	0

6. **a)** Create a list of eight numbers from 0 to 12 having the following characteristics:
    - the mean is 7
    - the median is 7
    - the mode is 5
    - no number appears more than twice

    b) Alter no more than two numbers so that the mean is 7, the median is 7, and the mode is 6.

7. Mary Craig receives the following marks in the first five out of six history tests: 63, 75, 60, 56, 72.

    a) What is the lowest mark Mary can receive on her sixth test in order to receive a mean mark of 70%?

    b) Based on her previous test scores, is such a mark realistic?

8. The following table lists salaries for the executives of Lifeline Enterprises Inc.

Position	Salary
President	$240,000
1st Vice President	$ 90,000
2nd Vice President	$ 90,000
Supervising Manager	$ 75,000
Accounting Manager	$ 60,000
Personnel Manager	$ 60,000

Find the mean, median, and mode. Which measure of central tendency seems to best describe the "average" executive salary for the company?

9. Last month, Mrs. Venucci, a grocer, stocked several can sizes of Ruby
    Tomato Sauce. The sales figures for the month are shown in the table
    below.

Size of Can	Number of Cans Sold
213 mL	10
284 mL	20
398 mL	44
680 mL	61

a) Calculate the mean, median, and mode of the data.

b) Mrs. Vernucci wishes to cut back the variety of sizes and stock
    one size only. What measure of central tendency should she use
    to decide which size to keep? Explain your answer.

10. The following table lists the number of Canadians who were
    unemployed during the years 1996 to 2000.

Year	1996	1997	1998	1999	2000
Number of Unemployed	1 436 900	1 378 600	1 277 300	1 190 100	1 089 600

a) A federal agency wishes to demonstrate that the government's
    policies and practices have caused a dramatic decrease in
    unemployment. Construct a bar graph that emphasizes the
    differences in the values from 1996 to 2000.

b) A member of the opposition wants to point out that the decrease
    in unemployment is really quite insignificant. Devise a bar graph
    that minimizes the differences in the data.

c) Create a bar graph that represents the data fairly and accurately.

11. The following table breaks down the populations of British
Columbia, Nunavut, Northwest Territories, Yukon, and Manitoba
into three age groups.

Age Group	British Columbia	Nunavut	Northwest Territories	Yukon	Manitoba
0–14 years	725 003	10 350	10 923	6 091	238 293
15–64 years	2 830 272	17 068	28 207	22 077	756 272
65 and older	540 659	741	1 730	1 717	155 469
Total	4 095 934	28 159	40 860	29 885	1 150 034

a) Draw five circle graphs: one each for the British Columbia,
Manitoba, Northwest Territories, Nunavut, and Yukon statistics.
For each graph, include a title and an appropriate legend.

b) Based on the circle graphs, Paddy remarked that Nunavut has
more than twice the number of children aged 0 to 14 years that
BC does. How would you respond to his comment?

c) Consider the statistics for people aged 65 and older. Why do you
think the percentages for this age bracket are so low for Yukon,
Nunavut, and Northwest Territories compared to the percentages
for Manitoba and British Columbia?

Project Presentation

Prepare a poster containing a collage of materials from the items you added to your project file. Your poster should contain the following elements:

- a title indicating the theme of your poster
- the data table you selected, along with its source and some of the statistical analysis you completed
- a line plot, a bar graph, and circle graph displaying your data
- examples of graphs that present biased and unbiased representation of the data.

Case Study

Supermarket Scenario

Mr. Khan is the owner of the RightPrice grocery store chain. He was uncertain about the profitability of the CutWell brand of cold meats that his stores carry. Mr. Khan asked his purchasing manager, Ralph Johnson, to investigate the product line and to recommend whether or not the company should continue to carry the line. In response, Ralph looked into the chain's sales history of CutWell cold meats, and conducted a popularity poll of the product in all seven stores.

Ralph presented his boss with the following data analysis.

Report on CutWell Products

Prepared by Ralph Johnson

Sales History

The following bar graph illustrates overall sales of the CutWell product over the last five years. I asked each store meat manager for the store's total sales. For each year, I then graphed the mean sales of all 7 stores.

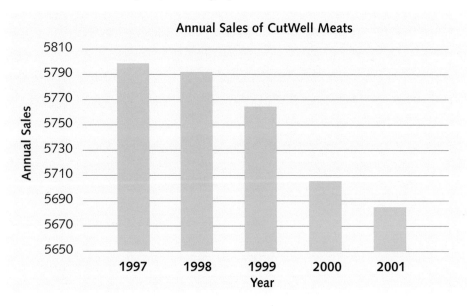

You can see from the bar graph that the total sales of this line are definitely on the decline.

Customer Poll

Each store conducted its own poll to test the popularity of the CutWell line of meats.

I asked each store's assistant meat department manager to interview at least 10 customers on Saturday, January 19, 2002. Because of restricted store space, the surveys took place in the health food department of each store. In each case, the interviewer was the store's health foods assistant manager.

The survey question was as follows.

"How would you rate the quality of CutWell cold meats over the last five years?"

A total of 44 customers were interviewed. The following circle graph illustrates their responses.

Customer Rating of CutWell Meats

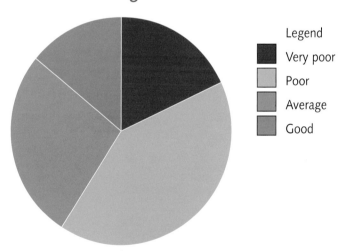

Legend
- Very poor
- Poor
- Average
- Good

On the basis of these statistics, I recommend that we discontinue the CutWell Meats products line.

Respectfully submitted,
Ralph Johnson
RightPrice Purchasing Manager

Mr. Khan was disturbed with the findings. Although he personally thought that CutWell Meats was a fine product, he could not ignore such negative statistics. After all, more than 50% of those surveyed said that the product was "below average." As well, it was obvious from the sales graph that CutWell Meats were on the decline.

Assume you are a product vendor for CutWell Meats. Do a critique of Ralph Johnson's data analysis and interpretation that you hope will convince Mr. Khan to continue selling the product in his store.

Chapter 3
Owning and Operating a Vehicle

A Vehicle of Your Own

In Canada today, vehicles are an essential means of transportation for most people. Vehicles are used for both pleasure and work. In most parts of Canada, people rely on automobiles as their primary means of transportation. In the north, however, snow machines and all-terrain vehicles are more commonly used for transportation. Purchasing and operating a vehicle of your own is a major expense. This chapter looks at the costs involved in owning and operating a vehicle.

Goals

In this chapter, you will learn how to choose a vehicle that suits your needs and to calculate the costs of buying and operating a vehicle and depreciation. You will consider the advantages and disadvantages of new vs. used vehicles, and about financing options and leasing arrangements.

New Terms

operating costs: the operating costs of a vehicle include the costs of fuel, regular maintenance, and repairs, as well as the registration and insurance costs.

Chapter Project

In the project for this chapter, you will choose a new and a used vehicle that you would consider buying. You will research what it would cost to own and operate each of these vehicles.

As you complete the project activities, you will add the following items to your project file:

1. A description of the new and used vehicles you choose to research.

2. An estimate of the fuel costs for each vehicle.

3. An estimate of the typical maintenance costs for each vehicle.

4. A calculation of the typical insurance and registration costs for each vehicle.

5. A list of the cost of options, freight, and other charges required to purchase a new vehicle.

6. An estimate of the value of each vehicle after 1, 2, and 3 years.

7. An estimate of the costs of a loan and other charges required to purchase the new vehicle and the used vehicle.

8. The total costs of purchasing and operating each of the vehicles you have chosen.

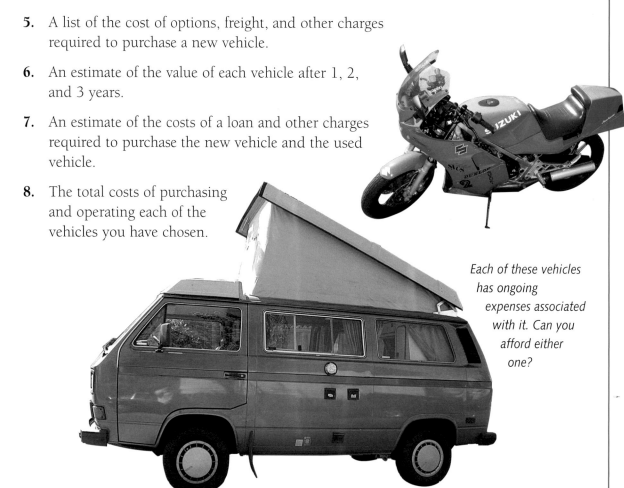

Each of these vehicles has ongoing expenses associated with it. Can you afford either one?

The Selkirk College Aviation program uses Cesna 172s for training flights.

Exploration 1

Choosing a Vehicle

Buying a vehicle is a major purchase involving many decisions. Since a lot of money is spent on a vehicle, it is important to make an informed choice. Choosing the right vehicle demands some time and effort for research. Price, style, gas consumption, maintenance costs, reliability, safety, resale value, and insurance rates should all be considered to make an informed decision.

Small Group Activity

Obtain a copy of a consumer guide magazine or a guidebook on vehicles. Make a list of what is important to look for in a vehicle, for example, the braking system, fuel economy, rusting, resale value, and safety features.

Example 1

If you wish to borrow money to purchase a car, financial planners generally advise that your total monthly debt repayments should be no more than 40% of your net income. If your monthly net income is $1,200.00, what is the maximum monthly debt repayment you can afford?

Solution

40% of $1,200
= 0.4 × $1,200
= $480.00
You can afford a maximum monthly debt repayment of $480.00.

Goals

In this exploration, you will begin to explore how to choose a vehicle and investigate some of the costs of financing a purchase.

Example 2

What is the minimum monthly net income that is needed if you wish to take a loan with monthly repayments of $600?

Solution

40% × N = $600, where N = net income
0.4N = $600

Divide both sides of the equation by 0.4 to find N.

N = $1,500

You should earn at least $1,500 net per month to be able to repay this loan.

GST and PST must be paid on a new or used vehicle purchased from a dealer. In Manitoba and British Columbia, a vehicle purchased privately requires payment only of PST. GST is 7% for all provinces and territories in Canada. Refer to the map on p. 51 to find the PST rates for the provinces and territories.

Example 3

A new SUV is purchased from a dealer in St. Boniface, MB for $45,000. What are the taxes on this purchase? What is the total amount paid?

Solution

The total taxes are:

7% GST + 7% PST = 14%

14% of $45,000
= 0.14 x $45,000
= $6,300

The taxes are $6,300.
The total cost is:
$45,000 + $6,300 = $51,300.

Mental Math

a) Convert the following percents to decimals:

   i) 40%   ii) 8%

b) Convert the following decimals to percents:

   i) 0.5   ii) 1.45   iii) 0.06

Project Activity

a) What is important to you in a vehicle? Before you select a vehicle, decide on your needs as well as the features you would like to have. Use this information to select the vehicles you will research.

b) Make a list of the makes and models of vehicle you would consider buying. Check the internet for information. Try to find consumer reports or consumer guidebooks that describe the type of vehicle you want. What are the advantages and disadvantages of each vehicle?

c) Look through newspapers or magazines or on the internet and choose a new and a used vehicle that you would like to buy. Cut out or find pictures of the vehicles you have chosen and record the make, model, and price of each vehicle you have selected.

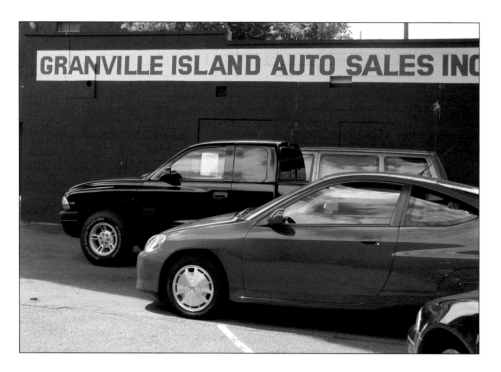

Technology

1. Use "automobile consumer reports" as a search string in a search engine.

2. Check out: http://autosmart.nrcan.gc.ca/

3. The Canadian Automobile Association web site is at www.caa.ca.

Notebook Assignment

1. Are you planning to purchase a vehicle in the near future? About how much are you planning to spend on the vehicle? Do you currently have a job? If you do have a job, how much do you earn on average each month? How much of this will you save each month to buy your vehicle?

2. List as many safety features of a vehicle as you can.

3. What is the maximum debt repayment that is recommended for the following monthly net incomes?

    a) $1,250

    b) $2,050

    c) $3,250

    d) $4,500

    e) $980

4. What is the minimum income that is recommended for each of the following debts?

    a) $350 a month

    b) $520 a month

    c) $680 a month

    d) $850 a month

    e) $1,200 a month

5. A new motorcycle is bought from a BC dealer for $27,480. What are the taxes on this purchase? What is the total cost of the vehicle?

6. A new snowmobile is bought from a dealer for $8,500 in Yukon. What are the taxes on this purchase? What is the total paid?

7. A used truck is bought privately in Manitoba for $25,500. What are the taxes on this purchase? What is the total paid?

8. A used all-terrain vehicle is bought privately for $8,300 in Nunavut. What are the taxes? What is the total paid?

9. A new car is bought from a dealer in Manitoba for $32,500. What are the taxes? What is the total paid?

Extension

10. If you bought a new vehicle for $24,500 in Northwest Territories, Nunavut, or Yukon instead of in Manitoba or British Columbia, how much would you save on taxes? What disadvantages might there be in buying a vehicle from Northwest Territories, Nunavut, or Yukon instead of Manitoba or British Columbia? Do you think a vehicle would cost the same before taxes in all 5 provinces or territories listed? Explain your reasoning.

Exploration 2

Operating a Vehicle: Fuel Economy

A major cost of operating a vehicle is the fuel cost. Different vehicles require different amounts of fuel to drive the same distance. The number of litres of fuel a vehicle needs to travel 100 kilometres is defined as its fuel economy. In the imperial system, fuel consumption is expressed as miles per gallon.

Class Discussion

Brainstorm to find typical gas prices in your region. What are the most and least expensive prices? What different grades of gasoline are available? Why do you think gas prices change over time? What other fuels can be used for vehicles? How much do they cost?

Small Group Activity

Examine a map of Canada that includes a chart showing the distances between major cities. Estimate the following distances.

a) How far is it from your house to your school?

b) Pick several towns or cities in your province or territory and estimate the distances between them.

c) Estimate the driving distance across Canada from the east to the west coast.

d) Estimate the driving distance from the northernmost town accessible by road in Canada to the town which is furthest south.

Goals

In this exploration, you will learn about fuel economy and how to calculate the fuel costs for operating a vehicle.

New Terms

fuel economy: a vehicle that has good fuel economy burns less fuel and therefore costs less to operate than other vehicles. Fuel economy in the metric system is expressed as the number of litres of fuel required to travel 100 kilometres. The formula for fuel economy is:

$$\text{fuel economy} = \frac{\text{litres of fuel used} \times 100}{\text{km driven}}$$

Example 1

A car requires 52 litres of gasoline to fill the tank. If the cost of gasoline is 58.8 cents a litre, calculate the cost to fill the tank.

Solution

58.8¢ a litre = $0.588 a litre.

52 litres cost:

52 × $0.588 = $30.576 or $30.58 (rounded to the nearest cent)

Example 2

Calculate the distance travelled in kilometres, given the following odometer readings:

Initial reading: 012862.8   Final reading: 013639.7

Solution

013639.7 – 012862.8 = 776.9 km travelled

Example 3

Which car has the best fuel economy?
Car A: 8L/100 km
Car B: 6.8L/100 km
Car C: 11.5L/100 km

Hints

Remember to change cents per litre into dollars per litre by dividing by 100. For example:

65.9¢ = 65.9 ÷ 100 = $0.659.

If you know the fuel economy, and the distance travelled in km, you can calculate the amount of fuel required by using the formula:

$$\text{litres of fuel used} = \frac{\text{fuel economy} \times \text{km driven}}{100}$$

Mental Math

a) Change the following amounts given in cents to dollars:

   i) 53.5 cents   ii) 7 cents   iii) 65.8 cents

b) Change the following amounts given in dollars to cents:

   i) $1.25   ii) $0.05   iii) $120

Solution

Car B has the best fuel economy because it only needs 6.8 litres of fuel to travel 100 km. The lower the consumption, the better the fuel economy.

Example 4

A car with a full tank of gas travelled 572 km before stopping at a gas station. If the car requires 41.2 litres of gas to fill the tank, find the fuel economy and the cost of the fuel for the trip if the cost per litre is 56.3¢.

Solution

Use the following formula to calculate the fuel economy:

$$\text{fuel economy} = \frac{\text{litres} \times 100}{\text{kilometres driven}}$$

$$41.2 \times \frac{100}{572} = 7.2 \text{ L/100 km}$$

The cost for fuel is:

$$41.2 \times \$0.563 = \$23.1956 \text{ or } \$23.20 \text{ (rounded to the nearest cent)}$$

It costs \$23.20 to travel 572 km.

Example 5

Gina travelled a total of 350 km in the city, and 200 km on the highway during one week of driving. Her car has a fuel economy of 10.5 L/100 km in the city, and 7.4 L/100 km on the highway. Gasoline costs 62.5 cents per litre. Calculate the number of litres of fuel she used, and the cost of the fuel.

Solution

Use the following formula to calculate the number of litres of fuel required for driving in the city, and for driving on the highway:

$$\text{Litres needed for city} = \frac{10.5}{100} \times 350 = 36.75 \text{ L}$$

$$\text{Litres needed for highway} = \frac{7.4 \text{ L}}{100} \times 200 = 14.8 \text{ L}$$

$$\text{Total litres needed} = 36.75 + 14.8 = 51.55$$

Calculate the cost by multiplying the total litres needed by the cost per litre.
62.5 cents = \$0.625.
Total cost = 51.55 × \$0.625 = \$32.22 (rounded to the nearest cent)

Project Activity

a) Find the fuel economy of the two vehicles you have chosen to research. You may do this by asking a local dealership or by referring to Transport Canada's Fuel Consumption Guide. You may also estimate the fuel consumption by referring to the table below.

Approximate Fuel Economies for Different Types of Vehicles

Type of Vehicle	Fuel Economy–City L/100 km	Fuel Economy–Highway L/100 km
Subcompact	4.5	3.8
Compact	5.4	4.3
Mid-size	6.8	5.5
Full-size	10.5	7.3
Sports	13.4	8.8
Luxury	11.4	8.0
Mini-van	11.7	8.2
4-wheel drive SUV	12.4	8.6
Light-duty truck	6.9	5.8
Heavy-duty truck	16.1	11.2
Moped	2.8	2.8
Motorcycle	4.2	3.5
Snowmobile	n/a	14
All-terrain vehicle	n/a	6.5
Bicycle	0	0

b) Determine the type of fuel used in each vehicle, and the cost per litre for this fuel.

c) Assume that you are driving 32 km each way to work and an average of 50 km each weekend. Calculate the total distance driven in one year, based on 50 weeks of driving to and from work and 50 weekends of driving. Then calculate the distance travelled for a two-week road trip to a destination in Canada. Choose a destination and establish the distance from your home. Complete a table like the one on p. 145 for your project file.

Technology

The web site for the Transport Canada Fuel Consumption Guide is http://autosmart.nrcan.gc.ca/pubs/fcg3_e.cfm

Estimate of Annual Distance Travelled

Day	Distance Travelled
1. Monday to Friday (daily distance × 5)	
2. Saturday and Sunday	
3. Total distance travelled for 1 week (Lines 1+2)	
4. Total distance travelled for 50 weeks (Line 3 x 50)	
5. Distance travelled on 2-week road trip	
6. Total distance travelled in one year (Lines 4 + 5)	

d) Use the fuel economy figures for each of your vehicles and the cost of fuel to estimate both the total number of litres used in one year and the total cost of fuel for one year for each of the vehicles you chose.

e) Divide the total yearly fuel cost from part d) above by 12 to determine the average monthly cost for fuel for each vehicle.

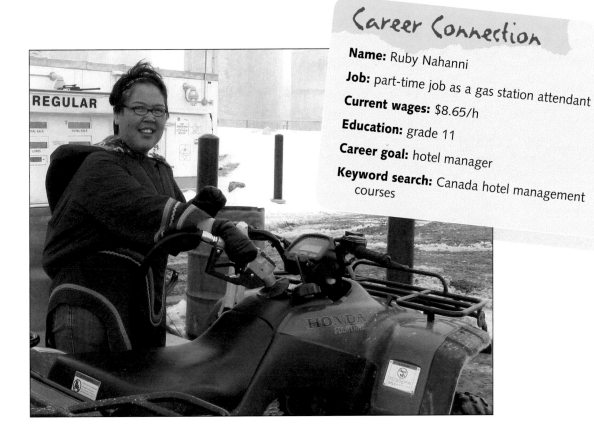

Career Connection

Name: Ruby Nahanni

Job: part-time job as a gas station attendant

Current wages: $8.65/h

Education: grade 11

Career goal: hotel manager

Keyword search: Canada hotel management courses

Notebook Assignment

1. Why do you think a vehicle uses more fuel in the city than on the highway?

2. What is the most expensive price for gas you have seen this year? What is the cheapest? What are some reasons that fuel prices change over a year?

3. Find the cost for each of the following:

	Litres	Cost/Litre	Total Cost
a)	90	55.7¢	
b)	18	46.2¢	
c)	51.3	47.4¢	
d)	87.4	45.2¢	
e)	118	53.4¢	

4. Determine the distance travelled using the odometer readings given below.

a)	Initial reading: 039287.6	Final reading: 040324.3
b)	Initial reading: 076543.2	Final reading: 076956.7
c)	Initial reading: 001279.8	Final reading: 001454.3
d)	Initial reading: 003883.3	Final reading: 007375.2
e)	Initial reading: 123914.5	Final reading: 124721.3

5. Determine the fuel economy for each of the following trips using the odometer readings given.

	Initial	Final	Distance	Litres Used	Fuel Economy
a)	071416.0	071739.0		57.6	
b)	023165.2	023721.9		54.8	
c)	087158.1	088031.4		97.2	
d)	015632.1	016341.8		37.2	
e)	0135714.8	0136028.3		43.9	

6. A pick-up truck travels 92 km on 10 L of gasoline when driven on a smooth, paved road. The truck is only able to travel 78 km on the same amount of gasoline when driven on a gravel road.

    a) Determine the fuel economy of the truck on the paved road.

    b) Determine the fuel economy of the truck on the gravel road.

7. In the city, an SUV requires 29.8 L to travel a distance of 250 km. On the highway, it requires 31.8 L to travel a distance of 340 km.

    a) Determine the fuel economy of the SUV in the city.

    b) Determine the fuel economy of the SUV on the highway.

8. A van requires 46.1 L to drive 380 kilometres.

    a) Determine the fuel economy of the van.

    b) If the cost of gasoline is 58.6¢ per litre, find the cost of driving the van 380 kilometres.

9. Francis travelled a total of 500 km in the city and 1200 km on the highway. His car has a fuel economy of 11.9 L/100 km in the city, and 7.5 L/100 km on the highway. Gasoline costs 60.0 cents per litre. Calculate the number of litres of fuel used, and the cost for the fuel.

10. While on holiday, Qajaq travelled a total of 800 km in the city, and 1000 km on the highway. Her car has a fuel economy of 13.9 L/100 km in the city, and 8.6 L/100 km on the highway. Gasoline costs 65.2 cents per litre. Calculate the number of litres of fuel used, and the cost for the fuel.

Extension

11. Bill travelled in his minivan to a ski area in British Columbia. He kept track of his gas purchases. He left on December 26 with a full tank of gas and an odometer reading of 051372. Use the information in the table to answer the questions that follow.

	Final Reading	Km Driven Since Last Fill	Litres	Cost per Litre	Cost for Gas
a)	051570		27.2	58.3¢	
b)	051727		27.2	58.1¢	
c)	051947		41.8	56.3¢	
d)	052280		51.3	56.3¢	
e)	052565		52.2	55.9¢	
f)	052 848		59.1	55.6¢	
g)	053056		33.1	54.3¢	
	Totals				

a) What was the total quantity of gas purchased?

b) What was the total cost?

c) What was the average fuel economy for the whole trip?

d) What was the average cost per 100 km for the whole trip?

e) Are the gas prices given in this question close to gas prices in your community this month?

f) How much cheaper or more expensive would the trip be using current gas prices?

Exploration 3

Maintaining a Vehicle

An important expense to consider when operating a vehicle is the cost for repairs and maintenance. The older a vehicle, the more likely it is to need repairs. A newer vehicle may be under warranty so that the cost of repairs is covered. However, all vehicles need regular maintenance and servicing. When a vehicle is serviced or repaired, the total bill is based on three factors: parts cost, labour cost, and taxes.

Small Group Activity

Divide the repairs on the list below into 3 categories: routine maintenance, minor repairs, and major repairs. Estimate how much each repair would cost. Does each vary with the type of vehicle? Can you list other maintenance tasks and repairs?

oil change	flush the cooling system
new tires	replace oil filter
replace transmission	replace muffler
tune-up	replace exhaust system
seasonal service	wheel balance
replace wiper blades	replace antifreeze
replace brake pads	replace shocks and springs

Goals

In this exploration, you will consider the costs for the routine maintenance of a vehicle, and the costs for major repairs.

New Terms

warranty: an agreement by the vehicle dealership to pay the costs for repairing a new vehicle if there is a mechanical fault within a specified period of time. Common warranties are three-year warranties and five-year warranties.

labour cost: the amount paid for labour; is normally found by multiplying hours by the rate charged by the repair shop.

Example 1

Jane took her vehicle to a car dealer in Manitoba for servicing. The oil and the oil filter were changed, and new wiper blades were installed. The costs for parts were as follows:

4 litres of oil	$2.05 a litre
1 oil filter	$5.60
2 wiper blades	$14.75 a pair

The time required to service Jane's vehicle was 0.6 hours. The shop rate for labour was $59.00 an hour. How much is this service going to cost Jane? No PST is charged on labour or services in Manitoba.

Solution

Litres of oil (4 × $2.05)	$ 8.20
Oil filter	$ 5.60
Wiper blades	$14.75
Subtotal	**$28.55**
GST ($28.55 × 0.07)	$ 2.00
PST ($28.55 × 0.07)	$ 2.00
Total parts	**$32.55**
Labour ($59.00 × 0.6)	$35.40
GST ($35.40 × 0.07)	$ 2.48
Total labour	**$37.88**
Total cost ($32.55 + $37.88)	**$70.43**

Some garages offer special packages, such as an oil change for $19.95. Such packages may include oil, filter, and labour costs. PST and GST are added to this charge.

New Terms

shop rate: This is the hourly rate charged by a garage to work on a vehicle.

Hints

Although PST is not charged on labour costs in Manitoba, it is added to labour costs in BC.

Career Connection

Name: Ilcia Diaz

Job: vehicle mechanic

Current wages: $23.60/h

Education: grade 12, 3-year diesel/mechanic trades course at community college; currently enrolled in helicopter mechanics course at The British Columbia Institute of Technology

Career goal: helicopter mechanic

Keyword search: helicopter mechanic courses Canada

Project Activity

Determine approximate costs for one year of repairs and maintenance for each of the two vehicles you chose. You may research prices at a local automotive shop or you may estimate the costs using the Automotive Repair Price List. Record your choices in your project file.

a) For your new vehicle, you must change the oil and filters three times, replace the antifreeze once, replace the windshield wipers once, and have a tune-up once during the course of one year.

b) For the used vehicle you must do all of the above, plus you must include one major repair (your choice).

Automotive Repair Price List*

Basic Maintenance

oil change and replace filter	$30 – $70
tune-up	$80 – $185
seasonal service	$30 – $70
wiper blades	$10 – $30
replace antifreeze	$80 – $150

Major Replacement Costs

brakes	$300 – $750
transmission	$1500 – $3,000
suspension	$300 – $500
cooling system	$150 – $320

* approximate costs, including parts and labour

Notebook Assignment

1. What type of vehicles do you think are most expensive to repair, domestic vehicles manufactured by North American companies, or foreign vehicles? Explain your answer.

2. Complete the following chart and calculate the total cost of repairs if the labour costs are $60 an hour. Remember to add the taxes that are applicable in your province or territory.

Item	Number Required	Unit Price	Parts Cost	GST	PST	Installation Time (h)	Labour Cost	GST	PST	Item Total
Oil	4 L	$2.45/L				0.1				
Fuel filter	1	$21.00				0.3				
Air filter	1	$7.00				0.4				
Antifreeze	8 L	$1.98/L				0.1				
Fan belts	2	$29.00				0.2				

Total Cost: $

3. Complete the following chart and calculate the total cost of repairs for an ATV in Nunavut if the labour costs are $85 an hour.

Item	Number Required	Unit Price	Parts Cost	GST	Installation Time (hrs)	Labour Cost	GST	Item Total
Oil	1 L	$3.75/L			0.1			
Oil filter	1	$16.75			0.2			
Muffler	1	$250.00			0.6			
New tires (installed)	4	$80.00			0.4			
Headlights	2	$10.00			0.3			

Total Cost: $

4. Find the total cost of servicing a vehicle in British Columbia that requires two headlights at $28.50 each, an exhaust pipe at $130, and a muffler and tailpipe at $55.50. The time required for servicing the vehicle is 1.6 hours. The rate the service station charges for labour is $55 an hour.

5. Find the total cost of servicing a vehicle in Yukon that requires two litres of oil at $4.10 per litre, two wiper blades at $11.25 a pair, and two fan belts at $35.50 each. The time required to service the vehicle is 0.8 hour. The rate the service station charges for labour is $70.00 an hour.

Extension

6. Use the information in question 3 above. Calculate what the total price, with taxes, would be if these repairs were completed in British Columbia.

Exploration 4

Insuring and Registering Your Vehicle

When you purchase a vehicle you are required by law to register it and to buy licence plates for it, as well as buy insurance for it. Vehicle insurance systems and regulations vary depending on your location. In Manitoba and British Columbia, basic coverage must be purchased from the provincial insurance system: Autopac in Manitoba and ICBC (Insurance Corporation of BC) in British Columbia. In Northwest Territories, Nunavut, and Yukon you may purchase vehicle insurance through private insurance companies.

When you buy vehicle insurance, you pay a premium. The amount of your basic premium depends on how you use your vehicle, where you live, and your claim record. The way you use your vehicle is called its rate class. Typical rate classes are: pleasure use only, driving to and from work or school, and business use. The area where you live is called a territory, and it affects your rates—city rates and rural rates are different. Your driving record is also a big factor that affects your premiums. If you make no at-fault claims over a period of time, your premiums will be reduced. If you have made insurance claims where you are at fault, your premiums will be higher.

Goals

In this exploration, you will learn how vehicle insurance works and how to calculate the costs for insuring and registering your vehicle.

There is a minimum requirement of $200,000 third party liability insurance. This means that if you are responsible for vehicle damage or personal injury to another person, your insurance company will pay the expenses up to the amount of coverage you have. Many people choose higher amounts, and pay higher premiums for the extra coverage.

You can also choose to insure your vehicle against collision and other mishaps such as vandalism, theft, flooding, and so forth. This coverage is called comprehensive or all-perils insurance, and it is optional.

Insurance companies have books of printed tables that can be used to calculate insurance premiums for a particular vehicle and driver. Most calculations, however, are computerized. Insurance brokers enter the relevant information and a computer calculates the premium.
Each province and territory has different prices for registration and licence plates, and the costs vary from year to year. The amount you pay depends upon the type of vehicle and the way it is used.

New Terms

at-fault claims: when you make an insurance claim for an accident that you caused.

basic coverage: the minimum insurance required by law.

collision insurance: this optional insurance covers damages to your vehicle due to a collision.

comprehensive (all-perils) insurance: this optional insurance covers all damages and mishaps (other than collision) that can happen to your vehicle, for example, vandalism, theft, or water damage.

premium: the amount you pay for insurance.

rate class: an insurance category that depends on the area where you live; your rate class affects the cost of your insurance.

rate group: this is a category that depends on the type of vehicle you are insuring; the rate group affects your optional insurance premiums.

third party liability: legal financial responsibility for damage to another person's property, or for personal injury or death; third party insurance will pay for this up to the amount of coverage you choose.

Example 1

Eve buys a four-door, six-cylinder Ford Taurus that has a book value of
$12,550. She wants to use the car to drive to work and for personal use.
In the past five years, she has made no at-fault insurance claims. She
would like a $200 collision deductible, $500 comprehensive deductible
and $3,000,000 third party liability. She lives in a rural area with a
population less than 10 000.

   Determine Eve's annual insurance costs by consulting tables from a
local insurance company and following the instructions given. If her
registration and licence plates cost $35, what will Eve pay for
registration, plates, and insurance?

Solution

The form below shows one example of a completed insurance estimate form. Using a form
from a local insurance company or the internet, look up Eve's territory (rural) and her rate
group (driving to work) and fill in the premium costs for the coverage Eve has selected.

Western INSURANCE COMPANY

Form 1 Insurance Estimate Form

Rate class: 002   Territory: rural   Rate group: 5

Line	Item	Details	Premium Cost
1	Basic coverage	mandatory	$790
2	Third party liability	$3,000,000	$100
3	Collision deductible	$200	$138
4	Comprehensive (all-perils) deductible	$500	$36
5	**Total (without safe driver discount)**		**$1,064**
6	Safe driver discount	– 40%	-$425.60
7	**Total payable**		**$638.40**

The total for registration, licence plates, and insurance is:
$638.40 + $35 = $673.40

New Terms

deductible: when you make a claim on your collision or comprehensive insurance you must pay
the deductible amount yourself; the insurance company pays the balance of the costs.

safe driver discount: a discount you receive if you have a claim-free record over a given period
of time.

Class Activity

Interview at least three people who have vehicles. They can be someone in your family, one of your friends, someone with a private business, someone who has a government vehicle, or someone who has a bus or a taxi.

Ask the following questions:

1. What type of vehicle do you own?

2. What year is this vehicle?

3. Do you have collision and/or comprehensive insurance?

4. Do you get any safe driving discount? If so, what percent discount do you get?

5. What is the total cost for your vehicle's registration and insurance?

    As a class, make a summary of what you learned in your interviews.

Small Group Activity

1. Using an internet search engine, type in the keywords "auto insurance" followed by the name of your province or territory. Research the following questions:

    a) Why is it important to take out insurance on cars, trucks, motorcycles, ATVs, and other vehicles?

    b) What does "third party liability" mean?

    c) What does "comprehensive insurance" mean?

    d) What does "collision insurance" mean?

    e) What does "deductible" mean?

    f) Find out at least two more pieces of information about vehicle insurance.

Technology

Manitoba has a web site where you can estimate insurance premiums by entering details about yourself and your vehicle. It is called an Insurance Rate Calculator. The web site is:

www.mpi.mb.ca/irc/intro.asp?Lang=0

Other useful web sites for research on vehicle insurance are:

1. British Columbia ICBC Insurance: www.icbc.com/Insurance

2. Manitoba Autopac: www.mpi.mb.ca

3. General Information web site: www.royalsunalliance.ca/royalsun/sections/auto_insurance/

2. Determine the annual insurance cost for each vehicle you chose. Assume you have a 10% safe driver discount. Obtain the necessary information by getting a set of insurance tables from a local insurance agency or by going online.

Notebook Assignment

Refer to a set of insurance tables to complete this assignment.

1. If you could choose your own vanity plates, what would you have on them?

2. Why do you think it is important to have third party liability insurance?

3. Looking at insurance company collision tables, which costs more, $200 deductible or $100 deductible? Why do you think this is so?

4. Why do you think insurance costs more in a city than it does in a small town or rural area?

5. Why do you think insurance costs less for pleasure use than for commuting to and from work?

6. How do you think driving safely can affect your insurance premiums?

Auto manufacturers use dummies to test the safety of their vehicles. Crash tests are done to determine the impact of a collision when travelling at different speeds and in different road conditions.

New Terms

book value: a number of different books contain car prices; the black book lists vehicles made in last five years; the red book lists older vehicles; the gold book lists exotic vehicles; the blue book lists older classic vehicles. The book value of a vehicle is the standard price given in these books for a particular vehicle. It may not be the same as the actual selling price.

vanity plates: licence plates that have personalized information rather than an assigned licence number.

7. Andrew has a two-door, six-cylinder Ford Probe GT with a book value of $15,650. He uses this car only for pleasure since he lives within walking distance of his work. He has a 20% safe driver discount and would like basic coverage with $1,000,000 third party liability. He lives in a city with a population of 200 000. What are his insurance costs? If his vehicle registration and plates cost $35, what is the total cost for registration, licence plates, and insurance?

8. Ellen has a station wagon, four-cylinder, Suzuki Tracker with a book value of $4,875. She has no safe driver discounts. She would like $200 deductible collision insurance and $2,000,000 third party liability. She lives in a town with a population of 15 000. What will her insurance costs be if she needs her vehicle to go to and from work? If her registration and plates cost $45, what will the total cost for registration, licence plates, and insurance be?

9. Samantha owns a four-door, six-cylinder, Jeep Cherokee with a book value of $15,680. She lives in a rural area with a population of 6000. She has a 30% safe driver discount. She wants $200 deductible collision insurance, $100 deductible comprehensive insurance, and $2,000,000 third party liability. She wants the coverage for a pleasure vehicle. What will her insurance costs be? If her registration and licence plates cost $35, what will the total cost for registration, plates, and insurance be?

Exploration 5

Buying a New Vehicle

Many decisions must be made before a new vehicle is purchased. There are many makes and models of vehicles, and most have a variety of optional equipment that can be selected. Options are often grouped into option packages for purchasers to select, although options can also be purchased separately. Packages are usually less expensive.

New vehicles are expensive, and it is important to understand all the charges. The charges include the base price, options, freight charges, and a federal air tax, if applicable. (The tax on air-conditioning is also known as the Federal Excise Tax.) Dealerships also charge a documentation fee and they may subtract an allowance for a trade-in vehicle, if you have one.

The sticker price is the full price of the vehicle plus the chosen options. The sticker price of a particular vehicle model is the same at different dealerships, but the actual selling price may vary from dealership to dealership. Special discounts may be offered or consumers may be able to negotiate a lower price. As a consumer, you should check more than one dealership before purchasing a new vehicle.

Goals

In this exploration, you will calculate the total costs for purchasing a new vehicle.

New Terms

base price: the cost of a vehicle with standard equipment.

documentation fee: what you have to pay the dealership for doing the paperwork involved in purchasing a vehicle.

freight charges: the cost of transporting a vehicle from the manufacturer to the dealership.

optional equipment: extras that you can add on to a vehicle.

preferred equipment package: this is a set of optional equipment that can be bought as a "package" for a discounted price.

sticker price: the full asking price of a vehicle suggested by the manufacturer, including the base price plus options plus freight plus an air-conditioning tax if applicable; also called the manufacturer's suggested retail price.

trade-in allowance: the amount that the dealership will give you for your old vehicle.

Small Group Discussion

In small groups, brainstorm and list the advantages and disadvantages of buying a new over a used car. Create a list of possible options that are available on new vehicles. Each group should report back to the class.

Example 1

Find the sticker price for the following two-door Mustang. The base price is $25,880 and it has the following optional equipment:

- a preferred equipment package costing $1,260
- a four-speed automatic transmission costing $995
- an AM/FM stereo with CD player costing $200
  An air tax of $100 and freight of $620 will also be charged.

Solution

Base price	$25,880
Optional equipment ($1,260 + $995 + $200)	$2,455
Air tax	$100
Freight charge	$620
Total price	**$29,055**

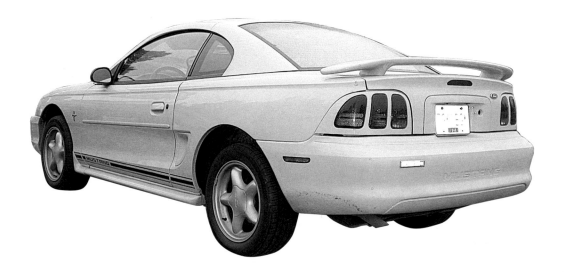

Example 2

Dez is going to buy a two-door Camaro Z28 sport coupe. The base price
is $20,798. He adds an options package that costs $1,585, plus he wants
an automatic transmission for an additional $695. Freight on the car is
$655. The dealership will give him a trade-in allowance of $5,000 on his
old car. There is a documentation fee of $150. Dez lives in Manitoba.
What is the total price he will pay?

Solution

Base price		$20,798
Total options	$1,585 + $695 =	$2,280
Freight charge		$655
Sticker price	$20,798 + $2,280 + $655 =	$23,733
Add documentation fee	$23,733 + $150 =	$23,883
Less trade-in	$23,883 − $5,000 =	$18,883
PST	$18,883 × 0.07 =	$1,321.81
GST	$18,883 × 0.07 =	$1,321.81
Total price	**$18,883 + $1321.81 + $1321.81 =**	**$21,526.62**

Hints

Don't forget that if you choose to have air-
conditioning in your vehicle, you must pay a
federal tax of approximately $100.

Technology

If you wish to find information on the internet
about a particular make and model of vehicle
and its options, go to a search engine, and
then type in the make of the vehicle you wish
to research.

Project Activity

1. Investigate the costs of various options for the new vehicle you chose to research. Most automobile-makers have a web site where you can select a car and options, and find out how much they cost, or you may contact a dealership directly. Pick the options you want and the costs for these options and record your choices in your project file.

2. Research the freight charges, and any other charges applicable on your vehicle.

3. Calculate the sticker price.

4. Research the documentation fee.

5. Imagine that you have a trade-in allowance of $5,000. Calculate the total price of your new vehicle before taxes.

6. Imagine that you manage to negotiate a "deal" for 2% less than the sticker price. Calculate the total price before taxes.

7. Calculate the total price including taxes. Use the tax rates for the province or territory where you live.

Notebook Assignment

1. What is your "dream" vehicle? What options would it have? Draw or describe it.

2. Find the sticker price for the following coupe. The base price is $14,765. Its optional equipment package consists of a preferred equipment package costing $1,730, a three-speed automatic transmission costing $765, an AM/FM stereo with CD player costing $350, a 15-inch steering wheel costing $170, power mirrors costing $150, and a tachometer costing $40. In addition, there is an air tax of $100 and a freight charge of $760.

3. You are buying a new truck. You would like it to have an AM/FM CD stereo system. Your dealer indicates that it is available in the Premier Equipment Package which includes the stereo, automatic transmission, power antenna, and rust protection. This package costs an additional $2,300. What could you do to help you make a decision?

4. Calculate the purchase price of each of the following vehicles if you live in British Columbia.

Vehicle	Base Price	Options & Freight	Sticker Price	Documentation	Cost of Vehicle	Trade-in	PST	GST	Total Price
1	$19,400	$2,230		$150		$5,700			
2	$27,960	$2,760		$185		$9,000			
3	$15,275	$975		$125		$7,200			
4	$22,740	$1,525		$155		$10,000			

5. Sheila lives in Manitoba. She buys a light duty Nissan truck with a base price of $17,218. She gets an option package worth $2,490 plus an optional stereo system for $665. There is a freight charge of $830 and a federal tax of $100 on the air-conditioning unit. How much will she pay for this car including taxes?

6. Andy, who lives in British Columbia, decides to buy a Mustang two-door convertible. He pays the base price of $24,673 and takes an option package worth $2,614. He adds on the automatic transmission for an extra $695. There is a freight charge of $795 and the options package he selects has air conditioning. Andy receives a trade-in allowance of $4,500 for his old car. How much will he pay for his car?

7. Sue, who lives in Nunavut, wants a Tracker. The base price is $19,796. She would like power windows and power locks for an extra $300 and $285 respectively. There is a freight charge of 10% of the base price. She does not require air conditioning. How much will she pay for the vehicle?

Extension

8. A family friend is planning on starting a taxi service in your community. He asks for your recommendations about buying a suitable vehicle. Cost is an important factor, and he hopes to spend less than $25,000. Form a discussion group and reach a consensus on the recommendations you will make to your friend. Justify your recommendations.

Exploration 6

Vehicle Depreciation

All vehicles lose value as they become older. This is called depreciation. A new car often depreciates by between 20% and 30% in its first year, and then by 15% each year after that. The depreciation rate for minivans, trucks, and SUVs may be between 20% and 30% in the first year and 10% each year after that. As a vehicle depreciates, its resale value decreases.

Class Discussion

What does the term depreciation mean? What do you know about depreciation? How might depreciation be a disadvantage when buying a new car?

Goals

In this exploration, you will learn how vehicles lose their value as they get older. You will learn how to calculate the resale value of a vehicle after a given number of years.

New Terms

depreciation: a decrease in the value of something as it gets older.

depreciation rate: the percent rate by which something loses value.

resale value: the value of something after it has depreciated.

Example 1

A new car is sold for $35,000. Calculate the depreciation and the car's resale value at the end of the first three years. The depreciation rate is 20% for the first year and 15% for each year after that.

Solution

First Year:

Depreciation: $35,000 × 0.20 = $7,000
Resale value after 1 year: $35,000 − $7,000 = $28,000

Second Year:

Depreciation: $28,000 × 0.15 = $4,200
Resale value after 2 years: $28,000 − $4,200 = $23,800

Third Year:

Depreciation: $23,800 × 0.15 = $3,570
Resale value after 3 years: $23,800 − $3,750 = $20,230

Example 2

What is the total depreciation after three years for the car in Example 1 above?

Solution

The total depreciation is the original price minus the final value after three years.
$35,000 − $20,230 = $14,770

The car has depreciated $14,770 after 3 years.

Mental Math

Find 10% of the following amounts:

a) $23,500

b) 8500

c) $800

Example 3

Sam purchases a 4-year-old used truck for $10,500. What will Sam's truck be worth after two years if the depreciation rate for this model of truck is 10% a year? What is the total depreciation after two years?

Solution

First year after purchase:

Depreciation: $10,500 × 0.10 = $1,050
Resale value after first year: $10,500 − $1,050 = $9,450

Second year after purchase:

Depreciation: $9,450 × 0.10 = $945
Resale value after second year: $9,450 − $945 = $8,505

Total depreciation: $10,500 − $8,505 = $1,995

Project Activity

Determine the depreciation and the resale values after each of the first three years for each of the vehicles you selected to research. Also determine the total depreciation after three years. Assume a depreciation rate of 25% for the first year of a new vehicle. Assume a depreciation rate of 10% a year after the first year for a minivan, truck, or SUV and 15% a year after the first year for other vehicles.

Notebook Assignment

1. Determine the resale value of the following new vehicles for the years and depreciation rates given.

    a) $17,000 Vibe at the end of three years (first year 20%, 15% a year thereafter).

    b) $16,408 Cavalier at the end of two years (first year 25%, 15% a year thereafter).

    c) $26,433 S10 4WD Extended Cab at the end of five years (first year 20%, 10% a year thereafter).

    d) $38,699 Windstar at the end of four years (first year 30%, 10% a year thereafter).

2. Determine the total depreciation for each of the vehicles in question 1.

3. Determine the resale value of the following used vehicles for the years and depreciation rates given.

    a) $6,000 Nissan light truck three years after purchase (10% depreciation each year).

    b) $3,500 Chevy Impala two years after purchase (15% depreciation each year).

    c) $9,800 Subaru station wagon four years after purchase (10% depreciation each year).

    d) $15,500 Mazda Miata three years after purchase (15% depreciation each year).

Extension

4. A formula for the resale value (V) of a vehicle with price (P) given a depreciation rate (r) as a percent for time (t) years, is given by:

$$V = P(1 - \frac{r}{100})^t$$

Use the formula to calculate the following:

    a) the resale value after six years of a used Toyota Tercel worth $12,800 if the depreciation rate is 15% per year.

    b) the resale value after five years of a new Subaru Outback worth $35,600 if the depreciation rate is 25% for the first year and 10% per year thereafter.

Problem Analysis

Traffic Impedance

Construction on a new high-rise building has resulted in an increased traffic flow from Acme Construction headquarters to the construction site. In the following diagram, 'A' represents Acme Construction headquarters and 'B' represents the construction site. How many different ways are there for Acme Construction workers to get to the construction site if all traffic travels south or east on the streets shown?

Looking at a Simpler Case

Before solving the larger problem, let us look at some simpler cases. To keep track of the possible paths, put a number in each intersection to represent the number of ways traffic can get to that intersection travelling only south or east.

1. How many ways are there to get from A to X?

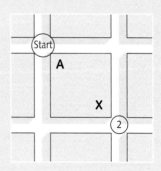

2. How many ways are there to get from A to Y? Explain your answer.

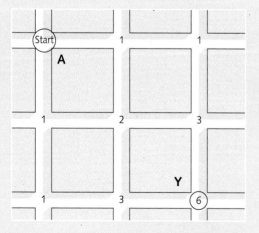

3. Complete the numbers in the grid to find the number of ways from A to B.

4. What pattern(s) do you notice in the numbers at the intersections of these maps?

5. Although traffic in the area is heavy, suppose that street repairs must be made to each intersection in the neighbourhood. One intersection is to be closed on a particular day.

   a) Which intersection should be closed to have the least effect on traffic flowing from Acme Construction to the construction site?

   b) Is there another intersection that, if it were closed, would result in the same minimum traffic impedance? If so, which one(s)?

   c) Which intersection, if closed, would have the greatest effect on the traffic flowing from Acme Construction to the construction site?

   d) Is there another intersection that, if it were closed, would result in the same maximum traffic impedance? If so, which one(s)?

6. Suppose that street repairs must be made to each street in the neighbourhood. One block of street is to be closed on a particular day.

   a) Which block of street should be closed to have the least effect on traffic flowing from Acme Construction to the construction site?

   b) Is there another block of street that, if it were closed, would result in the same minimum traffic impedance? If so, which one(s)?

   c) Which block(s) of street, if closed, would have the greatest effect on the traffic flowing from Acme Construction to the construction site?

   d) Is there another block(s) of street that, if closed, would result in the same maximum traffic impedance? If so, which one(s)?

Exploration 7

●●●●●●●●●●●●●●●●●●

Buying a Used Vehicle

Since a new vehicle depreciates so much in its first year, many people prefer to buy a one- or two-year-old used vehicle. A used vehicle can be difficult to buy for someone who is inexperienced. You must be careful not to buy a "lemon." You can buy a used vehicle from a dealership or privately. When you buy from a dealership it may cost more money than buying privately, but an advantage is that qualified mechanics will have looked over the vehicle. If you buy privately, it is wise to have any car you are considering checked over by a mechanic.

When you buy from a dealership you must pay GST and PST. When you buy privately, you only pay PST. Before you purchase a vehicle, make certain that there are no liens against the vehicle. A lien is a claim on the vehicle by another person to whom the owner owes money. A lien search can be done through a bank and costs about $26.00. When you buy a used vehicle, make sure you have a written contract.

Look over the vehicle carefully. Check for dents and other damage, the mileage, the condition of the tires, and whether the seat belts and instruments work properly. Ask for a test drive. Look for blue smoke from the exhaust, a sign that the engine is burning oil and may be damaged. Get advice by reading through consumer buyers guides such as *Lemon Aid* or *Canadian Consumer.* When in doubt, walk away from the vehicle—there are many more out there waiting for you.

Goals

In this exploration, you will find the total cost for buying used vehicles from a dealer and privately.

New Terms

lien search: a search to see if there is a claim on a vehicle by another person to whom the owner owes money.

If you are buying a car privately the following steps are suggested for calculating what it will cost you:

Step 1 Start with the cost of the vehicle.

Step 2 Will a diagnostic test or any repairs need to be done on the vehicle? Add these costs + PST + GST to the total.

Step 3 Add the PST to the book value of the vehicle (you must pay this when you licence the car).

Step 4 Do you need to carry out a safety check on the vehicle? Add $40.00 + GST.

Step 5 Do you need to do a lien search? Add $26 (including tax).

Step 6 Find the total.

Class Discussion

Brainstorm the advantages and disadvantages of buying a used vehicle rather than a new one, and what to look out for when buying a used vehicle. Make a checklist that shows how to avoid buying a "lemon."

Example 1

Les goes to a reputable dealer in Killarney, MB to buy his car. The sticker price for his car is $5,500. How much will this car cost him?

Solution

The dealer has already checked to ensure there is no lien on the car and that it is in good working order. When purchasing from a dealer, the buyer must pay both PST and GST.

PST: $5,500 \times 0.07 = $385
GST: $5,500 \times 0.07 = $385

The total cost for the car is $5,500 + $385 + $385 = $6,270.

New Terms

diagnostic test: an inspection by a mechanic to evaluate a vehicle.

Example 2

Gordie lives in Victoria, BC. He wants to buy a used car from a private owner, who is asking $1,995 for the car. Gordie needs to do a lien search, which will cost $26. Since he is not a mechanic, he decides to have a $30 diagnostic test done. The mechanic tells him that the car needs some engine work that will cost $650, including labour. When he gets the car licensed, he must pay PST on the book value of the car. The book value is $2,500. He will also have to take the car for a safety inspection. This will be an added $40 plus GST. How much will this car cost Gordie?

Solution

Step 1:	Vehicle Cost	$1,995.00
Step 2:	Diagnostic & Repairs $30.00 + $650.00	$680.00
	GST $680 × 0.07	$47.60
	PST $680 × 0.075	$51.00
	Total Diagnostic/Repair	$778.60
Step 3:	PST on Book Value $2,500 × 0.075	$187.50
Step 4:	Safety Check	$40.00
	GST on Safety Check 40 × 0.07	$2.80
	Total for Safety Check	$42.80
Step 5:	Lien Search	$ 26.00
Step 6:	Total: $1,995.00 + $778.60 + $187.50 + $42.80 + $26	$3,029.90

Project Activity

Calculate the total cost for the used vehicle you chose to research. If you selected a vehicle for sale privately, include the costs for a lien search, a vehicle inspection, and for new brake pads. Include all relevant taxes for your province or territory. You may consider the book value to be the same as the price asked for the vehicle. If you selected a used vehicle for sale through a dealer, you need only include the relevant taxes.

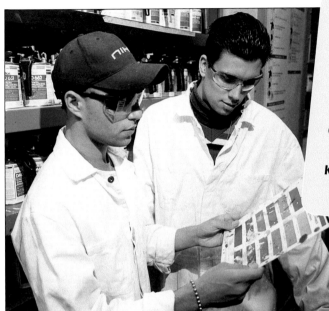

Notebook Assignment

1. If you were choosing a used vehicle, what make and model would you pick?

2. What are the advantages and disadvantages of buying a used vehicle privately rather than through a dealer?

3. Charlene goes to a dealer in Winnipeg to buy a used car. The price for the car is $12,430. How much does she pay including taxes?

4. Calculate the total purchase price of a used truck listed at $7,450 at a licensed automobile dealership in Port Moody, BC.

5. Harry has found a car in Churchill, MB that he likes and wants to buy through a private sale. The price of the car is $2,495. Harry's friend examines the car and recommends that Harry install a new battery for $129 and get a tune-up for a cost of $85. The safety check will cost $40 plus GST. The book value for this car is $2,200. How much will this car cost Harry?

6. Linda buys a car to drive to Yukon College in Carcross, YT. The car itself costs $4,500, a diagnostic test costs $35, and a $26 lien search is done. The safety check costs $40 plus GST. The book value for this car is $5,000. If this car is bought through a private sale, what is the total cost?

7. Scott wants to buy an older car in Prince George, BC. The owner is asking $800. When he has finished repairing the car the following expenses are recorded before taxes: engine work, $700; electrical work, $150; stereo system, $450; tires, $420; interior, $900; exterior, $600; suspension, $150; exhaust, $140; and other repairs, $190. The safety check will cost $40 plus GST. The book value for this car is $1,000. How much will Scott have paid in total for this car? He requires a lien search.

8. Michel wants to buy a fairly new used car. He lives in Coquitlam, BC, and found one in the *Auto Trader* for $9,595. A diagnostic check was done for $35 and a lien search for $26. A safety check was done for $40 plus GST. The book value of this car was $9,600. What will Michel pay?

9. Calculate the total purchase price of a used mid-sized automobile sold privately in Iqaluit. The vendor is asking $5,500. A diagnostic test costs $35. The mechanic reports the automobile does not need any repairs. A safety check costs $40. A lien search costs $26. The book value of the automobile is $5,850.

10. Calculate the total purchase price of a used vehicle sold privately in Inuvik, NT. The vendor is asking $3,600 for the vehicle. A lien search costs $26, and a diagnostic test costs $35. The mechanic reports that the car needs the following repairs: engine work, $50; electrical, $275; suspension, $250; exhaust, $170; and tires, $680. A safety check costs $40. The book value of the vehicle is $3,775.

Extension

11. Elik in Cambridge Bay, NU, has a choice of two all-terrain vehicles. The first is a used ATV sold privately. The price the vendor is asking is $8,000 but the book value of the ATV is $9,500. Elik pays a mechanic $75 to do a diagnostic test on the ATV. The mechanic reports the machine needs engine work for $300 and the front bearings replaced for $250. The second ATV Elik is considering is very similar to the first one, but is available through a dealership. The dealership is listing the ATV at $9,250.

a) Calculate the total purchase price of the ATV sold privately.

b) Calculate the total purchase price of the ATV sold at the dealership.

c) Which ATV is less expensive and by how much?

d) Which of the two ATVs would you choose? Give reasons for your answer.

Dogsleds used to be the standard method of winter travel in Nunavut. Today, snowmobiles and ATVs are more common.

Exploration 8

Taking Out a Loan to Purchase a Vehicle

When you have found a vehicle you wish to buy, and you know the total price, you must decide on how you will pay for it. You can pay for it with cash, or you may finance the vehicle with a loan from a bank, credit union, or through the dealership. You may wish to make a down payment for part of the cost, and then borrow the rest.

Class Discussion

Where can you obtain loans for vehicles? What are typical rates for loans from banks and credit unions? What are typical rates for loans from automobile dealerships? Can you get a better interest rate to buy a new vehicle from a bank or from a dealership? Why do you think dealerships offer such low interest rates for loans on new vehicles?

Dealerships compete aggressively for vehicle buyers.

Goals

In this exploration, you will learn how to find the monthly payment, the total paid, and the finance charge involved when purchasing a vehicle.

New Terms

down payment: an amount paid in cash which goes toward paying for the vehicle; the amount borrowed for a loan is equal to the cost of the car minus the down payment.

Example 1

You wish to take a loan for $15,500 to purchase a used truck. Your monthly payment is $364 for a four-year loan. Calculate the total paid and the financing charge.

Solution

Multiply 4 years by the number of months to get the total number of payments:
4 × 12 = 48 months

Multiply the number of months by the payment amount:
48 months × $364 = $17,472.00

Calculate the finance charge:
$17,472 − $15,500 = $1,972.00

The total paid is $17,472.00 and the financing charge is $1,972.00.

Qualifying for a vehicle loan may be easy, but the monthly payments may be high.

Example 2

Moira makes a down payment of $5,000 on a new mid-sized automobile she purchases for $20,703.54. To finance the remaining amount, she takes out a three-year loan at a fixed interest rate of 8.25% annually. The monthly payment for a $1,000 loan at 8.25% is $31.46.

- **a)** Calculate the principal for the loan she requires.

- **b)** Calculate her monthly payment for the loan.

- **c)** Calculate the total paid for the loan.

- **d)** Calculate her finance charge for the loan.

- **e)** Calculate the total cost of the automobile, including her down payment.

Solution

a) Amount of the loan: $20,703.54 – $5,000 = $15,703.54

b) Since the loan Moira requires is for $15,703.54, the value of $31.46 must be multiplied by $15,703.54 ÷ 1000.

Moira's monthly payment is: $31.46 × $15,703.54 ÷ 1000 = $494.03.

c) Since Moira is repaying the loan in three years, and there are 12 months in a year, she makes a total of 12 × 3 = 36 payments.

The total amount Moira pays for her loan at the end of three years is:
$494.03 × 36 = $17,785.08.

d) The finance charge is: $17,785.08 – $15,703.54 = $2,081.54.

Moira pays an additional $2,081.54 in interest over the three-year period of the loan.

e) The total she pays for the vehicle is the total paid for the loan plus her down payment:
$17,785.08 + $5,000 = $22,785.08

Project Activity

1. For your new vehicle, research the financing rates offered by the dealership you selected. Imagine that you have a down payment of 10% of the purchase price. Use the purchase price of the new car you chose to calculate the following:

   a) the down payment

   b) the amount to be borrowed

   c) the monthly payment

   d) the total paid for the loan

   e) the financing charge

   f) the total paid for the vehicle, including your down payment

   If you cannot find out the financing rate from a dealership, choose one of the following options: 3.0% annually for 2 years or 5.5% annually for 4 years. State the rate you choose.

2. For your used vehicle, imagine you have saved 10% of the cost. Determine the amount you will need to borrow from the bank to finance the balance. Research current bank interest rates for consumer loans. Use the price of the used vehicle you chose to calculate the following:

   a) the down payment

   b) the amount to be borrowed

   c) the monthly payment

   d) the total paid for the loan

   e) the finance charge

   f) the total paid for the vehicle (including your down payment)

   If you cannot find the interest rate for a loan from a bank, use either 6.5% annually over two years or 7.5% annually over four years. State the percent and time period of the loan you are using.

Hints

To calculate the loan payment for a principal of P, multiply the monthly payment found in the table on p. 59 by $P \div 1000$.

Total paid for loan = monthly payment × number of months of loan

Total paid for vehicle = total paid for loan + down payment

Notebook Assignment

1. How much per month can you currently afford to pay for a vehicle loan? Do you have enough for a new or a used vehicle, or can you afford any vehicle right now? Be realistic.

2. Why do you think that vehicle dealerships offer such low interest rates compared to financial institutions?

3. You wish to take a loan for $8,500 to purchase a used car. Your monthly payment is $379 for a two-year loan. Calculate the total paid and the finance charge.

4. Emily wishes to take a loan for $25,535.88 to purchase a new car. Her monthly payment is $800 for a three-year loan. Calculate the total paid and the finance charge.

5. Phil wishes to take a loan for $12,680.25 to purchase a used car. His monthly payment is $306.60 for a four-year loan. Calculate the total paid and the finance charge.

6. Inuujaq is able to make a down payment of $3,000 on a new snowmobile she purchases for $14,500. In order to finance the remaining amount, she takes out a four-year vehicle loan from the dealership at a fixed interest rate of 4.0% annually.

   a) Calculate the principal (amount borrowed) for the loan she requires.

   b) Calculate her monthly payment for the loan.

   c) Calculate the total paid for the loan.

   d) Calculate the finance charge for the loan.

   e) Calculate the total she pays for the snowmobile (including the down payment)

Hints

To calculate 10% of the vehicle price, multiply the price by 0.10. A quick way to do this is to move the decimal point in the price one place to the left. To calculate a loan amount, subtract the down payment from the price of the vehicle.

Mental Math

Calculate 10% of the following amounts:

a) $22,655.20   b) $45,560

7. Sara is able to make a down payment of $6,000 on a new automobile she purchases for $35,265.40. In order to finance the remaining amount, she takes out the dealership's three-year car loan at a fixed interest rate of 3.75% annually.

   a) Calculate the principal for the loan she requires.

   b) Calculate her monthly payment for the loan.

   c) Calculate the total paid for the loan.

   d) Calculate the finance charge for the loan.

   e) Calculate the total she pays for the automobile including the down payment.

8. Chad wishes to purchase a new kayak for $2,800.00. He will make no down payment. He takes out a three-year loan at a fixed interest rate of 3.25% annually from the dealership.

   a) Calculate his monthly payment for the loan.

   b) Calculate the total paid for the loan.

   c) Calculate his finance charge for the loan.

   d) What is the total he pays for the boat?

Extension

9. David wishes to buy a new vehicle from a dealership. He has three options:

   - Pay $32,525 cash for the car.
   - Borrow $32,525 in cash from his bank at 4.5% annually over three years and pay this cash amount to the dealer.
   - Pay $32,525 for the car and finance it through the dealership at 4.5% annually over four years.

   Calculate the total paid for each option. Give the advantages and disadvantages of each option. Which option would you choose and why?

Exploration 9

Leasing a Vehicle

Leasing a vehicle is a popular way to finance a vehicle, especially for businesses. Instead of purchasing a vehicle outright, you can lease a vehicle. When you lease a vehicle you pay a set amount each month for a specified number of months. At the end of this time you can either purchase the vehicle or lease another one. If you choose to purchase the vehicle, you must pay a set price called the residual value.

Advantages to leasing a vehicle are a low or no down payment and low monthly lease payments compared to loans. For businesses, there is also a tax advantage because the monthly payments are a business expense that lowers income tax. With a leased vehicle, you always have a newer vehicle under warranty. A disadvantage is that you do not actually own the vehicle during the time you are leasing, and the vehicle can be more expensive if you choose to buy it outright at the end of the lease term.

If you prefer a new vehicle every two or three years, leasing may be an attractive option. If you plan to keep your vehicle for longer periods of time, then it may be better to buy rather than lease, or lease to buy.

Goals

In this exploration, you will calculate the cost of leasing a vehicle. You will compare the cost of buying to the cost of leasing the same vehicle with an option to purchase.

New Terms

lease term: the time period of a lease in months; common terms are 2 years (24 months) and 3 years (36 months).

lease payment: the monthly payment for the lease; a taxable amount.

residual value: the predicted value of a vehicle at the end of a lease.

Small Group Activity

Obtain newspaper or magazine advertisements offering vehicle leasing. Make a list of the leasing offers for various vehicles. Include the monthly payments, the term of the lease, and the guaranteed residual value from each ad.

Example 1

The following describes a new SUV in Nanaimo, BC. The cost of the vehicle is $34,000 plus taxes (freight is included in this price). The monthly lease payment is $349 plus taxes for a lease term of 36 months. For leasing, a down payment of $3,850 is required. As well, a refundable security deposit of $500 and the first month's payment must be made when the lease is signed. The residual value rate is 75% after three years.

a) Calculate the total monthly lease payment including taxes.

b) Calculate the total lease payment.

c) Calculate the amount which must be paid at the start of the lease.

Solution

a) Total monthly payment: monthly payment + taxes
Taxes are: $349 × 7.5% (PST) = $26.18 and $349 × 7% (GST) = $24.43
Total monthly payment: $349.00 + $26.18 + $24.43 = $399.61

b) Total lease payment: down payment + total payments
Total payments: 36 × $399.61 = $14,385.96
Total lease payment: $3,850 + $14,385.96 = $18,235.96

c) The total to be paid at the start of the lease: down payment + security deposit + one month's payment
Total to be paid at the start: $ 3,850 + $500 + $399.61 = $4,749.61

New Terms

residual value rate: the percent rate used to determine the residual value.

security deposit: a refundable deposit used to pay for the repair of scratches or dents when you return the vehicle.

Example 2

For the vehicle in Example 1 the residual value rate is 75% after 3 years. Calculate the residual value of the vehicle after 3 years (including taxes).

Solution

Residual value = cost of vehicle × residual value rate
              = $34,000 × 0.75 = $25,500

GST on the residual value is $25,500 × 0.07 = $1,785
PST is $25,500 × 0.075 = $1,912.50
Residual value plus tax: $25,500 + $1,785 + $1,912.50 = $29,197.50

Example 3

For the vehicle in Example 1 above, at the end of the three-year lease you have the option of returning the vehicle or purchasing it for its residual value. Calculate the total price you would pay for the vehicle if you purchase it after the three-year lease is over.

Solution

Total cost of purchasing leased vehicle is:
total lease payment (incl. taxes) + residual value (incl. taxes)
$18,235.96 + $29,197.50 = $47,433.46

Hints

a) Total monthly payment: monthly payment + taxes.

b) Total lease payment: down payment + number of months × total monthly payment.

c) Total residual value: price of vehicle × residual value rate (as a decimal) + taxes.

d) Total cost to purchase: total residual value + total lease payment.

Notebook Assignment

1. A vehicle in Steinbach, MB, has the following lease agreement:

Down payment	$3,000
Lease payment	$250 a month
Lease term	24 months
Security deposit	$500

   a) Calculate the total monthly lease payment including taxes.

   b) Calculate the total lease payment.

   c) Calculate the amount that must be paid at the start of the lease.

2. A vehicle in Whitehorse has the following lease agreement:

Down payment	$2,500
Lease payment	$195 a month
Lease term	36 months
Security deposit	$500

   a) Calculate the total monthly lease payment including taxes.

   b) Calculate the total lease payment.

   c) Calculate the amount that must be paid at the start of the lease.

3. A lease vehicle in Flin Flon, MB, is priced at $35,500. The residual value rate is 70% after four years. What is the residual value including taxes?

4. A lease vehicle is priced at $28,800 in Salmon Arm, BC. The residual value rate is 75% after two years. What is the residual value including taxes?

5. A government-leased vehicle in Wha Ti, NT, has a residual value of $29,552.77 (taxes included) and total lease payments of $16,545.15 (taxes included). What will be the total cost of purchasing this leased vehicle after the lease term ends?

6. An SUV in Iqaluit sells for $34,200 and leases for $348 per month plus tax for a 48-month lease. A down payment of $3,500 is required. The guaranteed residual value of the SUV at the end of the lease is $16,526. Determine the total lease payment and the total cost of the SUV if it is purchased at the end of the lease.

7. A 4 x 4 pickup in Rankin Inlet, NT, leases for $329 a month plus taxes for a lease term of 30 months. A down payment of $3,500 is required. The sale price is $30,050 and the guaranteed residual value rate is 75%.

    a) Calculate the total lease monthly payment.

    b) Calculate the total lease payment over the term of the lease.

    c) Calculate the guaranteed residual value.

    d) Calculate the total cost if the vehicle is purchased outright at the end of the lease.

    e) Calculate the difference between the total cost if the vehicle is purchased outright at the end of the lease and the cost of the vehicle if it is purchased outright at time of purchase.

Extension

8. A Honda Odyssey minivan in Prince George, BC, leases for $260 per month plus taxes for a four-year lease. A down payment of $2,800 is required. The residual value of the vehicle at the end of the lease is $15,602 before taxes.

    a) Determine the total lease payment and the total cost if the vehicle is purchased at the end of the lease.

    b) The selling price for the Honda Odyssey is $25,500 plus taxes. Honda is currently offering a four-year loan at 4.5% with a down payment of $2,000. Calculate the total cost of this vehicle if it is paid for by this loan.

    c) If you had to choose between leasing this vehicle and then purchasing it at the end of the lease period or buying it with the loan, which would you do? Explain your answer.

    d) What do you think are the advantages and disadvantages of leasing a vehicle?

Chapter Review

1. What minimum monthly net income is recommended if you wish to take out a loan with payments of $580 a month?

2. A car with a full tank of gas travelled 600 km before stopping for gas. The car required 50 litres of gas and the cost of gas was 65.5 cents per litre. Find the fuel economy and the cost per 100 km.

3. A car with a fuel economy of 15 litres per 100 km in the city travels 80 km during a one-week period. The cost for gas is 54.8 cents per litre. Find the number of litres of gas used, and the cost of the gas.

4. Toby took his car in for servicing in Pelican Narrows, MB. The oil and filter were changed, and the vehicle had a routine inspection. It was found that the brakes needed adjustment. Four litres of oil at $2.55 per litre were needed. The filter cost was $6.75. It took 1.75 hours for the routine inspection, brake adjustment, and the oil and filter change. The shop rate for labour was $63 per hour. Calculate the total bill including taxes that Toby had to pay.

5. Estimate the cost of registration and insurance using an insurance estimate form for a truck with a book value of $8,550 which is used for business purposes in a rural area in B.C. You wish to take out $1,000,000 third party liability insurance, and to have $200 collision deductible and $500 comprehensive deductible. You have a safe driver discount of 30%. The registration and licence plate costs are $35.00.

6. An NHL hockey player in Vancouver, BC would like to buy a Porsche Boxster. The base price is $75,300. He wants heated leather seats, a leather steering wheel, a four-speaker CD player, and automatic air-conditioning and temperature control. These options cost a total of $5,500. There is an air tax of $100, a freight charge of $750, and a documentation fee of $180. Calculate the sticker price, and the total price after taxes.

7. A new car worth $31,400 depreciates by 20% in its first year, and then by 15% a year after that. What is the value of the car after 4 years? What is the total depreciation after 4 years?

8. You have a choice of two cars in Naramata, BC. One is a private sale for $4,465. A diagnostic check would need to be done for $35 and a lien search for $26. You will have to buy two new tires for $275. A safety check that costs $40 plus GST will need to be done. The book value of this car is $5,000. The other car can be bought through a used car dealer on sale for $4,900. Which is the better buy and by how much? Which car would you buy?

9. Catherine wishes to buy a car. She is considering the following two options:

    • A new Subaru Outback through a dealership for a total of $31,450. The dealership offers financing at 3% annually over three years. There is a five-year warranty on this vehicle. She has a down payment of $3,000.
    • A two-year-old used Subaru Outback for a total of $24,800. She has a down payment of $3,000, but will have to borrow the rest from her bank at 5.5% annually for three years. There are three years left on the warranty for this vehicle.

    Calculate the total paid for each option. State the advantages and disadvantages of each option. Which option would you choose, and why?

10. The monthly lease payment on a two-door sedan in Fort Simpson, NT, is $203.79 a month plus taxes for a term of 60 months. A down payment of $2,175 is required. The sale price is $25,000 and the guaranteed residual value is 58%.

    a) Calculate the total lease payment over the term of the lease.

    b) Calculate the total cost if the sedan is purchased outright at the end of the lease.

Project Presentation

For each of the two vehicles you chose to research, organize the information from your project file as indicated below:

1. description of vehicles (year, make, model)

2. ad for vehicles

3. list of options purchased, freight charges, and documentation fee (for the new vehicle only)

4. cost for lien search, vehicle inspection, and brake pads (for the used vehicle bought privately only)

5. total purchase prices including taxes

6. total cost per month and cost per year to purchase and operate the vehicles. Fill in a table like the one below:

	New Vehicle		Used Vehicle	
	Cost per month	Cost per year	Cost per month	Cost per year
Loan payment				
Insurance				
Fuel				
Maintenance and repairs				
Total				

7. Determine answers for each of the following:

   a) the value of vehicles after each year for three years

   b) information on fuel economy

   c) estimated distance travelled in one year

   d) any other information on the vehicles you feel is pertinent to the project.

8. If you had to purchase one of your vehicles, which one would you select? Why? Give multiple reasons.

Case Study

● ● ● ● ● ● ● ● ● ● ● ● ● ● ●

8-YEAR-OLD FORD BRONCO, 180,000 km, good condition, little rust. $5,500 obo. Contact David Snowbird in Qualicum Beach, BC: 250-314-1592.

1. Landon wishes to purchase the vehicle in this ad privately. He manages to reduce the asking price by 5%. What will he be able to buy the car for before tax? How much must he pay for the car including tax? Note that when you buy a used vehicle privately in BC you pay PST but not GST.

2. He must do a lien search for $26 and have a vehicle inspection for $30. The inspection shows that he must have $350 worth of repairs done. This price includes shop time and parts. How much will it cost for the lien search, inspection, and repairs if he has to pay taxes on the inspection and repairs?

3. How much will the vehicle cost including the lien search as well as the inspection and repairs?

4. Landon has saved $1,000, but he must borrow the balance from his bank at 6.5% annually, paid monthly. How much does he need to borrow? What will his monthly payment be if the loan is for 1 year? How much will he pay in total for the loan?

5. Landon lives in Parksville, BC, a small town of 4000 people. He wishes to use his vehicle for pleasure only, and he has a 10% discount. He wishes to extend his third party liability to $1,000,000 and to have a $200 collision deductible and a $200 comprehensive deductible. It costs $45 for registration and licence plates. What will his total cost for insurance, registration, and plates for the year be?

6. Landon's car averages 8.5 litres/100 km and he plans to drive approximately 14 000 km in one year. What will his fuel costs for the year be? Use current fuel prices for your area.

7. He estimates that his regular maintenance and repairs will be $600 a year. What will his total costs for the year be, including his loan, insurance, fuel, and maintenance and repairs?

8. His vehicle depreciates by 10% per year. What will it be worth after one year?

Chapter 4
Measurement Technology

From Feet to Metres

Many aspects of our lives involve measurement. How far can you throw a baseball? How tall are you?

Two measurement systems are commonly used in Canada, the *Système internationale d'unités,* known as the metric system, and the imperial system. In the imperial system, used in the United States and Great Britain, measurements are made using units such as feet, pounds, and gallons. Canada uses the metric system, as do most other countries around the world. In the metric system, measurements are made in metres, grams, and litres.

Measurements can be estimated or determined through the use of appropriate technology. Many occupations require the accurate use of this technology to determine measurements.

Measuring tapes used for sewing commonly have both metric and imperial measurements.

Goals

In this chapter, you will practise making measurements in both the metric and imperial systems, and you will convert measurements from one system to the other. You will use rulers, Vernier calipers, and micrometers to find exact measurements.

Chapter Project

In this project, you will play the role of a student wildlife technician at a wildlife park. Your job is to conduct a simulation experiment that demonstrates the effects of the pesticide DDT on the thickness of eggshells. The thickness of eggshells has an important impact on whether the chicks inside will survive or not.

You will display the results of your experiment on an informational poster that will be posted in the park's information kiosk.

As you work on the project, you will add the following items to your project file:

1. A report on the effects of the pesticide DDT on bird populations.

2. The results of an experiment that simulates the effects of DDT on egg size.

3. The results of an experiment that simulates the effects of DDT on eggshell thickness.

Career Connection

Name: Kevin Jacobson

Job: forestry technician

Current wages: $15.50/hour

Education: high school graduation; Forest Resource Technician diploma at British Columbia Institute of Technology

Career goal: owner of an ecotourism company

Keyword search: Canada college forestry technician course

Exploration 1

• • • • • • • • • • • • • • • • • •

The History of Measurement

When people first began to take measurements, they used parts of their bodies as measuring devices, for example, their fingers, hands, and feet. Some measurements that were developed based on human bodies included: a digit, a hand, a span, and a cubit.

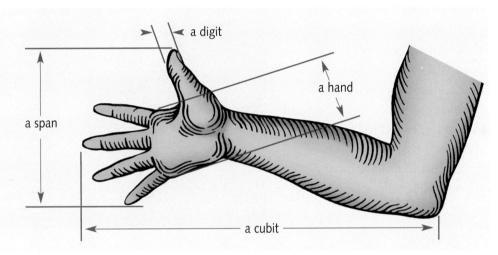

This kind of measurement lacks consistency because people's bodies are of varying sizes. Gradually, these units of measurement were standardized. For example, the ancient Egyptians used the cubit in two forms. The short cubit was about 45 centimetres long and the royal cubit was about 52 centimetres long. The royal cubit was used to make measurements while the pyramids were built.

Two systems became widely used in the modern world, the imperial system, and the *Système internationale d'unités*, or metric system. Today, the metric system is the dominant system in Canada but until 1980, Canadians mainly used the imperial system. Canadians still use the imperial system for certain measurements because the United States, an important trade partner for Canada, uses this system.

Goals

In this exploration, you will learn about the history of measurement systems.

The Imperial System

The primary unit for measuring length in the imperial system is the foot, which is subdivided into 12 equal parts called inches. Another unit of the imperial system is the yard, which is three feet long. Longer distances in the imperial system are measured in miles. A mile is 5280 feet long.

Some other units of measurement based on the human body are still used today but are less well known. For example, the height of horses is measured in "hands." At one time, a hand would have varied but it has now been standardized at four inches.

The fathom is a measurement unit once used to measure the depth of water from a boat. A stone or piece of lead would be attached to a rope and thrown into the sea. As it was pulled out, a sailor would measure it by counting off lengths of his outstretched arms. A fathom was standardized at six feet.

Classroom Activity

Measure the items listed below using the original body parts that underlay the measurement units listed. Record the measurements made by each person on the board and compare them. Did everyone get the same measure? How could you measure each of the items so that everyone gets the same measure?

Oreo, Rachel's National Show Horse, is 15.3 hands high, measured to her withers. Rachel is 17.1 hands high, measured to the top of her head.

Distance	Unit	Class Measure
distance around the class	fathom	
height of classroom door	span	
length of the spine of this book	digit	
height of teacher's desk	hand	

The Système internationale d'unités or Metric System

The *Système internationale d'unités* was developed in France because of a widespread desire to create a uniform system of measurement. It is abbreviated "SI" but is often called the metric system in English. The metric system was gradually adopted by most other countries and today, most countries use it to make measurements.

The metric system is an efficient system because it is based on decimal numbering. This means that metric measurements are multiples of 10 and can easily be converted from one unit to another by multiplying or dividing by a factor of 10.

The primary unit for measuring length is the metre. Listed below are prefixes used before the word "metre" in the metric system to indicate other measures in the system and their relationship to the metre. For example, the prefix "centi" means one-hundredth and a centimetre is one-hundredth of a metre. "Milli" means one-thousandth and a millimetre is one-thousandth of a metre. "Kilo," on the other hand, means a thousand times, so a kilometre is one thousand metres. Refer to a ruler calibrated in metric units and examine the length of a centimetre and a millimetre.

Metric System Prefixes	Prefix Factor
tera	1 000 000 000 000
giga	1 000 000 000
mega	1 000 000
kilo	1 000
hecto	100
deca	10
deci	0.1
centi	0.01
milli	0.001
micro	0.000 001
nano	0.000 000 001
pico	0.000 000 000 001

Career Connection

Name: Mike Tanchak

Job: roofer

Current wages: $11.50 an hour

Education: high school graduation; certificate program in Carpentry and Residential Construction, Malaspina University–College, Nanaimo, BC

Career goal: to operate his own roofing business

Keyword search: Canada college carpentry and construction program

Project Activity

You will begin the project by researching the effects of the pesticide DDT on bird populations. You may use books or the internet to conduct your research. One important book on this topic is *Silent Spring,* written by Rachel Carson and published in 1962. Compile the results of your research into a short report on the historical effects of DDT on bird populations.

Notebook Assignment

1. Estimate which of the following lengths is greater. Then measure with a string to find out which is actually greater:

    a) your foot length or the length around your ankle

    b) your arm span or your height

    c) your hand span or your foot length

2. Compare the following measures to those of the metric measuring system. Write a statement expressing these comparisons:

    a) the length of your pace compared to a metre

    b) the width of your small fingernail compared to a centimetre

3. Compare the following measures to those of the imperial measuring system. Write a statement expressing these comparisons:

    a) the width of your thumb compared to an inch

    b) the length of your foot compared to a foot

    c) the distance from your nose to the fingertip of your outstretched hand compared to a yard

    d) the width of your hand compared to the hand used to measure horses

4. One way you can estimate measurement is to use a reference that will represent one unit of measure. Identify a reference for each of the following measurements in the metric system. You can use this reference to estimate when you do not have a measuring device. An example of a reference is "the length of my pace is equal to one metre."

    a) metre

    b) centimetre

    c) millimetre

5. Identify a reference for each of the following measurements in the imperial system.

    a) foot

    b) inch

    c) yard

6. Describe how you might estimate the following:

   a) the width of a textbook

   b) the distance around a city block

   c) the height of a tree

7. Determine the most suitable units in both the metric and imperial systems for measuring the following items:

   a) the height of a person

   b) the width of a television screen

   c) the length of a staple

   d) the distance from Brandon, MB, to Portage la Prairie, MB

   e) the height of a pop can

   f) the length of a sheet of curling ice

Extension

8. Samuel Langhorne Clemens is the well-known author of the classic tale *Tom Sawyer*. He is better known by his pen name of Mark Twain. He derived his name from a term used by the riverboat captains. The riverboats continuously checked the depth of the water on the river. They could not continue if the depth of the water was less than two fathoms. When they found the depth of the water was two fathoms deep, they would call out "mark twain," meaning mark two fathoms. Clemens chose Mark Twain as his pen name. How many feet do two fathoms of water represent? What do you think the draft of the ship might be?

Measuring the depth of the water is important for fishing trawlers as well as riverboats.

Exploration 2

•••••••••••••••••••••

Measurement in the Metric and Imperial Systems

Shown below is a ruler marked with the common units of linear measurement in both centimetres and inches. Note that each centimetre ($\frac{1}{100}$ of a metre) is subdivided into 10 parts, allowing for measurements to the nearest millimetre ($\frac{1}{1000}$ of a metre). Note also that each inch is subdivided into 16 parts, indicating that measurements can be made to the nearest $\frac{1}{16}$ of an inch. Longer tick marks are used to indicate $\frac{1}{8}$, $\frac{1}{4}$, and $\frac{1}{2}$ of each inch.

Calculations in the imperial system require you to manipulate fractions. These calculations can be done using the $\boxed{A\frac{b}{c}}$ key on a scientific calculator.

Goals

In this exploration, you will measure lengths in both the metric and imperial systems and solve measurement problems in both metric and imperial units.

Example 1

Find the measurements represented by each of the arrows on the ruler below.

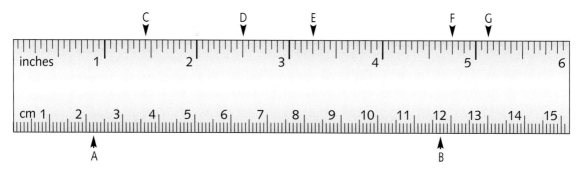

Solution

A represents a measurement of 22 mm.

B represents a measurement of 117 mm.

C represents a measurement of $1\frac{7}{16}$".

D represents a measurement of $2\frac{1}{2}$".

E represents a measurement of $3\frac{1}{4}$".

F represents a measurement of $4\frac{3}{4}$".

G represents a measurement of $5\frac{1}{8}$".

Example 2

Perform the indicated operations on the following fractions using a scientific calculator.

a) $\dfrac{5}{16} + \dfrac{7}{16}$

b) $\dfrac{3}{8} + \dfrac{1}{2}$

c) $1\dfrac{1}{2} \times 3\dfrac{11}{16}$

Solution

a) Calculations with fractions can be performed with a scientific calculator having a $\boxed{A^b/_c}$ key. To enter the fraction $\dfrac{5}{16}$ using such a calculator, press the following keys:

5 $\boxed{A^b/_c}$ 16 $\boxed{=}$

The display of the calculator indicates the fraction $\dfrac{5}{16}$ by 5 $\boxed{\lrcorner}$ 16. To add $\dfrac{5}{16}$ and $\dfrac{7}{16}$, press the keys:

5 $\boxed{A^b/_c}$ 16 $\boxed{+}$ 7 $\boxed{A^b/_c}$ 16 $\boxed{=}$

The display on your calculator will read 3 $\boxed{\lrcorner}$ 4, showing that the answer is a fraction.

b) You can add the fractions in b) by pressing the following keys on your calculator:

3 $\boxed{A^b/_c}$ 8 $\boxed{+}$ 1 $\boxed{A^b/_c}$ 2 $\boxed{=}$

The display on your calculator will read 7 $\boxed{\lrcorner}$ 8, indicating an answer of $\dfrac{7}{8}$.

c) You can add the fractions in c) by pressing the following keys on your calculator:

1 $\boxed{A^b/_c}$ 1 $\boxed{A^b/_c}$ 2 $\boxed{\times}$ 3 $\boxed{A^b/_c}$ 11 $\boxed{A^b/_c}$ 16 $\boxed{=}$

The display on your calculator will read 5 $\boxed{\lrcorner}$ 17 $\boxed{\lrcorner}$ 32, indicating an answer 5$\dfrac{17}{32}$.

Example 3

Find the area of the figure below to the nearest $\frac{1}{16}$ in^2.

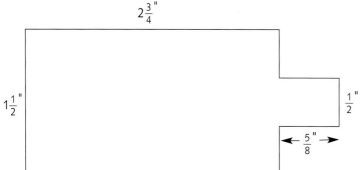

Solution

Divide the area of the figure into two rectangular regions, Area 1 and Area 2. The area of a rectangular region is found by multiplying the length times the width, A = *l* x w.

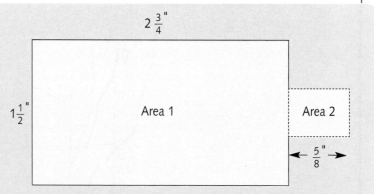

Area 1 = *l* x w

$= (2\frac{3}{4}$ in) x $(1\frac{1}{2}$ in)

= 2 [A♭/c] 3 [A♭/c] 4 [x] 1 [A♭/c] 1 [A♭/c] 2 [=]

= 4 [⌐] 1 [⌐] 8

$= 4\frac{1}{8}$ in^2

Area 2 = *l* x w

$= (\frac{1}{2}$ in) x $(\frac{5}{8}$ in)

= 1 [A♭/c] 2 [x] 5 [A♭/c] 8 [=]

= 5 [⌐] 16

$= \frac{5}{16}$ in^2

To find the area of the entire figure, add Area 1 and Area 2:

4 [A♭/c] 1 [A♭/c] 8 [+] 5 [A♭/c] 16 [=]

= 4 [⌐] 7 [⌐] 16

$= 4\frac{7}{16}$ in^2

Notebook Assignment

1. Perform the indicated operations on the following fractions using a scientific calculator:

   a) $\dfrac{7}{16} + \dfrac{3}{16}$

   b) $\dfrac{1}{4} + \dfrac{3}{8}$

   c) $2\dfrac{5}{16} + \dfrac{3}{4}$

   d) $\dfrac{3}{8} \times \dfrac{3}{4}$

   e) $1\dfrac{1}{2} \times 1\dfrac{1}{8}$

2. Examine the figures below and answer the questions.

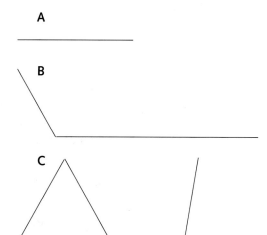

A

B

C

a) Estimate the length of each figure in both metric and imperial units.

b) Measure each line to the nearest millimetre, using a metric ruler.

c) Measure each line to the nearest ¹⁄₁₆", using an imperial ruler.

3. Find the perimeter of the following figure to the nearest ¹⁄₁₆", using an imperial ruler.

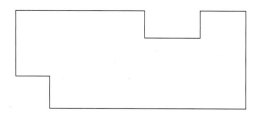

4. Find the perimeter of the following figure to the nearest millimetre, using a metric ruler.

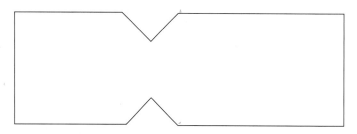

5. Measure the dimensions of the following figure to the nearest millimetre and calculate its area to the nearest square millimetre.

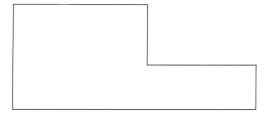

6. Measure the dimensions of the following figure and calculate its area to the nearest $\frac{1}{16}$ in^2.

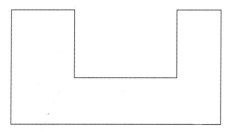

7. Measure the following right-angled triangle to the nearest millimetre and calculate its area to the nearest square millimetre. The formula for area of a triangle is $\frac{1}{2} \times$ base $\times$ height (A $= \frac{1}{2}bh$).

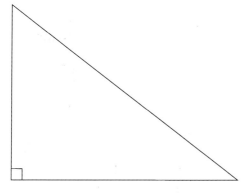

8. **a)** Estimate the perimeter of the following figure.

    b) Calculate the perimeter of the following figure to the nearest millimetre, using a metric ruler.

    c) Calculate the area of the shaded region. Round your answer to the nearest square millimetre.

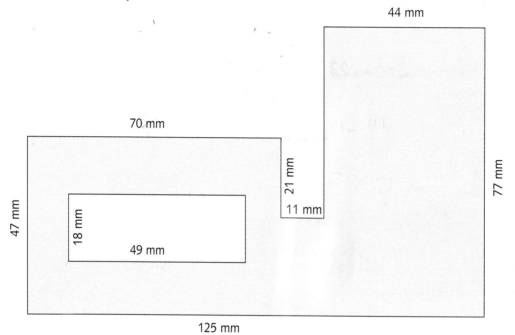

Extension

9. Calculate the area of the basketball court, the volleyball court, and the badminton court in your school in both the imperial and metric systems.

Exploration 3

Conversions within Systems

We are often given measurements in varying units: centimetres and metres, for example, or inches and feet. We may need to convert these measurements into common units before we can solve measurement problems. The following chart contains the most commonly used units.

Metric		
10 millimetres (10 mm)	=	1 centimetre (1 cm)
100 cm	=	1 metre (1 m)
1000 m	=	1 kilometre (1 km)
Imperial		
12 inches (12 in or 12")	=	1 foot (1 ft or 1')
36 in or 3 ft	=	1 yard (1 yd)
5280 ft or 1760 yd	=	1 mile (1 mi)

Goals

In this exploration, you will learn to perform conversions within both imperial and metric systems of measurement.

Example 1

You have decided to replace all the wire to the signal lamps on a boat trailer. After carefully measuring each wire, you determine that you require 485 cm of wire. Electrical wire is only sold by the metre. How many metres of wire must you purchase?

Solution

To find the number of metres you need, convert centimetres to metres:

485 cm x 0.01 = 4.85 m

You will need to buy 5 m of wire, since the store only sells wire by the metre.

Another method for converting from one unit to another is by using a unit conversion ratio. A unit conversion ratio is a fraction equal to 1. Examples of unit conversion ratios are:

$$\frac{10 \text{ millimetres}}{1 \text{ centimetre}} \quad \text{and} \quad \frac{12 \text{ inches}}{1 \text{ foot}}$$

The numerator of the fraction contains the unit to which you want to convert. The denominator of the fraction contains the original units in which the measurement was taken. To find the appropriate unit conversion ratio, refer to the table on the previous page, and consider the following example.

Example 2

A plank measures 6 ft, 4 in. How many inches long is the plank?

Solution

First convert six feet to inches. Since you are converting from feet to inches, inches will be in the numerator and feet in the denominator of the conversion ratio:

$$\frac{12\ inches}{1\ foot}$$

Multiply six feet by the unit conversion ratio to find the number of inches:

$$6' \times \frac{12"}{1'} = 72"$$

On a calculator, the key strokes are:

6 [×] 12 [A$\frac{b}{c}$] 1 [=]

To find the total length, add 72 inches to 4 inches:
72 in + 4 in = 76 in
The total length of the plank is 76 inches.

Example 3

A living room has a length of 5 yards, 2 feet. What is the length of the room in inches?

Solution

= (5 yds × 36 in/yd) + (2 ft × 12 in/ft)
= 180 in + 24 in
= 204 inches

Example 4

Perform the following calculation:

2 km – 820 m

Solution

You can either convert 2 km to m or 820 m to km. If you choose to convert 2 km to m, the unit conversion ratio is:

$$\frac{1000 \text{ m}}{1 \text{ km}}$$

$$2 \text{ km} \times \frac{1000 \text{ m}}{1 \text{ km}} = 2000 \text{ m}$$

Therefore, 2 km – 820 m = 2000 m – 820 m = 1180 m.

Note that conversion from one unit to another in the metric system requires you to multiply or divide by a factor of 10.

Notebook Assignment

1. Determine the unit conversion ratios for converting from:

   a) kilometres to metres

   b) inches to yards

   c) feet to miles

   d) centimetres to millimetres

   e) yards to miles

   f) metres to millimetres

2. Convert the following:

   a) 2 m   = _____ mm

   b) 3 ft   = _____ in

   c) 7500 m   = _____ km

   d) 2 miles   = _____ ft

   e) 4.7 cm   = _____ mm

   f) 7650 cm   = _____ m

   g) 3520 yds   = _____ mi

   h) 720 000 cm   = _____ km

3. Convert the following

   a) 3 cm, 5 mm   = _____ mm

   b) 10 ft, 2 in   = _____ in

   c) 1 mi, 300 ft = _____ ft

   d) 7 yds, 5 ft   = _____ in

   e) 5 m, 32 cm   = _____ cm

   f) 5 m, 32 cm   = _____ mm

   g) 8 yds, 2 ft   = _____ ft

   h) 8 yds, 2 ft   = _____ in

4. Perform the following calculations in the metric system:

   a)   2 m + 60 cm

   b)   5 km + 8 m

   c)   3 cm – 5 mm

   d)   1 m – 9 cm

   e)   2 km – 100 m

   f)   8 cm – 12 mm

5. Perform the following calculations in the imperial system:

   a)   4 ft, 5 in + 7 ft, 3 in

   b)   6 yd, 2 ft + 5 yd, 1 ft

   c)   2 mi, 3000 ft + 4000 ft

   d)   12 ft, 8 in + 10 ft, 7 in

   e)   8 yd, 1 ft – 3 yd, 2 ft

   f)   6 ft, 4 in – 3 ft, 11 in

   g)   2 mi – 1000 ft

   h)   9 ft – 10 in

6. A florist requires 10 inches of ribbon for each bouquet of flowers she creates. How many bouquets will she be able to create from five yards of ribbon?

7. An airline will accept luggage whose length, width, and height add up to no more than 62 inches. Will the airline accept a box on its flight if it has the following dimensions: length, 2 ft, 3 in; width, 2 ft; and height 1 ft, 4 in?

8. One piece of wire 2 ft, 3 in is attached to another piece of wire 1 yd, 1 ft, 8 in long. What is the length of the new piece if the wires overlap by one inch?

Extension

9. Wayne is running the Vancouver Marathon which is 26 miles. If Wayne knows he can average a speed of 10 km/h how long will it take him to complete the marathon?

Exploration 4

Conversions Between Systems

Because we interact so much with our American neighbours, both imperial and metric measurements are commonly used in Canada. For example, most people in Canada know their height and weight in the imperial system, but think of temperature, volume, and lengths in metric measurements. An understanding of imperial and metric units and the process of converting between the two measurement systems is an important skill in many occupations.

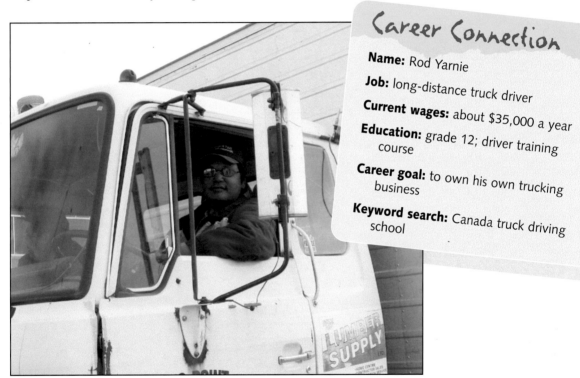

Career Connection

Name: Rod Yarnie

Job: long-distance truck driver

Current wages: about $35,000 a year

Education: grade 12; driver training course

Career goal: to own his own trucking business

Keyword search: Canada truck driving school

Goals

In this exploration, you will learn to convert units from the metric system to the imperial system, and from the imperial system to the metric system of measurement.

Technology

Use a search engine on the internet, and type in the keywords "conversion calculator." There are many sites with conversion calculators, and they will help you find instant conversions, or to check your answers. One such web site is:

http://interactive.usask.ca/skinteractive/modules/factfig/convert/convcalc.html

Conversion Table

Length

metric	imperial
1 millimetre [mm]	0.0394 in
1 centimetre [cm] 10mm	0.3937 in
1 metre [m] 100 cm	1.0936 yd
1 kilometre [km] 1000 m	0.6214 mi
imperial	metric
1 inch [in]	2.54 cm
1 foot [ft] 12 in	0.3048 m
1 yard [yd] 3 ft	0.9144 m
1 mile (1760 yd)	1.6093 km
1 int nautical mile (2025.4 yd)	1.852 km

Area

metric	imperial
1 sq cm [cm^2] 100 mm^2	0.1550 in^2
1 sq m [m^2] 10,000 cm^2	1.1960 yd^2
1 hectare [ha] 10,000 m^2	2.4711 acres
1 sq km [km^2] 100 ha	0.3861 mi^2
imperial	metric
1 sq inch [in^2]	6.4516 cm^2
1 sq foot [ft^2] 144 in^2	0.0929 m^2
1 sq yd [yd^2] 9 ft^2	0.8361 m^2
1 acre (4840 $yd^{2)}$	4046.9 m^2
1 sq mile [mi^2] 640 acres	2.59 km^2

Volume

imperial	metric
1 cubic inch	16.4 cu cm
1 cu foot [ft^3] 1728 cu in	0.0283 cu m
1 cu yard [yd^3] 27 cu ft	0.765 cu m

Capacity

imperial	metric
1 fluid oz	28.41 mL
1 pint (20 fl oz)	568.26 mL
1 quart (2 pints)	1.1365 L
1 gallon (4 quarts)	4.546 L

Example 1

You and your family decide to travel to the United States. After crossing the border, you notice speed limit signs saying the maximum speed is 70. The driver slows down to 70 km/hour, but everyone is passing you. At a posted speed of 70 miles/hour, what is the speed in kilometres/hour?

Solution

The United States uses the imperial system, so you will have to convert from the imperial to metric system. Refer to the conversion table on the previous page, and find the number you will need to multiply the miles by to find kilometres.

70 mi/h × 1.6093 km/mi = 112.65 km/h

70 miles/hour is about 113 kilometres/hour (rounded).

Example 2

Your dining room measures 5 m by 8 m. You have found the perfect carpet for the room, but it is sold in square yards. How many square yards do you need?

Solution

Refer to the conversion tables on the previous page. Note that 1 square metre equals 1.196 square yards.

You will need 40 m^2 (5 x 8), so apply that to the conversion formula.

40 m^2 × 1.196 yd^2/m^2 = 47.84 yd^2

You will need 48 square yards of carpet.

Notebook Assignment

Use the conversion tables on p. 216 to complete the following problems.

1. Convert:

   a) 216 cm = _____ feet

   b) 25 yards = _____ m

   c) 6 feet = _____ cm

   d) 160 miles = _____ km

   e) 2200 km = _____ miles

2. Convert:

   a) 5 m^2 = _____ yd^2

   b) 6 yd^2 = _____ m^2

   c) 1 yd^3 = _____ feet^3

   d) 30 yd^3 = _____ m^3

   e) 8 m^3 = _____ yd^3

   f) 120 m^3 = _____ yd^3

3. The trip from Prince Rupert to Seattle is 1033 miles. How many kilometres is this? Approximately how many hours would this drive take? What assumptions have you made?

4. The trip from Whitehorse to Inuvik is 1227 kilometres. Find this distance in miles. Approximately how many hours would this drive take? What assumptions have you made?

5. A low bridge has a posted height of 7' 6". Your truck is 2.3 m high. Will it fit under the bridge? Calculate how much over—under—you will be.

Extension

6. A $1.00 coin is $2\frac{1}{2}$ cm wide. Your class is conducting a fund-raising event to help needy families. The coins are laid out in a row on double-sided tape in a mall. At the end of the day, your strip of coins is 50 yards long. Calculate how many coins your class collected.

7. You have an aquarium which measures 75 cm × 30 cm × 20 cm. While you are filling it with water, you wonder just how many litres it will take. Knowing that 1 cm^3 = 1 mL, find the number of litres needed to fill the aquarium. If one gallon of water weighs approximately 10 pounds, how much does the water in your aquarium weigh?

Problem Analysis

Dinner with the Wellingtons

The Wellington family went out to dinner yesterday evening. Tim, Marilyn, Heather, Brittany, and Stephanie each ordered a different main course. Ham, chicken, pork, salmon, and steak were the only main courses on the menu. Each family member also ordered a baked potato, salad, and a different vegetable. The five vegetables on the menu were carrots, corn, peas, broccoli, and beans. Use the information below to determine what main course and vegetable each family member had.

1. The person who had steak and corn sat on the left of Tim and on the right of Stephanie.

2. The person who had chicken doesn't play tennis; but the person who had ham, the person who had broccoli, and Heather played doubles tennis yesterday with Stephanie.

3. The person who had broccoli did not have it with pork; Brittany did not order pork either.

4. The person who had ham recently saw Tim; the person who had broccoli helped Tim wrap a present for Tim's father.

5. Marilyn's and Stephanie's vegetables begin with the same letter as do the vegetables of Tim and Heather.

To solve this logic problem, it is helpful to organize the information in a grid such as the one shown here.

To use this grid, place an X wherever you can say yes and O where it is clearly no. For example, statement 3 tells us that Brittany did not eat pork, so we can place an O at the intersection of Brittany and pork. Use the clues provided to fill in the grid with Xs and Os.

	ham	chicken	pork	salmon	steak	carrots	corn	peas	broccoli	beans
Tim										
Marilyn										
Heather										
Brittany			O							
Stephanie										
carrots										
corn										
peas										
broccoli										
beans										

Games

Numsquare

Objective

To avoid ending with four 0s in the middle squares.

Instructions

Place any four numbers
in the four corner squares.
Place the difference of the
two numbers in the square
between them. Continue.

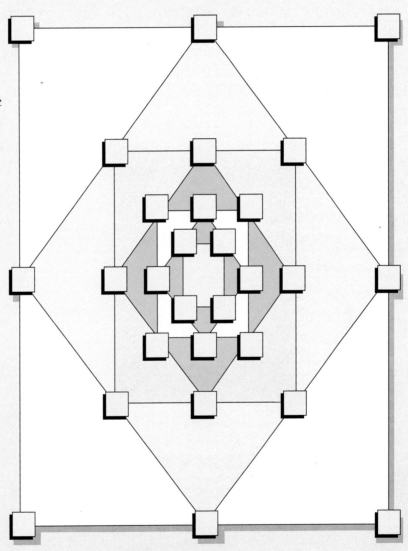

Exploration 5

Measuring with Vernier Calipers

Many industries require extremely precise measurements. Manufacturing of aircraft, busses, and scientific instruments are just a few examples of industries in which precise measurements are essential. Machinists — who make things to fit specific dimensions—must make very precise measurements.

Vernier calipers were invented by a French engineer named Pierre Vernier in 1631. They have a main scale, showing to the nearest millimetre, but also a Vernier scale that offers an even more precise measurement.

Career Connection

Name: Julius Delgato

Job: apprentice machinist

Current wages: $15.75 an hour

Education: grade 12; community college program

Career goal: tool-and-die maker

Keyword search: Canada college machinist apprentice tool-and-die maker

Goals

In this exploration, you will learn to read Vernier calipers in the metric system.

New Terms

Vernier calipers: an instrument for making accurate linear measurments.

Vernier Calipers

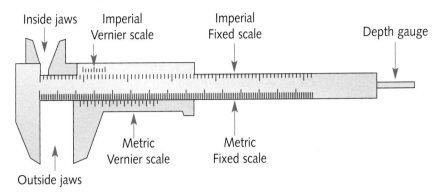

This instrument has various parts, including

- three devices for measuring:
  outside jaws are used to measure outer dimensions of objects, for example, the outer diameter of a pipe
  inside jaws are used to measure inner dimensions of objects, for example, the inner diameter of a pipe
  a **stem or depth gauge** used to measure the depth of objects, for example, the depth of a small container
- two measurement scales
  a fixed scale (metric and imperial)
  a moving (Vernier) scale (metric and imperial)

Examine the various scales on the Vernier caliper. The fixed scale is as the name implies—it does not move and looks like a ruler. The moving scale is called the Vernier scale.

Vernier calipers have one or two systems of measurement: metric, imperial, or both. You will only be using Vernier calipers calibrated in metric units.

The fixed scale on Vernier calipers calibrated in metric units is divided into millimetres, that is, $\frac{1}{10}$ cm. The moving Vernier scale represents $\frac{1}{10} \times \frac{1}{10} = \frac{1}{100}$ cm. Therefore, measurements taken with Vernier calipers are precise to the nearest hundredth of a centimetre.

The following examples will help you in reading the measurements taken with Vernier calipers.

Technology

Web sites that allow interactive reading of Vernier calipers can be found using the search term "Vernier calipers."

Example 1

Read the following measurement made in metric units with Vernier calipers.

Solution

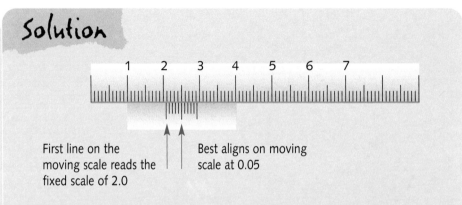

First line on the
moving scale reads the
fixed scale of 2.0

Best aligns on moving
scale at 0.05

First read the fixed scale, using the first line on the moving scale as a pointer. This line points to a place beyond 2.0 cm.
Now find the line on the moving scale that most closely aligns with a line on the fixed scale. The moving scale has 10 divisions, and each division represents 0.01 cm. The line that best matches is the fifth line on the moving scale; that is 0.05 cm.

Therefore the reading of the caliper is:
2.0 + 0.05 = 2.05 cm

To read Vernier calipers, note the following procedure:

a) Check where the first line on the moving scale lands. It will point to a place on the fixed scale. This position determines the first digits of the reading.

b) Find the last digit of the reading by examining which line on the moving scale aligns best with a line on the fixed scale. The line on the moving scale determines this last digit.

Example 2

Read the following Vernier calipers measurement.

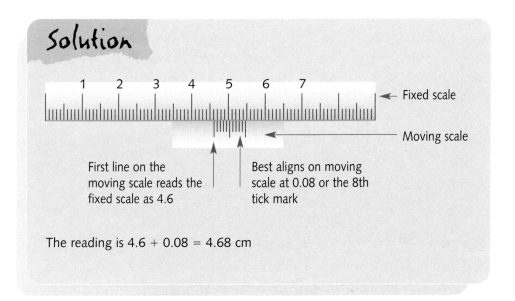

Solution

First line on the moving scale reads the fixed scale as 4.6

Best aligns on moving scale at 0.08 or the 8th tick mark

← Fixed scale

← Moving scale

The reading is 4.6 + 0.08 = 4.68 cm

Class Activity

Practise measuring objects with Vernier calipers. First, look around your classroom for items that could be measured using Vernier calipers. These might include finding the width of a pencil, a white board marker, the width of your index finger, the thickness of a textbook, the diameter (inside and outside) of the teacher's coffee cup, or the thickness of your desk.

Working in pairs, use Vernier calipers to measure the items you have selected and record your measurements. Place the object between the main jaws of the caliper. Then close the jaws until they just come into contact with the sides of the object. Read the caliper to find the measurement. Compare your findings with the rest of the class.

Project Activity

In this activity you will collect baseline and experimental data on eggshell dimensions and thickness using Vernier calipers. Each group will use one dozen boiled eggs to conduct their study.

Use a waterproof marker to label six eggs "control" and six eggs "experimental."

Use Vernier calipers to measure the length and width of the control and experimental eggs. Record these measurements as a data set.

Place the six experimental eggs in a vinegar solution for four hours.

At the end of four hours, remove the experimental eggs from the vinegar solution and wash them off with fresh water.

Use Vernier calipers to measure the length and width of each experimental egg. Present this as a data set.

Examine the data you have collected and discuss your findings with your group.

Mallard duck eggs may be affected by the pesticide DDT in the environment.

Notebook Assignment

1. Read the following Vernier calipers measurements. The scales have been enlarged for easier reading. The Vernier calipers are calibrated in metric units.

a)

b)

c)

d)

e)

f)

2. Read the following Vernier calipers measurements. The
measurements have been drawn to scale and are in metric units.

a)

b)

c)

d)

e)

f)

3. Measure the width of pencils from one package and record your answers in a table. Are there any variations in your measurements? What might cause any variations?

4. What types of objects are best to measure with Vernier calipers?

Extension

5. How are Vernier calipers used in your community?

The diameter of tree seedlings can be measured using Vernier calipers.

Exploration 6

Measuring with Micrometers

A micrometer is an even more precise measuring instrument than Vernier calipers. It measures smaller lengths, such as the thickness of the walls of pipes, rods, nuts and bolts, washers, and nails. Machinists use micrometers to find the thickness of materials. While Vernier calipers measure accurately to the nearest tenth of a millimetre, the micrometer can make measurements to the nearest hundredth of a millimetre.

Goals

In this exploration, you will learn to read micrometer measurements.

New Terms

micrometer: a gauge used to measure small distances or thicknesses to thousandths of a unit.

Reading a Micrometer

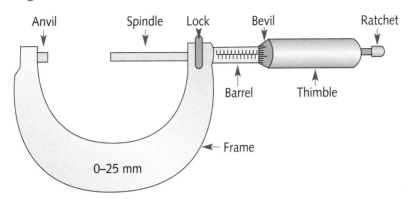

Note the following parts of the instrument:
- **measuring device**
  jaws (anvil and spindle) are used to measure small lengths
- **two measurement scales**
  a scale on the barrel (fixed scale)
  a scale on the thimble (moving scale)
- **one system of measurement units** (metric or imperial)

On a metric micrometer, the scales are as follows:
- **barrel:**
  The fixed scale on the barrel is divided into 25 main divisions. Each main division represents 1 mm. Each main division is divided in half, yielding 50 subdivisions in all. Each of these subdivisions represents 0.05 cm or 0.50 mm.
- **thimble:**
  The moving scale on the thimble is divided into 50 divisions. One complete rotation of the thimble represents $50 \times 0.01 = 0.50$ mm. Therefore, each division on the thimble represents $\frac{1}{1000}$ cm or 0.01 mm.

Using a Micrometer

Practise measuring with a micrometer by finding the width of different small objects such as coins. Place an object such as a penny between the jaws, then rotate the drum using the ratchet, until the object is secure and you hear three clicks.

Technology

Web sites that allow interactive reading of micrometers can be found by using the search item "micrometer applet" in an internet search engine.

Example 1

Read the following micrometer measurement.

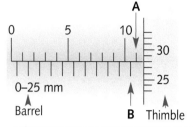

Solution

1. The measure of the last marking showing on the upper scale (indicated by arrow A) is 11 mm. Check the lower scale. The last marking showing on the lower scale (indicated by arrow B) is to the left of arrow A. In this case, the number from the barrel is read as 11 mm.
2. The thimble reading yields 0.28 mm.
3. The sum and resulting measurement is: 11 mm + 0.28 mm = 11.28 mm.

Example 2

Read the following micrometer measurement:

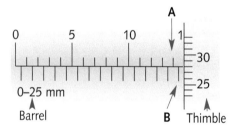

Solution

1. The measure of the last marking showing on the upper scale (indicated by arrow A) is 14 mm. Check the lower scale. The last marking showing on the lower scale (indicated by arrow B) is to the right of arrow A. In this case, 0.5 is added to the 14 mm, giving a barrel reading of 14.5.
2. The thimble reading yields 0.28 mm.
3. The sum and resulting measurement is: 14.5 mm + 0.28 mm = 14.78 mm.

Example 3

Read the following micrometer measurement:

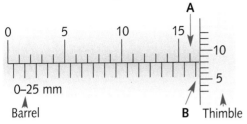

Solution

1. Read the number from the barrel as 16.5 mm. Note that the marking indicated by arrow B is to the right of the marking indicated by arrow A.
2. The thimble reading yields 0.08 mm.
3. The sum and resulting measurement is: 16.5 mm + 0.08 mm = 16.58 mm.

Example 4

Read the following micrometer measurement:

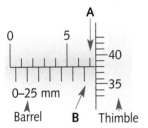

Solution

1. Read the number from the barrel as 7 mm (Note: the marking indicated by arrow B is to the left of the marking indicated by arrow A).
2. The thimble reading yields 0.38 mm.
3. The sum and resulting measurement is: 7 mm + 0.38 mm =7.38 mm.

Class Activity

Look around the room for items which could be measured with a micrometer. These could include the thickness of 25 sheets of paper, the thickness of your textbook cover, the thickness of a plastic cup, the thickness of a pen, or the diameter of a loonie. Working in pairs, use the micrometer to measure each of the items, and record your measurements. Compare your findings with those of the other groups.

Project Activity

In this activity, you will collect baseline and experimental data on eggshell dimensions and thickness using a micrometer. Each group will use one dozen boiled eggs for their study.

Use a waterproof marker to label six eggs "control" and six eggs "experimental." Place the six experimental eggs in a vinegar solution for four hours.

At the end of four hours, remove the experimental eggs from the vinegar solution and wash them off with fresh water.

Break a piece of eggshell off each of the eggs and use a micrometer to measure the thickness of the eggshell. Display your measurements as a data set.

Lesser Yellowlegs, medium-sized long-legged shorebirds, spend their summers in Yukon and Alaska and winters from Oregon to South America.

Notebook Assignment

1. Read the following micrometer measurements:

   a)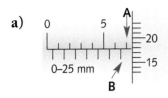

   b)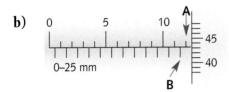

   c)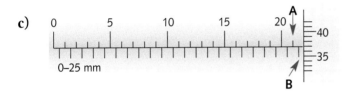

   d)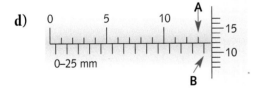

   e)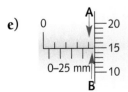

   f)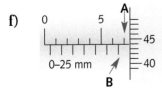

g)

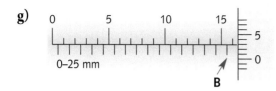

B

h)

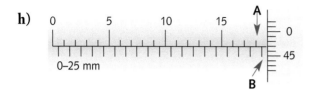

A

B

2. Read the following micrometer measurements:

a)

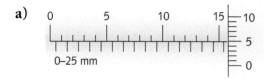

b)

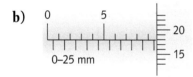

c)

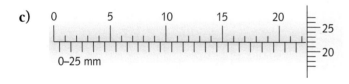

d)

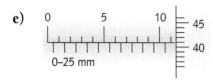

e)

f)

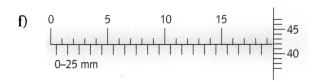

0–25 mm

g)

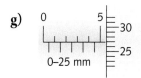

0–25 mm

h)

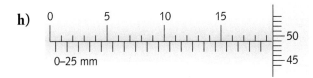

0–25 mm

3. Measure the width of pencils from one package and record your answers in a table. Are there any variations in your measurements? What might cause any variations?

4. Compare the measurements you determined by using the Vernier calipers with your answer to question 3. How do they compare?

5. What types of objects are best to measure with micrometers?

Extension

6. How are micrometers used in various trades and occupations?

Chapter Review

1. Using a ruler, measure each of the following objects to the nearest millimetre and the nearest $\frac{1}{16}$ of an inch:

   a) diameter of nickel

   b) diameter of dime

   c) diameter of loonie

   d) length of a 9 volt battery

   e) length of notebook

   f) length of pencil

   g) diameter of pencil

   h) length of paper clip

   i) width of paper clip

   j) inside diameter of washer

   k) outside diameter of washer

   l) length of wrench

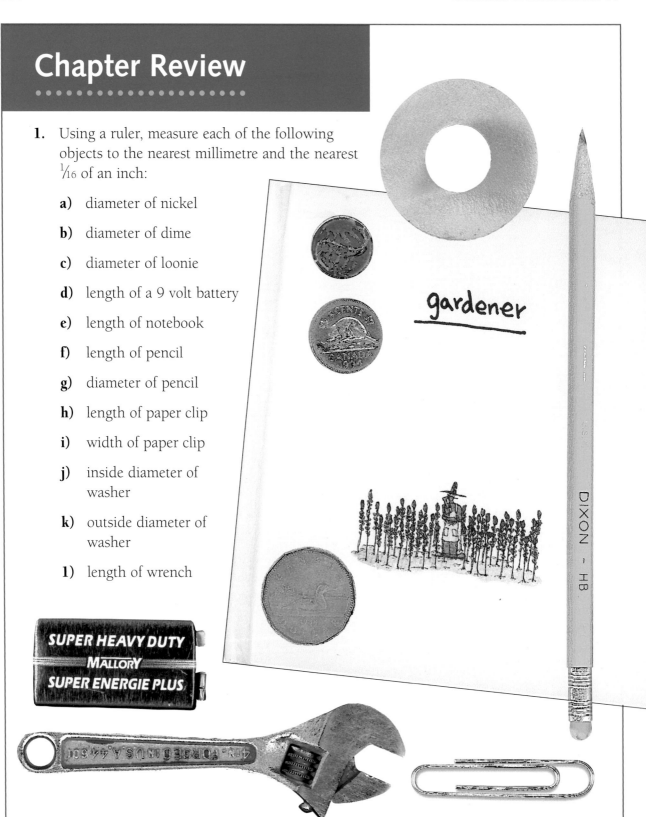

2. Explain why the metric system is a more efficient system of measurement than the imperial system.

3. Identify a familiar object as a reference for each of the following measurements, for example, millimetre—thickness of a dime:

   a) centimetre

   b) metre

   c) foot

   d) inch

4. a) Measure the dimensions of the following figure to the nearest tenth of a centimetre.

   b) Calculate its area. To what place value is it reasonable to round the area?

5. Convert the following.

   a) 6 m, 15 cm   = _____ cm

   b) 4 ft, 6 in   = _____ in

   c) 2 yd, 1 ft   = _____ ft

   d) 12 cm, 5 mm   = _____ cm

   e) 3 mi, 250 yd   = _____ ft

   f) 1 m, 8 cm   = _____ mm

6. Perform the following calculations.

   a) 3 m + 45 cm

   b) 6 ft, 8 in + 4 ft, 5 in

   c) 3 mi – 3 ft, 10 in

7. Read the following Vernier caliper measurement. The Vernier calipers have been calibrated in metric units.

8. Read the following Vernier caliper measurement. The Vernier calipers have been calibrated in metric units.

9. Read the following micrometer measurement. The micrometer has been calibrated in metric units.

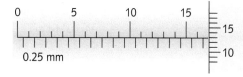

10. Read the following micrometer measurement. The micrometer has been calibrated in metric units.

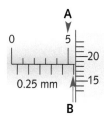

Project Presentation

Examine the data you have collected and discuss your findings in your small group.

Decide how you will present these findings on a poster to be mounted in a park kiosk. The purpose of the poster will be to inform the visiting public about the effects of DDT.

Prepare a poster that:

a) briefly explains the historical effects of the pesticide DDT on bird populations

b) reports on your two experimental simulations

c) includes an illustrated section that explains the measurement technology you used in your experiments

d) makes a recommendation about the use of DDT as a pesticide

e) contains both words and pictures or other graphical presentations of information.

Case Study

• • • • • • • • • • • • • •

The living room is in need of redecorating! New carpet, trendy wallpaper, and a fresh coat of paint will make the room look fabulous.

The rectangular-shaped room measures 20 feet by 30 feet. The walls are 8 feet high. You will need to calculate and convert various measurements, and find the cost of the materials in order to redecorate.

Carpet

a) What area will the carpet cover?

b) If 1 square yard contains 9 square feet, how many square yards of carpet are needed?

c) The store only sells carpet in square metres. Convert from square yards to square metres. How many square metres of carpet do you need?

d) The carpet you select costs $26.85/m^2. Find the total cost, including the taxes applicable in your community.

Wallpaper

a) You will wallpaper two walls—one shorter than the other. Find the measurements of each wall.

b) Calculate the area of these two walls.

c) One roll of wallpaper covers 10 m^2. How many rolls must you purchase?

d) If there were 2 windows, each measuring 6 feet by 4 feet, how many rolls of wallpaper would now be needed?

e) The product you like sells for $11.60 per roll, plus taxes. Find the total cost.

Paint

a) The two remaining walls will be painted. What are their measurements?

b) Calculate the area of these two walls.

c) 1 litre of paint will cover 20 m^2. How many litres will you need to buy?

d) The paint costs $7.95 per litre. Find the total cost, including taxes.

Total Cost

Find the total cost of your redecorating project.

Extension

a) List any incidental expenses you might incur for equipment and supplies.

b) You are not happy with the result! The new carpet you really want costs $31.20/m^2 and the new wallpaper costs $12.35/roll. Calculate how much extra it will cost to replace the carpet and the wallpaper.

Chapter 5
• • • • • • • • • • • •
Relations and Formulas

Representing and Interpreting Relations

There are many occasions in which you use relations and formulas. Do you have a part-time job where you are paid an hourly wage? If you do, you may calculate your gross pay using the formula "gross pay equals hourly rate multiplied by hours worked."

You have used formulas before. For example, in chapter 1, you used the formula $I = prt$ to calculate simple interest. In chapter 4, you used the formula to calculate the perimeter of a figure.

There are many ways in which two quantities can be related. When you are reading the newspaper, you often see graphs that illustrate a relation, such as the growth of a city's population over time or the increase in life expectancy over time.

The ability to interpret graphs is an important skill. Have you noticed how often graphs appear in magazines or newspapers? They appear frequently because they are an effective way to show a relation. Graphs are a picture of a relation and make that relation easier to see.

Goals	Technology	Hints
In this chapter, you will examine linear relations. You will learn to express them in words, with a table of values, as a graph, and as a formula. You will interpret the graphs of linear relations and determine their slope. You will also evaluate formulas.	A calculator will help you with the calculations required for the relations and formulas in this chapter.	Graph paper is required for this chapter.

Chapter Project

Some students obtain summer jobs planting trees in British Columbia and northern Manitoba. In addition to earning money, many of them find that spending a summer planting trees is challenging, improves the environment, and is a good way to meet other young people.

The project in this chapter is to role-play a student who spends a summer planting trees. Work with a group of 2-3 classmates to complete this project. Although this is a group project, each student must complete his or her own project file. As you work on this project, you will add the following items to your project file:

1. research information on the tree planting company you choose

2. graphs of earnings vs. trees planted

3. a list of expenses

4. a statement of the relation between fixed and variable expenses

Career Connection

Name: Amelia Gabriel

Job: summer job planting trees in northern British Columbia

Current wages: $4,500 during the summer

Education: grade 12 student; Renewable Resources Management Program, Yukon College, Yukon

Career goal: resource management officer

Keyword search: Canada college renewable resources management program

Exploration 1

Linear Relations between Quantities

Do you have a part-time job? Are you paid an hourly wage? How much do you earn? When you work more hours, your gross pay increases. When you work fewer hours, your gross pay decreases. A mathematical relation exists between the number of hours you work and your gross pay.

Example 1

Emma has a part-time job working at a bookstore and earns $8.00 an hour. Express this relation as a formula.

Solution

Emma's gross pay is equal to $8.00 multiplied by the number of hours she works.

gross pay = hourly rate of $8.00 × number of hours worked

You can write a shortened version of the formula by using letters to represent the key words. Choosing P to represent gross pay and h to represent the number of hours worked, write the formula as:

$P = 8 \times h$ or
$P = 8h$

The number of hours worked (h) and the gross pay (P) are called the variables in the relation. Since gross pay depends on the variable of hours worked, you call gross pay (P) the dependent variable and the hours worked (h) the independent variable.

Goals

In this exploration, you will examine linear relations whose graphs pass through the point of origin. You will express them in words, with a table of values, as a graph, and as a formula.

New Terms

dependent variable: relies on the values given to another variable.

independent variable: a variable whose values may be freely chosen.

origin: the point where the x and y axes intersect; the coordinates of the origin are (0, 0).

Example 2

Suppose that during the first week of November, Emma works the following hours:

Monday	4
Tuesday	0
Wednesday	2
Thursday	6
Friday	8

a) Express the relation between gross pay and hours as a table of values.

b) Express the relation between gross pay and hours as a graph.

Solution

a) Using the formula $P = 8h$, construct a table of values for the hours Emma works in the first week of November.

First, substitute the corresponding values for hours worked into the formula $P = 8h$. For example, to find Emma's gross pay for Monday, substitute the value of 4 into the formula.

$P = 8h$
$P = 8(4)$
$P = 32$

Then, calculate the rest of the values as follows:

Tuesday	Wednesday	Thursday	Friday
$P = 8h$	$P = 8h$	$P = 8h$	$P = 8h$
$P = 8(0)$	$P = 8(2)$	$P = 8(6)$	$P = 8(8)$
$P = 0$	$P = 16$	$P = 48$	$P = 64$

Enter these values for gross pay into a table of values as follows:

	Mon	Tues	Wed	Thurs	Fri
Hours worked	4	0	2	6	8
Gross pay ($)	32	0	16	48	64

b) On a graph, there are two axes, a horizontal axis (x-axis) and a vertical axis (y-axis). By plotting the hours worked on the horizontal axis and the gross pay on the vertical axis, you obtain a representation of the relation. Always plot the independent variable along the horizontal axis and the dependent variable along the vertical axis.

Plot the value of the number of hours worked and gross pay as one point on the graph. Refer to the table of values. On Monday, Emma works 4 hours and earns a gross pay of $32. Plot these two values as one point on the graph. The point is identified by the ordered pair (4, 32).

Plotting the remaining data from the table of values results in the following graph.

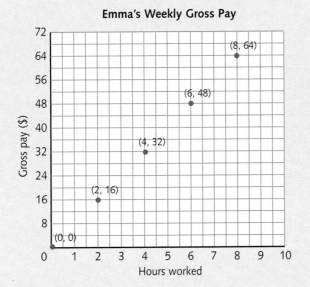

Emma's Weekly Gross Pay

continued on the next page

Hints

To graph a point, graph the first coordinate in the ordered pair with reference to the horizontal axis and the second coordinate with reference to the vertical axis.

The five plotted points appear to follow a straight line. Using a ruler, connect the points:

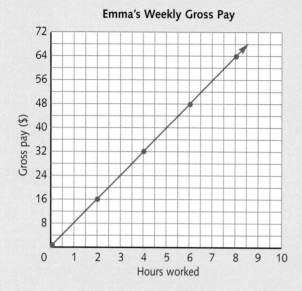

Emma's Weekly Gross Pay

Because the data produce a straight line, this type of relation is called a linear relation.

A graph is a convenient way to visualize a linear relation. Using a graph, you can find values between points and beyond points on the graph. The process of determining values between known points on a graph is called interpolation. The process of determining values beyond known points on the graph is called extrapolation.

Example 3

a) Use the graph to find Emma's gross pay if she works 3 hours.

b) Use the graph to find the number of hours Emma must work to earn a gross pay of $56.

New Terms

interpolation: the process of inferring intermediate values between existing data.

extrapolation: the process of inferring values beyond the existing data.

Solution

a) To find Emma's gross pay if she works 3 hours, locate point A on the line directly above 3 hours on the horizontal axis. The reading on the vertical axis that lines up with point A is $24. Therefore, Emma would earn $24 if she works 3 hours.

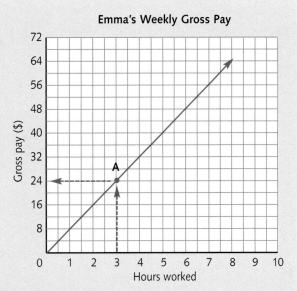

b) To find the number of hours Emma is required to work in order to earn $56, locate point B on the line directly to the right of $56 on the vertical axis. The reading on the horizontal axis that lines up with point B is 7 hours. Therefore, to earn gross pay of $56, Emma must work 7 hours.

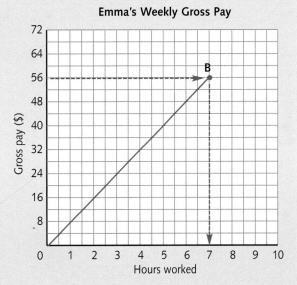

Mental Math

1. Use the formula $P = 10h$ to find P when:

   a) $h = 8$ b) $h = 0.5$ c) $h = 12.5$

Career Connection

Name: Shelley Podborski

Job: part-time job at a bookstore in Vancouver, BC

Current wage: $9.50 an hour

Education: grade 12 student; legal assistant program at Capilano College, North Vancouver, BC

Career goal: paralegal

Keyword search: Canada college legal assistant program

Project Activity

Research tree planting companies, using books or the internet. The following web sites may be helpful, or use the search string "tree+planting+Canada" in a search engine.

- www.canadiantreeplanting.com
- www.for.gov.bc.ca/hfp/planting/contract.htm

Using your research, assemble the following information and graph the linear relations it represents.

1. Decide on the company for whom you will work.

2. Identify and describe the location where you will plant trees.

3. What is the distance from where you live to where you will be planting trees?

4. How will you get to the location? Will you drive and/or fly?

5. When travelling to the location, at what rate (kilometres per hour) will you travel? Using this rate, draw a graph showing the relation between distance (kilometres) and time (hours). If you will be driving and flying, draw 2 graphs. From the graph, determine how long it will take you to arrive at your tree-planting location.

6. For the driving portion of your trip to the work site, you will need to give a reasonable estimate of the fuel consumption for an appropriate vehicle. (Refer to chapter 3.) How many kilometres does your vehicle travel on 1 litre of gasoline?

   Draw a graph showing the relation between the distance your vehicle travels (kilometres) and the amount of gasoline (litres) it requires. From the graph, determine how many litres of gasoline you will need for the trip. Determine how many litres of gasoline you will need for the return trip.

7. What is the cost of gasoline per litre? Draw a graph showing the relation between the cost of the gasoline (dollars) for the trip and the amount of gasoline required (litres). From the graph, calculate the cost of gasoline for the return trip.

Notebook Assignment

1. Identify the independent and dependent variables for the following relations:

   a) the number of words typed vs. the time spent at the keyboard

   b) the cost of stamps vs. the quantity of stamps purchased

   c) the commission income earned vs. the value of sales

   d) the number of paper clips vs. the mass of paper clips

2. During the second week of November, Emma works the following hours: Monday – 2; Tuesday – 0; Wednesday – 3; Thursday – 6; Friday – 5. Emma's hourly wage is $8/h.

   a) Express the relation between gross pay and hours worked with a table of values.

   b) Express the relation between gross pay and hours worked as a graph.

   c) How does your graph compare to the graph in example 2 on p. 250?

   d) If Emma works a different number of hours, how is the graph affected? Explain.

3. Under average road conditions, a particular vehicle can travel eight kilometres on one litre of gasoline. During the month of August, the vehicle uses the following amounts of gasoline: 30 litres, 45 litres, 10 litres, and 35 litres. Express the relation between the distance the vehicle travels and the amount of gasoline required to travel that distance:

   a) in words

   b) with a table of values

   c) as a formula (choose letters to represent the distance travelled and the amount of gasoline required)

4. Refer to the relation given in question 3.

   a) Identify the independent variable.

   b) Identify the dependent variable.

   c) Graph the relation.

5. A convenience store sells distilled water. The cost of one litre of distilled water is $3. Express the relation between the volume of distilled water sold and the cost of distilled water sold:

   a) in words

   b) with a table of values (choose your own values for the number of bottles sold)

   c) as a formula (choose letters to represent the volume and the cost)

6. Refer to the relation described in question 5.

   a) Identify the independent variable.

   b) Identify the dependent variable.

   c) Graph the relation.

7. Refer to the line graph of the relation given in question 6. Using the line graph and either interpolation or extrapolation, complete the following table.

Volume of water (litres)	Cost of water ($)
2.5	
8	
	$13.50
	$22.50

Extension

8. Name five scenarios that can be described using a linear relation. Choose one of the scenarios and complete the following.

   a) Identify the independent and dependent variables for the relation.

   b) Express the relation:
      - in words
      - with a table of values (choose your own values for the table)
      - as a graph
      - as a formula (choose letters to represent the variables)

Exploration 2

Slope of a Line

The graph of a relation is a visual representation of that relation. When you graphed the linear relations in the last exploration, the graphs were all straight lines.

However, the straight lines of different linear relations differed from each other. Some were drawn on a steeper incline than others. In this exploration, you examine the differences in steepness.

Example 1

Mario has been working in technical support at a call centre for two years and earns $15 an hour. His friend, Jason, has just started working there and earns $10 an hour. Graph these two relations.

Solution

Mario's gross pay can be expressed by the formula:

$P = 15h$, where P = gross pay and h = number of hours worked

Jason's gross pay can be expressed by the formula:

$P = 10h$

To graph these relations, first construct two tables of values. Choose your own values for the table whenever none are given. In this case, you could choose times of 0, 2, 4, 6, and 8 hours.

Goals

In this exploration, you will learn how to calculate the slope of a straight line.

New Terms

slope: the "steepness" of a line.

Mario

Table of values

Hours worked	0	2	4	6	8
Gross pay ($)	0	30	60	90	120

Jason

Table of values

Hours worked	0	2	4	6	8
Gross pay ($)	0	20	40	60	80

Plot the data from these tables of values to construct the following graphs.

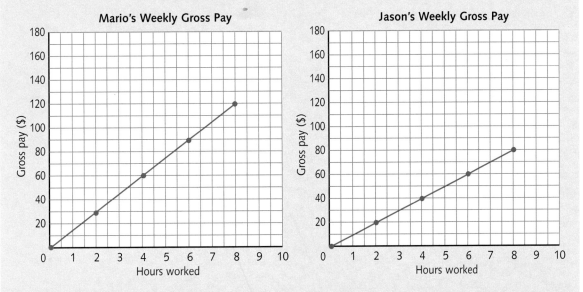

Compare the two graphs. Both graphs are straight lines. Both lines go through the point (0,0), known as the origin. The graph of $P = 15h$ seems to be steeper than the graph of $P = 10h$.

The "steepness" of a line is an important mathematical concept for which the mathematical term is slope. The slope of a line is a comparison. The slope of each of the lines above is the amount the gross pay has changed compared to the number of hours worked. In order to be able to make a more exact comparison of the slope of the lines, numerical values can be assigned to the slope.

Hints

Note that when comparing graphs, the scales of the axes must be the same.

Example 2

Determine the slope of the line that represents gross pay compared to hours worked for Mario.

Solution

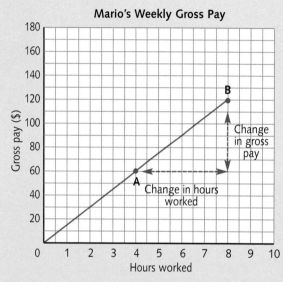

Follow the steps below to determine the slope of a line on a graph.

1. Choose two points on the line. It is most convenient to choose points that are on the intersection of two grid lines. Refer to the selected points as A and B.

   A represents a gross pay of $60 and 4 hours worked.
   B represents a gross pay of $120 and 8 hours worked.

2. Calculate the change in gross pay from A to B.

   $120 – $60 = $60

3. Calculate the change in hours worked from A to B.

   8 hours – 4 hours = 4 hours

Solution

4. Use the following formula to calculate the slope of the line:

$$\text{slope of the line} = \frac{\text{change in gross pay}}{\text{change in hours worked}}$$

$$= \frac{\$60}{4 \text{ h}}$$

$$= \frac{\$15}{1 \text{ h}}$$

$$= \$15 \text{ an hour}$$

The slope of this line is 15 and represents Mario's hourly rate of pay.

The slope in the example above is the amount the gross pay (or dependent variable) has changed compared to the amount the hours worked (or independent variable) has changed. Since the dependent variable is along the vertical axis, the change in the dependent variable is how much the line has increased vertically, or the rise. Since the independent variable is along the horizontal axis, the change in the independent variable is how much the line has increased horizontally, or the run.

In general, for all linear relations, the slope of a line can be determined using the formula:

$$\text{slope} = \frac{\text{change in the dependent variable (rise)}}{\text{change in the independent variable (run)}}$$

New Terms

rise: change in dependent variable.

run: change in independent variable.

Hints

Slope is equal to change in the dependent variable divided by change in the independent variable.

Example 3

a) Determine the slope of the line that represents gross pay compared to hours worked for Jason.

b) How does the slope of this line compare to the slope of the graph for Mario?

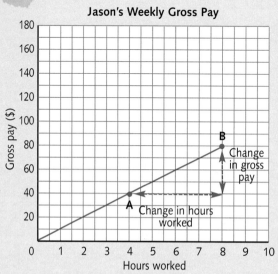

a) To determine the slope, choose two points on the line, A and B.

Calculate the change in the dependent variable (rise):

$80 - $40 = $40

Calculate the change in the independent variable (run):

8 hours – 4 hours = 4 hours

Calculate the slope:

$$\text{slope} = \frac{\text{change in the dependent variable (rise)}}{\text{change in the independent variable (run)}}$$

$$= \frac{\$40}{4 \text{ hours}}$$

$$= \frac{\$10}{1 \text{ hour}}$$

$$= \$10 \text{ an hour}$$

The slope of the line is 10.

b) The numerical value of the slope of the line representing Jason's weekly gross pay is 10, while the numerical value of the slope of the line representing Mario's weekly gross pay is 15. The slope of the line that appears steeper has a greater numerical value than the slope of the other line.

The slope represents the hourly rate of pay. The slope indicates how the two variables compare. In this example, the dependent variable (gross pay) is 10 times the independent variable (hours worked).

Hints

1. A slope can be indicated as follows:

- As an integer (example: 15)

- As a fraction (example: $\frac{5}{2}$)

- As a decimal (example: 2.5)

2. Slope $= \dfrac{\text{rise}}{\text{run}}$

Mental Math

1. Calculate the slope of the following lines:

a) line with a rise of 8 and a run of 2

b) line with a rise of 3 and a run of 6

c) line with a rise of 5 and a run of 5

Project Activity

Refer to the graphs you constructed in exploration 1.

1. Determine the slope for each of the lines.

2. What do the slopes represent?

Notebook Assignment

1. Examine the graph below and answer the questions that follow it.

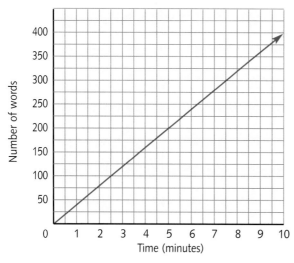

a) Choose two points on the line and find the slope of the line.

b) Choose another two points on the line and find the slope of the line.

c) Did the points you chose on the line affect the value of the slope? Explain.

2. Examine the following two graphs that model the mass in grams of
    paper clips.

Graph A

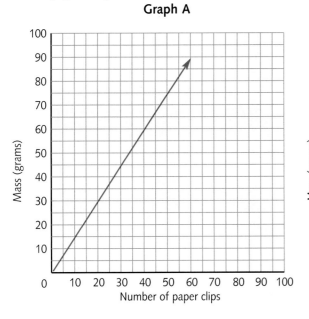

Graph B

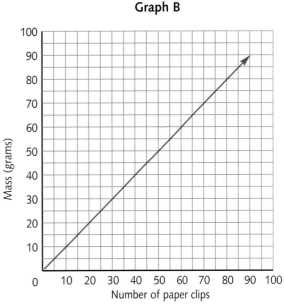

a) By observation, which line is steeper?
b) Calculate and compare the slopes of the two lines.
c) Explain what the two lines represent.
d) What can you tell about the paper clips?

3. Consider the following table of values that represents the speed of a
    skydiver in free fall after reaching terminal velocity.

Time (in seconds)	0	8	12	20
Speed (metres/second)	0	80	120	200

a) Identify the independent and dependent variables.

b) Graph the relation.

c) Calculate the slope of the line.

d) Explain what the slope of the line represents.

4. The following graph represents the relation between the number of boxes of chocolates a student sells for a school fundraiser and the profit she earns for the school.

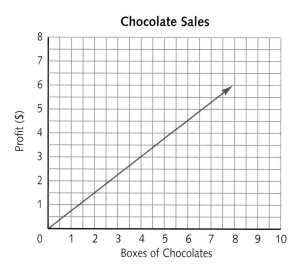

Chocolate Sales

a) Identify the independent and dependent variables.

b) Calculate the slope of the line.

c) What does the slope of the line represent?

5. Refer to the graph in question 4. Complete the following table of values using interpolation and extrapolation.

Boxes of chocolates	3		12	
Profit		$4.50		$10.50

Extension

6. What is the minimum hourly wage in your province or territory? Find the minimum hourly wage in two other provinces or territories.

a) Express the relation between gross pay and hours worked in each province or territory.

b) Graph the relations.

c) Compare the slopes.

d) How do the slopes of the relations relate to the hourly wages?

e) Is there a large difference between the hourly wages in the provinces or territories you have chosen? How do the graphs show this?

f) Why do you believe such a difference in the minimum wage between provinces and territories exists?

Exploration 3

Determining the Equation of a Line through the Origin

When you are given the formula of a linear relation, you can create a table of values and then you can graph the line representing the relation. Are you able to work the other way? If you are given the graph of a line, can you represent this relation as a formula?

Example 1

The following graph represents a relation between gross pay and hours worked. Express this relation as a formula.

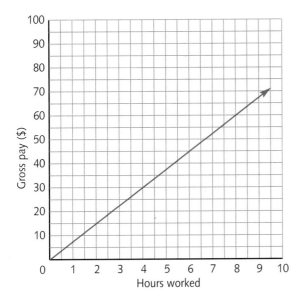

Goals

In this exploration, you will use the graph of a straight line that passes through the origin to determine the formula of the linear relation that the line represents.

Solution

The hourly rate of pay is the slope of the line. It can be identified as follows:

Locate two points on the line, A and B.

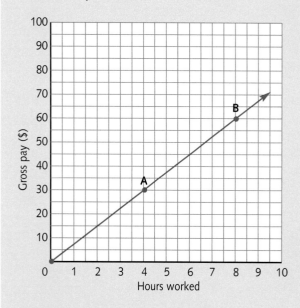

$$\text{slope} = \frac{\text{rise}}{\text{run}}$$

$$= \frac{\$60 - \$30}{8 \text{ hours} - 4 \text{ hours}}$$

$$= \frac{\$30}{4 \text{ hours}}$$

$$= \frac{\$7.50}{1 \text{ hour}}$$

$$= \$7.50 \text{ an hour}$$

The slope of the line is 7.5.

Therefore, the hourly rate of pay is $7.50 an hour.
The formula can be expressed by $P = 7.5h$.

This procedure can be used to find the formula for any linear relation that passes through the origin. Note that in the formula $P = 7.5h$, P is the dependent variable and h is the independent variable.

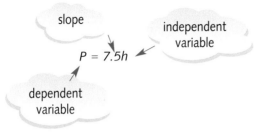

In general, the dependent variable equals slope times independent variable. Use this to find the formula for any line going through the origin. Consider the following example.

Example 2

A chemistry student examines a substance and finds the relation between its volume and its mass. She expresses the relation with the following graph.

a) Find the value of the slope of the line.

b) Express the relation represented by the graph as a formula.

c) What does the slope of the graph represent?

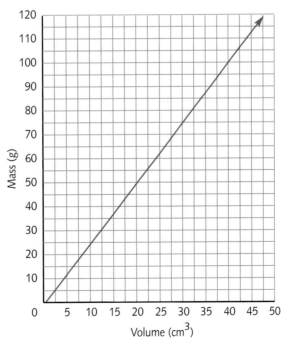

Solution

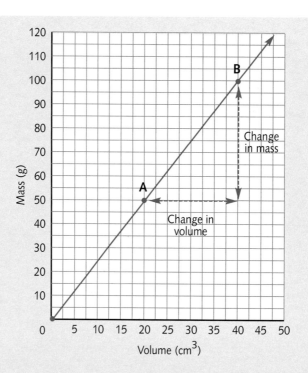

a) To find the slope, locate two points on the line, A and B. Calculate the change in the dependent variable:

100 − 50 = 50

Calculate the change in the independent variable:

40 − 20 = 20

Calculate the slope of the line:

$$\text{slope} = \frac{\text{rise}}{\text{run}} = \frac{50}{20} = \frac{5}{2}$$

The slope of the line is $\frac{5}{2}$ or 2.5.

b) Choose the letter m to represent the mass of the substance and the letter v to represent the volume of the object.

dependent variable = (slope)(independent variable)
$m = 2.5v$

c) The slope represents the mass of 1 cm³ of the substance. The scientific term for the mass of 1 cm³ of a substance is density. From the student's measurements, it is likely the substance is aluminum. Aluminum has a density of 2.699. The densities of some other substances are nickel—8.92, silver—10.49, and gold—19.32.

Bouncing Balls Activity

In the following activity, you will investigate the relationship between the height from which a ball is dropped and how high it bounces.

You will need the following equipment:

- metre stick
- masking tape
- a rubber ball
- transparent ruler
- graph paper

Working with one or two classmates, complete the following steps:

Step 1
Place the end of the metre stick on the floor and tape it to the wall.

Step 2
Place a piece of masking tape on the wall to mark 6 different drop heights. You must use 1 metre as one of your heights.

Step 3
Holding the bottom of the ball at the 1 m mark, drop the ball and record the height (cm) it bounces. Note: Try to measure the bounce from the bottom of the ball. Set up a chart where you can record the height from which you drop the ball and the height it bounces.

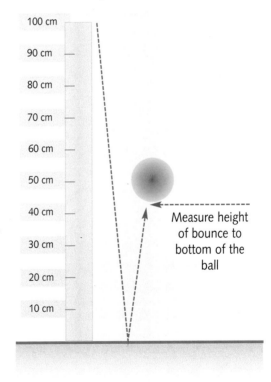

Measure height of bounce to bottom of the ball

Step 4
Drop the ball four more times from 1 m, recording its bounce height each time. Ignore any really wild bounces.

Step 5
Repeat steps 3 and 4 from 5 other drop heights, recording your data.

Step 6

For each drop height, cross off the highest and lowest bounce height values. Using the remaining three values, calculate the average bounce height and record this in the last column of your chart. Round this average to the nearest centimetre.

    The data that you have collected and recorded on your chart is a numerical model of the "bounciness" of your group's ball. In this form, the data may be difficult to interpret. To help visualize a pattern, draw a graph of these results.

Step 7

On your graph, plot drop height vs. average bounce height. The drop height is the independent variable and the bounce height is the dependent variable.

Step 8

Using your transparent ruler, draw the "line of best fit" for these points. Your points probably fall very closely along a straight line. However, if you just connect the dots, you will not get a perfectly straight line. There are several reasons why your points do not fall on a straight line:

- You may have made some errors in measurement.
- Your points may not be plotted properly.

In a situation like this, you can draw a line that passes through as many of the points as possible and comes as close as possible to the points that it misses. A line such as this is called the line of best fit. To draw the line of best fit for your graph, follow these steps:

    Adjust the position of a transparent ruler so that:

- its edge passes through as many points as possible.
- half the points that it does not touch are above the ruler.
- half the points that it does not touch are below the ruler.

The line that you have drawn is a graphical model of the relationship between the drop height of the ball and the bounce height.

New Terms	Hints
line of best fit: a straight line that best fits a set of data on a graph.	Remember that the independent variable is on the horizontal axis, while the dependent variable is on the vertical axis.

Step 9

Choose two points on your line of best fit and label them A and B. Find the slope of the line. What does this slope value represent?

Step 10

Use the values determined in step 9 to write the formula for the bounciness of your group's ball. Use the letters B for bounce height and D for drop height.

Both your graph and formula are models of the bounciness of your group's ball. Both can be used to make predictions of values not actually observed.

Step 11

Compare your results with those of other groups in your classroom.

Mental Math

Match the graph with the lines whose slope is $\frac{3}{2}$, 1, and $\frac{1}{3}$.

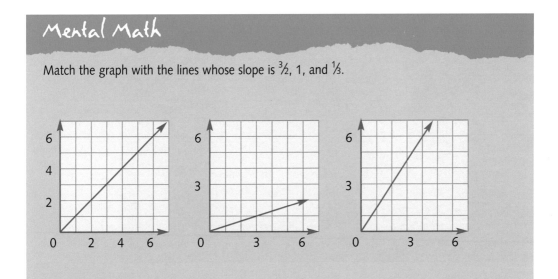

Project Activity

1. From your research, you probably found that the amount paid per tree varies depending on the company, the location, the type of tree, and the conditions of the soil. Often trees are delivered to tree-planters in bundles of 10.

    a) What amount will your company pay you for every 10 trees you plant?

    b) Draw a graph showing the relation between earnings ($) and the number of trees planted. Draw the graph for 0 to 200 trees.

    c) What is the slope of your line?

    d) What does this slope represent?

    e) Write a formula that describes this relation.

2. Suppose your group earns an additional 2 cents a tree.

   a) Draw a graph showing the relation between earnings ($) and the number of trees planted using this rate. Draw the graph for 0 to 200 trees.

   b) What is the slope of this line?

   c) What does this slope represent?

   d) Write the formula for this relation.

   e) How do the graphs of the two relations compare?

   f) How do the formulas expressing the two relations compare?

Notebook Assignment

1. The following graph represents a linear relation.

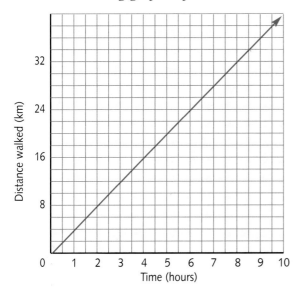

   a) Determine the dependent and independent variable of the relation.

   b) Determine the slope of the line.

   c) What is the meaning of the value of the slope?

   d) Write an equation (using letters) for the relation using the format below:

      dependent variable = slope × independent variable

2. The following graph represents a linear relation.

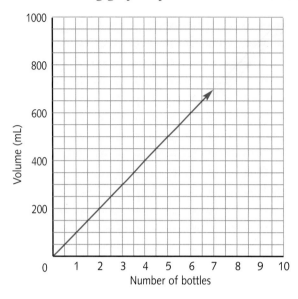

a) Determine the dependent and independent variables of the relation.

b) Use either interpolation or extrapolation to complete the following table.

Number of bottles		4		9
Volume (mL)	200		800	

c) Determine the slope of the line.

d) What is the meaning of the value of the slope?

e) Write an equation using letters for the relation.

3. Using the equation of the line from question 2e), complete the following table:

a)

Number of bottles		5		7
Volume (mL)	250		600	

b) What are the advantages and disadvantages of using a graph to solve linear relation problems?

c) What are the advantages and disadvantages of using a formula to solve linear relation problems?

4. A real estate agent's salary depends on the dollar value of all property sold. The agent earns 5% commission on all these sales.

    a) Identify the dependent and independent variables in this situation.

    b) Create a table for sales that shows $0 to $100,000 using increments of $20,000.

5. **a)** Construct a graph of the data from question 4.

    b) Determine the slope of the line.

    c) What does the slope represent?

    d) State the formula that describes the relationship among the dependent variable, the slope, and the independent variable (in words and using letters).

Extension

6. **a)** Draw any straight line through the origin and calculate its slope. Using letters to represent the independent and dependent variables, express the linear relation represented by the line as a formula. (Hint: Find the slope of the line.)

    b) Draw a second straight line going through the origin that is steeper than the first line. Choose the same letters for the independent and dependent variables. Express the linear relation represented by the line as a formula.

    c) How do the formulas compare?

Problem Analysis

Checking Drainage in Metroburg

Part of the job of a sanitation engineer consists of inspecting the underground drainage system of Metroburg. It is necessary that every section be inspected, and for obvious reasons the inspector does not wish to inspect any section more than once. Also, entry into and exit from the system are relatively inconvenient, and the inspector wishes to minimize the number of entrances and exits.

You may want to use coloured pencils to help you solve this problem. Reproduce the drawing and label different routes.

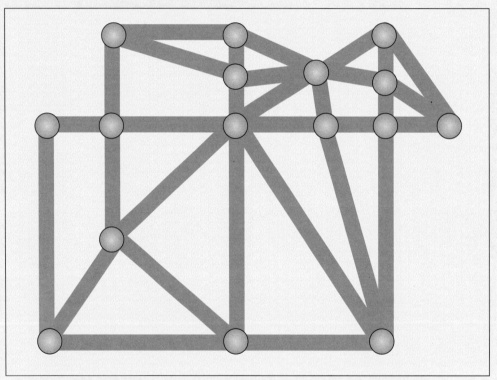

1. How many entrances and exits are required to give the inspector an opportunity to inspect each section of the system exactly once?

2. Find a path through the drainage system which has no more entrances and exits than required.

Games

The Peg Game
Can you find a winning pattern?

The board below shows two sets of pegs in slots. Black pegs are on the left and white pegs are on the right. There is an empty centre slot.

The object of the game is to exchange the positions of the black and white pegs.

Rules

- You can only move one peg at a time.
- You can only move "forward"; that is, black to right, white to left.
- You may move a peg into an adjacent empty slot, or
- You may jump exactly one peg of either colour into an empty slot.

Can you find a way to complete the task? There is a pattern of moves. Describe and explain the pattern.

Exploration 4

Linear Relations with a Fixed Value

In the previous explorations, the graph lines passed through the point (0,0) on the graph. You learned how to express these linear relations as a formula. What happens when a straight line does not go through the origin? How can you express it as a formula?

Consider the following examples. The first example shows a linear relation whose graph passes through the origin. The second example shows a linear relation whose graph does not pass through the origin. Note the similarities and differences between the two examples.

Example 1

A community centre has built a new banquet hall that they plan to rent out for weddings, socials, and other community events. The centre's budget is based on a charge of $4 per person. For any group renting the facility, the cost would thus depend upon the number of people who attend.

    a)   Create a table of values.

    b)   Graph the relation.

    c)   Determine the slope of the relation.

    d)   Write the formula for the relation.

Goals

In this exploration, you will use the graph of a straight line that does not pass through the origin to determine the formula of the linear relation represented by that line.

Solution

a) The independent variable is the number of people attending the event.

The dependent variable is the cost in dollars to rent the hall.

Number attending	0	20	40	60	80	100
Cost ($)	0	80	160	240	320	400

b) See the graph on the right.

c) slope $= \dfrac{\text{rise}}{\text{run}}$

$= \dfrac{\$400 - \$200}{100 - 50}$

$= \dfrac{\$200}{50 \text{ people}}$

$= \$4 \text{ a person}$

The slope of the line is 4. The slope represents the cost per person.

d) Use c to represent cost and n to represent the number of people attending the event. The formula can be expressed as:

dependent variable = (slope)(independent variable), or

$c = 4n$

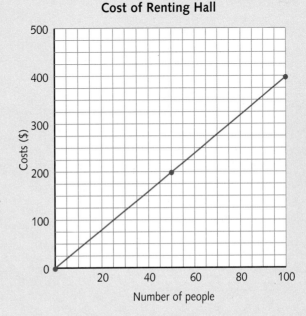

Cost of Renting Hall

Costs ($) / Number of people

Mental Math

1. A line has a slope of 2. Explain what this means.

2. A line has a slope of 20. Explain what this means.

3. How do the two lines compare?

Example 2

After a short while, the community centre finds that it is not making enough money to cover its expenses. In order to make a profit, it decides to charge renting groups $4 a person plus an additional charge of $50.

a) Complete a table of values for the community centre's new budget.

b) On the same graph as example 1, draw the graph of the data from this table of values.

c) Determine the slope of the new line.

d) How is the graph line of example 2 similar to the graph line of example 1? How is it different?

Solution

a)

Number Attending	0	20	40	60	80	100
Cost($)		50	130	210	290	370	450

b) See the graph on the right.

c) slope $= \dfrac{\text{rise}}{\text{(run)}}$

$= \dfrac{\$450 - \$250}{100 - 50}$

$= \dfrac{\$200}{50}$

$= \$4$ a person

The slope of the line is 4.

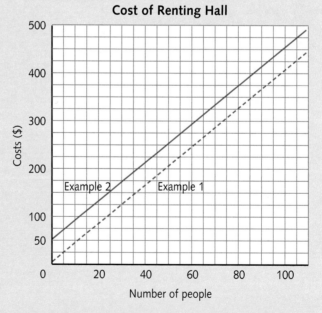

d) The two lines have the same slope of $4 a person. You can see this when you look at the graph. The two lines appear to have the same steepness and look to be parallel. The lines differ in where they cross the vertical axis. Adding an additional charge of $50 causes the line of example 2 to cross the vertical axis at $50.

Example 3

Find the formula for the relation represented by the line in example 2.

Solution

The formula for the relation of example 2 uses the same cost per person (slope) value as example 1. However, you must add the additional $50 to it. The two formulas will look like this:

Example 1	Example 2
Cost = $4 × number of people	Cost = $4 × number of people + $50
$C = 4n$	$C = 4n + 50

Example 2 represents a linear relation that does not pass through the origin. For this type of linear relation, the formula takes the following form:

dependent variable = (slope)(independent variable) + fixed value

Career Connection

Name: Kevin Gonzales

Job: concession stand at a community centre

Current wages: $7.25 an hour

Education: grade 11 student; Business Administration program, Assiniboine Community College, Brandon, MB

Career goal: entrepreneur

Keyword search: Canada college business administration

Project Activity

Although your group will earn money planting trees, it will also have expenses.

1. Estimate the cost of travelling to and from the work site. Refer to the activity in exploration 1. In addition to the cost of gasoline, include airfare if required, the maintenance costs of your vehicle, meals along the way, accommodation, and any other costs.

2. Estimate your clothing costs. These include items such as work gloves, steel-toed boots, a hard-hat, polypropylene underwear, and rain gear.

3. Estimate other expenses such as a tent, a bag to carry the trees, and bug repellent.

4. What is the daily living cost while you are planting trees?

5. Identify any other expenses you might incur.

Notebook Assignment

1. Two community centres rent banquet halls to private groups and charge the groups a fee based on the number of guests. The first community centre charges $5 for each guest; the second community centre charges $5 for each guest plus an additional fee of $100. Complete a table of values for each of the two community centres that includes the number of guests and the rental fee. Choose five numbers for each table of values.

2. **a)** Identify the independent variables of the relations in question 1.

    b) Identify the dependent variables of the relations in question 1.

    c) Draw the graphs for each of the relations described in question 1.

3. Refer to the two lines drawn in question 2.

    a) Does one line appear steeper than the other? Explain why or why not.

    b) Determine the value of the slope of each of the lines.

    c) How do the slopes of the lines compare to their steepness?

4. Refer to the two lines of question 2. Determine the formulas represented by each of the graphs.

5. The following two graphs model linear relations:

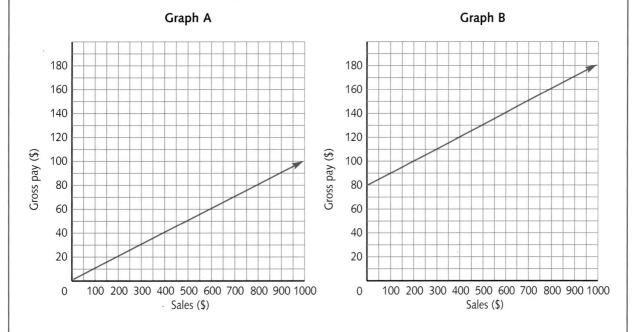

Graph A   Graph B

a) Identify the independent variables.

b) Identify the dependent variables.

c) What does the slope of each line represent?

d) Does one line appear steeper than the other?

e) Determine the slopes of each line.

f) How do the slopes of the lines compare?

6. Refer to the two lines on the graphs in question 5.

a) What is the fixed value for the line in Graph B?

b) What does the fixed value for the line in Graph B represent?

c) Determine the formulas for the lines in each graph.

7. A fitness centre charges its members a $50 registration fee when they join the centre. After that, they pay a monthly fee of $35.

   a) Express the relation between the cost of membership and the number of months of membership:

   - in words
   - with a table of values
   - as a graph
   - as a formula

   b) If you were promoting the centre, which method would you use to explain the costs? Why?

Extension

8. Suppose you own a video rental store and decide to hold the following promotion. You charge customers a fee for a special membership card that allows them to rent new releases at a reduced price. Choose an initial membership fee and a rental fee for the new releases. Choose fees in dollars or dollars plus fifty cents.

   a) Write a formula for the linear relation.

   b) Graph the linear relation.

   c) Give the graph to another student in the class and have him or her determine the formula expressed by your graph.

   d) Check to see whether the other student has found the correct formula.

Exploration 5

● ● ● ● ● ● ● ● ● ● ● ● ● ● ● ● ● ●

Applications of Linear Relations

When travelling, many people find it convenient to rent a vehicle. Suppose that you have a choice of renting a vehicle from one of two rental companies. How can you determine which company to rent from? An understanding of linear relations can help you make an informed decision.

When renting a vehicle, compare several companies' rates per day and per kilometre travelled.

Goals

In this exploration, you will use what you have learned about linear relations to solve real-world problems.

Example 1

Company A charges a car rental fee of $20 a day and $0.15/kilometre.
Company B charges a car rental fee of $30 a day and $0.10/kilometre.

a) Draw graphs representing car rentals from Company A and
Company B. Draw both lines on the same grid.

b) If you were going to drive 50 kilometres a day, which company
would be the better choice? Explain.

c) If you were going to drive 400 kilometres a day, which company
would be the better choice? Explain.

d) Where do the two lines cross? Explain the significance of this
crossover point.

Solution

a) Company A

Kilometres driven	0	100	200	300	400	500
Rental cost ($)	20	35	50	65	80	95

Company B

Kilometres driven	0	100	200	300	400	500
Rental cost ($)	30	40	50	60	70	80

Cost of Renting a Car from Companies A and B

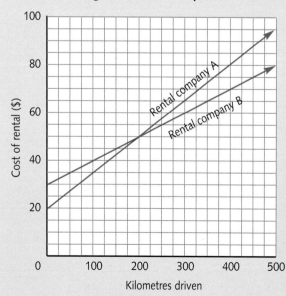

b)

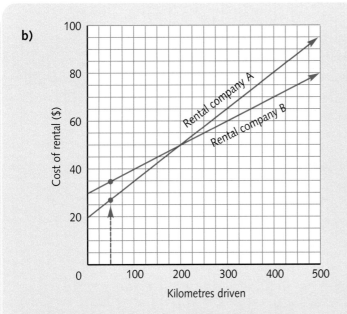

The cost of a car rental from Company A is lower when the distance driven (the independent variable) is 50 kilometres.

c)

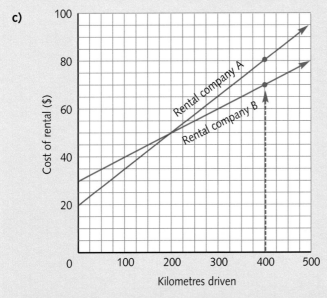

The cost of a car rental from Company B is lower when the distance driven is 400 kilometres.

d) The two lines cross at the point at which the independent variable is 200 kilometres and the dependent variable is $50. At this crossover point, the cost of renting from the two car rental companies is the same. On the left side of the crossover point, Company A is less expensive. On the right side of the crossover point, Company B is less expensive.

Example 2

The following graph represents the relationship between the Fahrenheit and Celsius temperature scales. Both scales are based on the freezing and boiling points of water. On the Fahrenheit scale, the freezing point is 32° and the boiling point is 212°. On the Celsius scale, the freezing point is 0° and the boiling point is 100°. The freezing point and boiling point are labelled on the line graph.

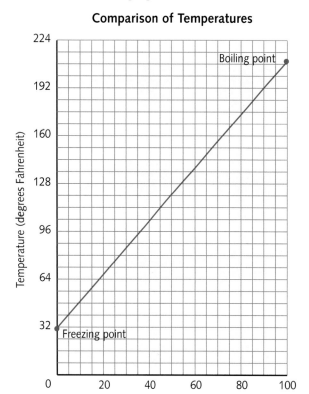

Comparison of Temperatures

a) Determine the slope of the line, using the freezing point and the boiling point.

b) Write a formula to represent the relation between degrees Fahrenheit and degrees Celsius. Use the letter F to represent degrees Fahrenheit and the letter C to represent degrees Celsius.

Solution

a) Locate the freezing point and the boiling point on the line.

$$\text{slope of the line} = \frac{\text{rise}}{\text{run}}$$

$$= \frac{212°F - 32°F}{100°C - 0°C}$$

$$= \frac{180°F}{100°C}$$

$$= \frac{9°F}{5°C}$$

The slope of the line is $\frac{9}{5}$ or 1.8.

b) The fixed value is the value of the dependent variable when the independent variable is 0. In this example, the fixed value is 32. Since dependent variable = (slope)(independent variable) + fixed value, $F = \frac{9}{5} C + 32$.

Project Activity

Refer to the list of expenses you created in exploration 4.

Some of these expenses, such as travel, clothing, and a bag for carrying trees are fixed. You have to pay them no matter how long you will be planting trees. Find the total of your fixed expenses.

Your living costs are variable, and the more days you stay the greater the cost will be.

1. Draw a graph showing the relation between expenses and the number of days you are on site.

2. Determine the slope of the graph.

3. What does the slope of your graph represent?

4. What is the fixed value?

5. What does it represent?

6. Write a formula that expresses the relation shown in your graph.

Notebook Assignment

1. Consider the following four graphs.

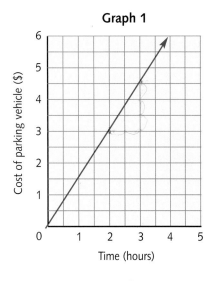

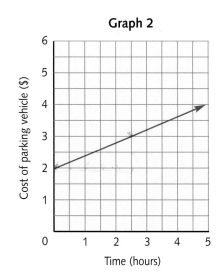

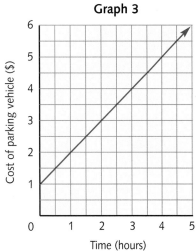

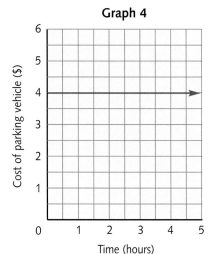

a) Identify the independent and dependent variables.
b) Determine the slope of each of the lines.
c) What does each slope represent?
d) Write the formulas for the lines.
e) Describe how the third and fourth graphs compare.

2. A school's soccer team is planning a trip. The team has determined the cost of the trip from two different travel agencies. Travel Agency A will charge the team $200 plus a cost of $45 per student. Travel Agency B will charge the team $250 plus a cost of $40 per student.

   a) Identify the independent and dependent variables of the relations.

   b) Using the letters C for cost and n for number of students, write a formula that represents Travel Agency A's total cost for the trip.

   c) Using the letters C for cost and n for number of students, write a formula that represents Travel Agency B's total cost for the trip.

3. Refer to the data provided in question 2.

   a) Draw the graphs of Travel Agency A and Travel Agency B on the same grid.

   b) If there were 5 students participating in the trip, which agency would have the lower cost? Explain.

   c) If there were 15 students participating in the trip, which agency would have the lower cost? Explain.

   d) Where do the line graphs cross? Explain the significance of this crossover point.

4. Consider the following line graph modelling the cost of a jacket sold at a discount department store.

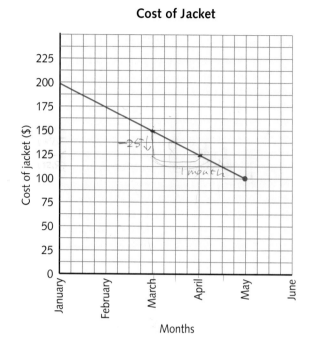

Cost of Jacket

a) Identify the independent and dependent variables.

b) Determine the slope of the line.

c) What does this slope represent?

d) Write a formula that represents the relationship between the cost of the jacket and the number of months.

Extension

5. The altimeter on a hot air balloon records the following altitudes.

Time	10:00	11:00	12:00	13:00	14:00	15:00	16:00	17:00	18:00
Altitude (m)	720	740	760	800	840	880	800	720	640

a) Identify the independent and dependent variables for the relation.

b) Plot these points on a grid.

c) Describe the flight of the hot air balloon from 10:00 to 18:00.

d) Calculate the slope of the line segments from:

  (i)   10:00 – 12:00
  (ii) 12:00 – 15:00
  (iii) 15:00 – 18:00

Exploration 6

Interpreting Graphs

In the previous explorations, you looked at graphs of linear relations. You learned that the graph of a linear relation is a line. There are many other possible relations between two variables. This exploration looks at the graphs of such relations.

Example 1

Nuka is a cross-country skier. On Saturday, she skied a trail near her home. The following graph shows her speed as she went along the trail. She started off along the trail at 10:00 a.m.

a) What is her speed at 10:20 am?

b) At what time is she going the fastest and what is her speed at that time?

c) What happens to her speed between 10:25 am and 10:35 am?

d) Describe her trip.

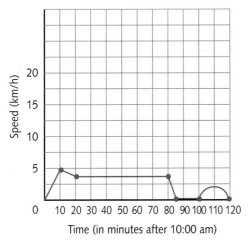

Nuka's Cross-Country Skiing Speed

Goals

In this exploration, you will examine and interpret graphs of relations that are not linear relations.

Solution

a) Her speed is about 4 km/h.

b) She is going the fastest at about 10:10 when she is going 5 km/h.

c) Her speed is constant.

d) As Nuka begins the trail, she increased in speed steadily for the first ten minutes to 5 km/h. She then slows down to 4 km/h and skis at that speed for about 60 minutes. Then, she slows to a stop over a 5-minute period. Nuka then takes a rest for 15 minutes. During the last 20 minutes of her trip, she gradually increases her speed to about 2 km/h and then gradually decreases to 0.

Example 2

A cafeteria has a large vending machine that contains soft drinks in cans. The graph below shows the varying number of cans in the machine on a typical day.

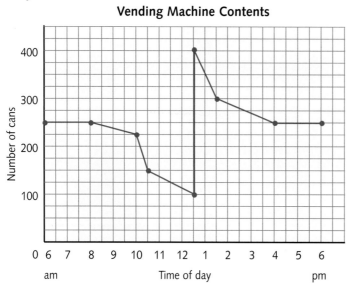

Vending Machine Contents

a) Describe how the number of cans in the machine varies during the day.

b) When is the morning coffee break, and when is lunch hour?

c) Can employees use the vending machine during working hours?

d) How many cans are sold during a typical working day?

Solution

a) Before 8:00 am, there are 250 cans in the machine. From 8:00 am to 10:00 am, 25 cans are purchased, and the number of cans decreases to 225. Between 10:00 am and 10:30 am, 75 cans are purchased. Between 10:30 am and 12:30 pm, 50 cans are purchased. At 12:30 pm, 300 cans are added to the machine. Between 12:30 pm and 1:30 pm, about 100 cans are purchased. From 1:30 to 4:00 pm, another 50 cans are purchased. The number of remaining cans in the machine is 250.

b) The number of drinks sold indicates that the morning coffee break is between 10:00 and 10:30 am, and the lunch hour is from 12:30 to 1:30 pm.

c) Employees can buy drinks during working hours.

d) 300 cans are sold during a typical working day.

The shape of a graph can tell you a great deal even if there are no numbers on the axes. Consider the following example.

Example 3

The following graphs show how interest rates have changed with time in three different countries. Describe how the interest rates have changed in each of the countries.

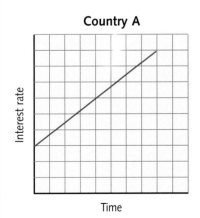
Country A

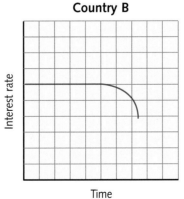
Country B

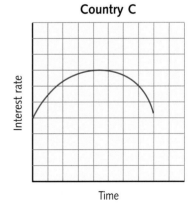
Country C

Solution

In Country A, interest rates rose steadily throughout the time period.

In Country B, interest rates were higher than in Country A at the beginning of the time period, remained constant for most of the time, and dropped rapidly for the last period of time.

In Country C, interest rates increased rapidly at first, then more slowly reached a maximum about halfway through the time period, and then decreased for the rest of the time period.

When you are interpreting graphs, check the value of the independent variable at zero. What is the value of the dependent variable at that point? Does it make sense?

As the value of the independent variable increases, check whether the value of the dependent variable increases or decreases. What does this mean for the particular variables? Does it make sense?

Check whether the value of the dependent variable changes at a steady rate. If it does not, how does it change? Is the change faster at first and slower later on, or is it slow at first and faster later on?

Example 4

Draw a graph to represent the following situation:

Sara walks from her home to the store. Halfway to the store, she realizes that she forgot to bring money, so she turns around, returns home, gets her money, and then walks all the way to the store. Graph time on the horizontal axis and distance from home on the vertical axis.

Solution

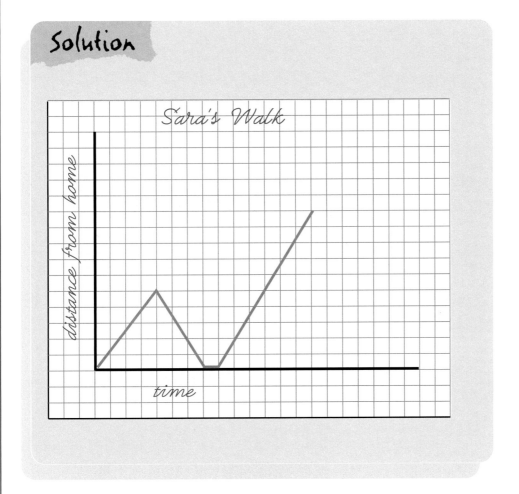

Project Activity

The number of trees you plant during a day will vary. There are times during the day when you will be more efficient than others. There are also times during the day when you will take breaks.

a) Draw a graph showing the number of trees you plant compared to the time of day.

b) Draw a graph showing the total number of trees you plant compared to the time.

c) How do the two graphs compare?

Notebook Assignment

1. Koihok types for three minutes at the rate of thirty-five words a minute. He takes a two-minute break and then types for three more minutes at the rate of twenty words a minute. Which graph best represents Koihok's time at the keyboard?

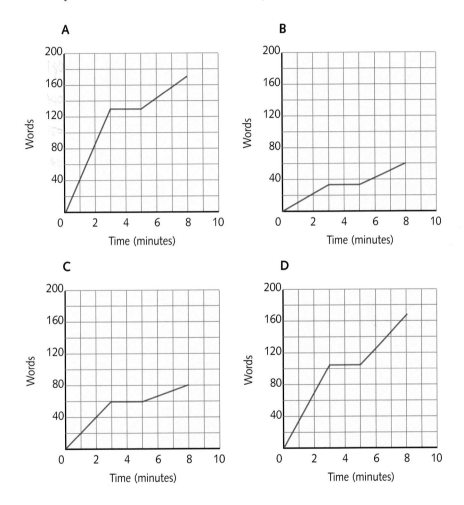

2.   The graph below shows the amount of gasoline in the gas tank during a recent trip.

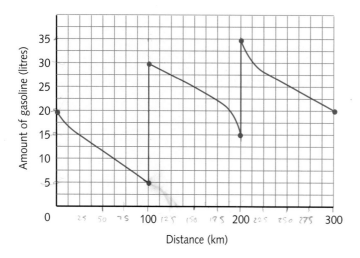

Distance (km)

a)   How many times did the driver fill up after the trip began?

b)   When was the most gasoline bought?

c)   How much gas was used for the entire trip?

d)   How much gasoline might the gas tank hold?

e)   If no stops had been made for gasoline fill-ups, how many kilometres after beginning would the car have run out of gasoline?

f)   Town driving uses more gasoline than country driving because you have to keep stopping and starting. Where were the towns located on this journey?

3.   The manager of a ski resort keeps a record of the depth of snow outside the lodge throughout the ski season. The graph below shows data collected during one week last winter.

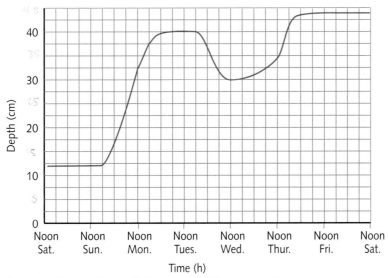

a) On which days of the week did it snow?

b) On which day did the greatest amount of snow fall?

c) Estimate the total depth of new snow which fell during the week.

d) It rained one day that week. On which day did it rain?

e) Estimate the amount of snow that melted on the rainy day.

f) If the snow had continued to melt at the same rate for one more day, what depth would have been left at the end of that day?

Ski resorts track the depth of snow on a daily basis.

4. Select the graph that best illustrates the situation described.

a) A car is travelling at a constant speed on a highway. It increases its speed to pass a second car, then returns to its original speed.

(i)

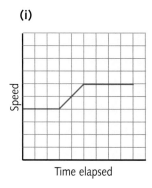

Time elapsed

(ii)

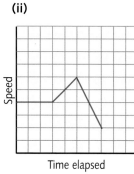

Time elapsed

(iii)

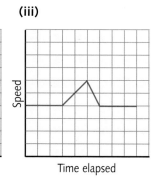

Time elapsed

(iv)

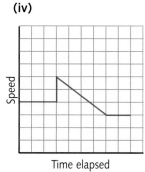

Time elapsed

b) A person is jogging, slows down and walks a while, and then slows down to a stop.

(i)

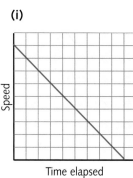

Time elapsed

(ii)

Time elapsed

(iii)

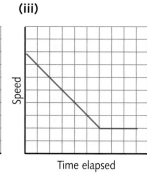

Time elapsed

(iv)

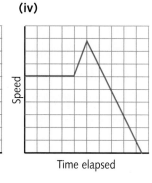

Time elapsed

c) A child climbs a hill at a steady pace and then runs down.

(i)

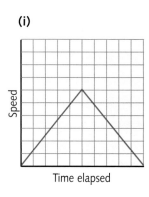

Time elapsed

(ii)

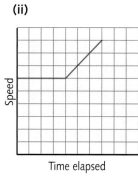

Time elapsed

(iii)

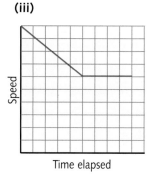

Time elapsed

(iv)

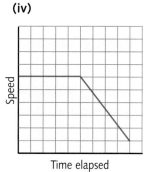

Time elapsed

d) A ball is thrown into the air from chest height and falls to the ground.

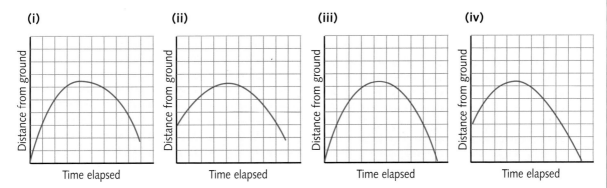

(i)   **(ii)**   **(iii)**   **(iv)**

e) A student takes a ride on a ferris wheel.

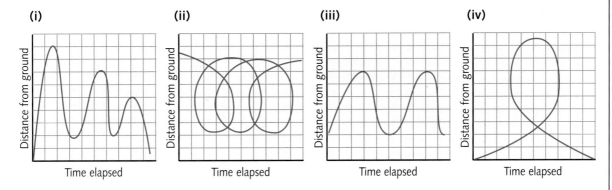

(i)   **(ii)**   **(iii)**   **(iv)**

5. Sketch a reasonable graph for each of the following statements:

    a) the height of a football compared to the number of seconds since it was kicked

    b) the temperature of a cup of coffee compared to the length of time it has been cooling

    c) the distance a yo-yo is from the ground compared to the time it is played with

    d) the number of pops per second a popcorn-maker makes compared to the time

6. Draw a graph to represent each of the following statements.

   a) Rashid is jumping on a trampoline. Graph the distance he is above the ground compared to the time he spends.

   b) Kendra is speeding along the highway and is stopped by a police officer. The officer gives her a ticket and then she continues on her way. Graph time on the horizontal axis and her speed on the vertical axis.

How does being stopped by the police affect Kendra's travelling speed?

   c) Carlos lives in a large city and travels to school on a local bus that stops every block to let passengers on and off.
     (i) Graph the speed of the bus compared to time.
     (ii) Graph the distance of the bus compared to time.

Extension

7. Describe a situation to match each of the following graphs. Label the dependent and independent variables on each graph.

(i)   **(ii)**   **(iii)**   **(iv)**

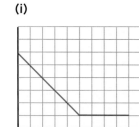 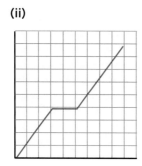 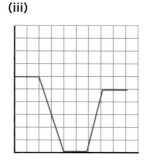 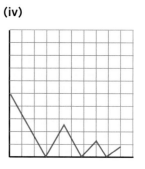

Exploration 7

Formulas

Formulas express relations. In this chapter, you have used formulas that express linear relations. There are also formulas that express other kinds of relations.

Many financial relations are expressed by formulas. You are familiar with the formula $I = prt$, the formula for calculating simple interest. This formula expresses the relationship between the amount of interest (I), the principal (p), the annual rate (r) of interest, and the length of time (t) in years. Because this relation involves more than two variables, it is not a linear relation. But since a relation exists among the four variables, you can solve for a missing variable when you are given the other three.

Many relationships in geometry can also be expressed using formulas. Most of these formulas do not express linear relations. For example, the area of a circle can be expressed as $A = \pi r^2$, where A is the area of the circle and r is the radius of the circle. Given one of the variables, you can solve for the other. Can you think of other formulas you have used in the past?

Goals	Hints	Mental Math
In this exploration, you will evaluate formulas.	Recall that you refer to the quantities in a formula as variables and represent them by letters.	Change the following percents to a decimal equivalent. **a)** 35% **b)** 90% **c)** 8% **d)** 0.5%

Example 1

A principal amount of $1,500 is invested in a financial institution that offers an interest rate of 4% per annum. Using the formula $I = prt$, calculate the interest earned at the end of five years.

Solution

$p = \$1,500 \qquad r = 0.04 \qquad t = 5 \qquad I = ?$

$I = prt$

$\quad = (1500)(0.04)(5)$

$\quad = 300$

After five years, the investment has earned $300.00 in interest.

Example 2

In a processing plant, a 10 cm-long bearing sleeve with a radius of 4 cm needs to be coated with Teflon. It costs $0.20/cm^2 to coat the sleeves. What is the total cost to coat 1000 sleeves?

The surface area of a cylinder (S) is found using the formula $S = 2\pi rh + 2\pi r^2$, where r is the radius of the cylinder and h is the height.

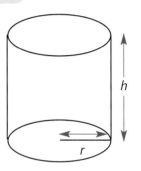

Solution

$S = 2\pi rh + 2\pi r^2$

$\quad = 2\pi(4)(10) + 2\pi(4)^2$

$\quad = 2\pi(40) + 2\pi(16) = 80\pi + 32\pi = 112\pi = 351.8583772$

The surface area of the cylinder rounded to two decimal places is 351.86 cm^2.

The cost is 351.86 cm^2 x $0.20/cm^2

$\quad = 351.86 \times 0.20$

$\quad = \$70.372$ to coat 1 sleeve

The total cost is $1000 \times \$70.372 = \$70,372$ to coat 1000 sleeves.

New Terms

irrational number: a number that cannot be expressed as a rational number.

Hints

π is an irrational number. Use the $\boxed{\pi}$ key on your calculator to evaluate expressions with π. π is approximately equal to 3.14.

Project Activity

1. Refer to the formulas you created in the project activity in exploration 3.

    a) Use the two formulas to find how much you would earn if you planted 1600 trees a day.

    b) Use the two formulas to find how much you would earn if you planted 2500 trees a day.

    c) How many trees would you need to plant to earn $500.00?

2. Referring to the project activity in exploration 4.

    a) Calculate your expenses if you are on site 50 days.

    b) Calculate your expenses if you are on site 70 days.

Members of a crew compete to see who plants the most trees per day.

Notebook Assignment

Solve the following problems by evaluating the formulas provided.

1. The formula for calculating the perimeter of a rectangle is $P = 2l + 2w$. Calculate the perimeter of a rectangle that has a length of 20 cm and a width of 15 cm.

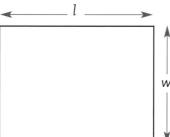

2. The formula for maximum heart rate has been defined as
   $r = 208 - (0.7)(a)$ where r is the heart rate and a is a person's age.

   a) Find the maximum heart rate recommended for a person
      aged 25.

   b) Find the maximum heart rate recommended for a person
      aged 40.

   c) Describe what happens to the recommended maximum heart rate
      as a person ages.

3. The relation between a vehicle's stopping distance (d) in metres and
   the vehicle's speed (s) in kilometres per hour is modelled by the
   formula
   $d = 0.0056s^2 + 0.14s$.

   a) Find the vehicle's stopping distance when its speed is 30
      kilometres per hour.

   b) Predict the vehicle's stopping distance when its speed is 60
      kilometres per hour.

   c) Find the vehicle's stopping distance when its speed is 60
      kilometres per hour.

   d) Was the vehicle's stopping distance at 60 kilometres per hour
      greater or less than you expected? Explain.

4. The world population in 1994 had just surpassed 6 billion. If the
   world population increases 1% a year on average, the population in
   future years is given by the formula $P = 6\ 000\ 000\ 000(1.01)^{t-1994}$
   (where P represents the population and t represents the year).

   a) Calculate the population predicted by the formula in the year
      2020.

   b) Calculate the population for 2002 using the formula.

   c) Find the actual population for 2002 using the internet. How
      does it compare to your calculation in b)? Is the world
      population increasing at 1%, more than 1%, or less than 1% per
      year?

5. The number of diagonals of a polygon with n sides can be found with the formula $d = \frac{n}{2}(n - 3)$. Find the number of diagonals for a polygon of 6 sides.

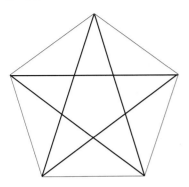

6. During a peak season, the rate at which a lemming population doubles can be expressed by the formula $P = N \times 2^t$, where N is the original number of lemmings, and t is the time in months. Determine how many lemmings would result from an original population of 500 lemmings after six months had passed.

7. In an electrical circuit, the total resistance, R_t, of two resistors, R_1 and R_2, in a parallel formation, is given by the formula:

$$\frac{1}{R_t} = \frac{1}{R_1} + \frac{1}{R_2}$$

Find the total resistance when the 2 resistors are 10 ohms and 20 ohms.

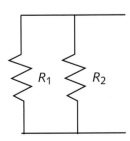

8. The theorem of Pythagoras states that the square of the hypotenuse, c, is equal to the sum of the squares of the other two sides, a and b. The theorem is expressed by the formula $c^2 = a^2 + b^2$. Find the hypotenuse of a triangle when side $a = 5$ and side $b = 12$.

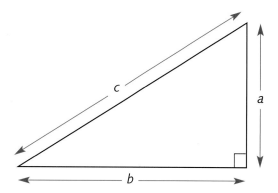

9. The height a rocket will reach in t seconds when it is propelled upwards with an initial speed of s metres per second is given by the formula $h = st - 4.9t^2$. Find the height a rocket will reach in five seconds when it is propelled upwards with an initial speed of 1000 metres per second.

Extension

10. The last term in an arithmetic sequence such as 1, 3, 5, 7, 9 . . . can be found using the formula $t_n = t_1 + (n - 1)d$, where t_n is the last term, t_1 is the first term, n is the number of terms, and d is the difference between the terms. Find the last term in the sequence 1, 3, 5, 7, . . . if the sequence has 100 terms.

11. The formula for calculating the final amount of an investment earning compound interest is $A = P(1 + r/n)^{nt}$. Use this formula to calculate the final amount (A) if a principal (P) of \$1,000 is invested at a rate (r) of 6% for 3 years (t), compounded semi-annually ($n = 2$).

Chapter Review

1. Match each of the formulas below with the appropriate line graph. The formulas and line graphs model the relation between the number of months members belong to a gym and the cost of membership.

i)

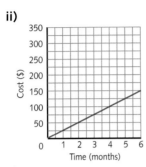

ii)

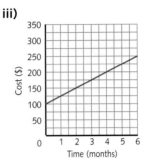

iii)

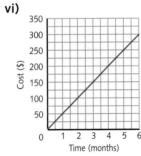

iv)

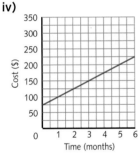

v)

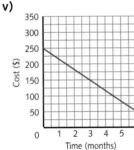

vi)

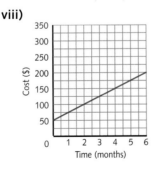

vii)

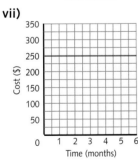

viii)

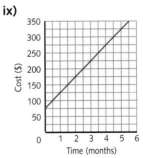

ix)

a) $C = 50n$

b) $C = 25n + 75$

c) $C = 50n + 75$

d) $C = 250$

e) $C = 25n + 50$

f) $C = 25n$

g) $C = 50n + 50$

2. A department store is selling all its goods at a 20% discount. Express the relation between the amount of the discount and the marked price:

  a) in words

  b) with a table of values (choose five of your own values)

  c) as a graph

  d) as a formula using the letter p for marked price and d for the amount of the discount

3. Refer to the graph you drew in question 2c). Complete the following table of values for the line graph, using interpolation or extrapolation.

Marked price	$30			$110	
Discount		$5			$26

4. Consider the following graph modelling the speed of a skydiver in free fall after a number of seconds.

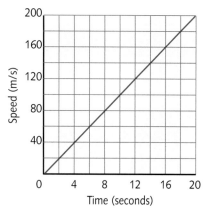

  a) Identify the independent variable.

  b) Identify the dependent variable.

  c) Complete the following table of values for the line graph, using interpolation or extrapolation.

Time (seconds)	5			12	
Speed (m/s)		100			140

5. Refer to the graph in question 4.

   a) What does the slope of the line represent?

   b) Determine the slope of the line.

   c) Determine the formula of the line graph. Choose the letters *s* for speed and *t* for time.

   d) Using the formula, complete the following table of values.

Time (seconds)	9	18	60
Speed (m/s)			

6. An electrical repair company charges its customers $50 plus an additional $20 for each half-hour of repairs. Express the relation between the cost of a repair and the time:

   a) in words

   b) with a table of values

   c) as a graph

   d) as a formula using the letter *c* for cost and *t* for time

7. Refer to the graph you drew in question 6c).

   a) Determine the slope of the line graph. Show your calculations.

   b) State the fixed value of the line graph.

   c) How do the slope and fixed value of the line graph compare with the formula you found in question 6?

8. Gabriel cycles to a friend's house but on the way his bike tire is punctured, and he has to walk the rest of the way there. At his friend's house, he repairs the puncture, and plays a video game. On the way back, he stops at a store for a snack. Use the following graph to answer the questions below.

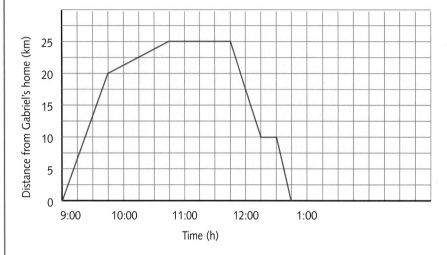

a) How far is it to his friend's house?

b) How far is it from his friend's house to the store?

c) At what time did his bike tire get punctured?

d) How long did he stay at his friend's house?

e) At what speed did he travel:
   (i) after the puncture to his friend's house?
   (ii) from his friend's house to the store?
   (iii) from the store back to his own home?

9. Thomas is travelling on the highway at 80 km/h. He enters a town and slows to 50 km/h. He then travels at 100 km/h. After a while, he stops to fill the car with gasoline. Once the car is filled with gasoline, he continues travelling at 100 km/h. Graph the speed at which Thomas travels compared to time.

10. Every morning at camp, one of the scouts hoists a flag to the top of the flagpole. The graphs below show the height of the flag as a function of time. Which do you think models the situation most realistically? If you think none of the graphs is realistic, draw your own version and explain it. Do any of the graphs represent an impossible situation?

a.

b.

c.

d.

e.

f.

11. The velocity of sound in air increases as the air temperature becomes warmer. The formula describing this relationship is $v = 330 + 0.6T$ where v is the velocity in *m/s* and T is the temperature in C°. Calculate the speed of sound at 16°C.

Project Presentation

Answer the following questions and place all your work, including any research you have done, in a portfolio.

1. Indicate the number of weeks you will be planting trees. Note that you plant trees 6 days each week.

2. Since you have not planted trees before, it will take some time until you can become efficient at it. Create a table that shows the number of trees you will be able to plant each week during the summer.

3. Calculate the amount you will earn from planting these trees.

4. Use the formula you created in the project activity of exploration 5 to calculate your expenses for tree planting.

5. How much money will you make after you deduct the expenses from your earnings?

6. Some students plant trees for a number of summers. They find that they are more efficient the next year compared to when they were beginners.

   a) If you decide to return and plant trees the next year, calculate how much money you would earn. Assume you could plant 30% more trees.

   b) Calculate your expenses. They may be less than the year before because you already have some of the equipment.

   c) How much money will you make after you deduct the expenses from your earnings?

7. a) Explain why you chose the company you did.

   b) What type of research did you do on the company?

   c) Are you confident it will be a good company to work for?

   d) Do they treat their rookies as well as the veterans?

Case Study

• • • • • • • • • • • • • •

Jordan is a university student from Winnipeg. He spent 6 summers planting trees in both northern Manitoba and northern British Columbia. He has written a book for students about tree planting. Two companies are interested in publishing his book.

Aura Publishing offers him royalties of 10% on book sales. McCreary Publishing offers him $1,500 for the rights to the book plus royalties of 5% on book sales. Each book sells for $15.00.

1. For each of the two publishing companies:

   a) Identify the independent and dependent variables of the relation.

   b) Create a table of values for the relation.

   c) Graph the relation.

   d) Determine the formula for the relation.

   e) Choose two points from the graph and find the slope of the relation.

   f) Explain what the slope of the relation represents.

2. **a)** Explain how the two relations are alike and how they are different.

   b) Explain how these similarities and differences are reflected in the graphs.

3. Each company is planning a first edition of 5000 books. The price of each book will be $15.00. Use the formulas you found in question 1 to answer the following questions. Show the formula, the substitution, and the answer.

   a) How much does Jordan earn with each company if all 5000 books are sold? Which publishing company pays Jordan more money? How much more?

   b) How much does Jordan earn with each company if only 2000 books are sold? Which publishing company pays Jordan more money? How much more?

4. Refer to your answers to questions 1–3 to decide which publishing company to select.

   a) Determine the value of the book sales at which both publishing companies pay Jordan the same amount of money.

   b) How many books would have to be sold for this amount of sales?

   c) Which company pays him more if sales are higher than this?

   d) Which company pays him more if sales are less than this?

5. Jordan decides to have the book published by McCreary Publishing. During the first week after the book is launched, sales are 50 books a day. During the next week, sales are 20 books a day. After that, sales remain constant at 5 books a day for the next 6 weeks. After an article appears in the newspaper about Jordan's book, sales increase to 30 books a day for the next week. Then they remain constant at 10 books a day for the next 4 weeks.

   a) Calculate the number of books that were sold in this time period.

   b) If sales were to continue at this rate, calculate the number of books that would be sold in a year.

   c) Is it realistic that the book would continue to sell at this rate? How could the company ensure that sales would continue at this rate?

   d) Did Jordan choose the publishing company that would pay him the greater amount of money? Explain.

Chapter 6

Applications of Probability

Understanding Probability

The popular French expression "bonne chance" means "good luck." Playing card games and board games or tossing coins all involve probability. Probability is also used to make decisions about the world. This chapter will teach you how to calculate the probability of specific events occurring: the next card being an ace, the next roll being a 7, getting a defective part for a car, or the chance of having a baby with blue eyes. This information can be used to develop strategies to take advantage of probability.

As you work through this chapter, you will flip coins, roll dice, and draw cards. These activities will help you learn how to calculate probability and odds, and to determine expected gains or losses. With this knowledge, perhaps you too will enjoy "bonne chance."

Goals

In this chapter, you will learn how to calculate probability and odds both theoretically and experimentally. You will also learn how to use probabilities to calculate expected gains and losses.

Career Connection

Name: Chris Lazlo

Job: computer retail sales clerk

Current wages: $10.50/h

Education: grade 12; self-taught computer geek

Career goal: software developer for computer games

Keyword search: Canada college computer

Chapter Project

The project for this chapter will be to create a game of chance to raise funds at a charitable event. Working individually or with a partner, you will design and demonstrate a unique game. You will calculate the probabilities of winning and losing. You will also calculate how much profit your game should generate using expected values. When you have completed the project, you will have the following information in your project file:

1. a description of the game and a statement of its objective

2. the rules for playing the game

3. a list of materials needed

4. a calculation of the probability and odds of winning

5. how much money it costs to play

6. payoffs for winning

7. expected values

The following diagram represents a standard deck of 52 playing cards.

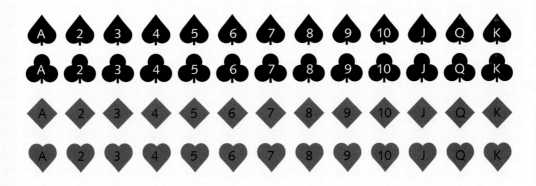

Exploration 1

Expressing Probabilities

Probability is an indication of the likelihood of an event occurring. It is expressed as a comparison of desired outcomes to total outcomes. Probabilities can be expressed in different ways. In this chapter we will use four of the most common: fractions, decimals, percents, and words. Many people use written expressions such as "one chance in ten" to express probability while others write $\frac{1}{10}$ to express the same probability.

Example 1

Determine the probability of drawing a spade from a deck of well-shuffled playing cards and state your answer as a fraction, a decimal, a percent, and in words. Refer to the diagram on p. 321.

Solution

There are 13 spades in a deck of 52 cards. This can be expressed in the following ways:

fraction: $\frac{13}{52}$ or $\frac{1}{4}$

decimal: 0.25

percent: 25%

in words: 13 out of 52 or one out of four

Goals

In this exploration, you will learn to express probabilities as fractions, decimals, percents, and in words.

Hints

$$\text{Probability} = \frac{\text{number of desired outcomes}}{\text{total possible outcomes}}$$

Pairs Activity

Work with a partner to design your own probability question based on your immediate surroundings. Examples might include:

- What is the probability that students are wearing jeans?
- What is the probability that girls have elastics in their hair?
- What is the probability that students are wearing sandals?

Estimate each probability. Express your probabilities as fractions, decimals, percents, and in words.

Career Connection

Name: Sarah Gatin

Job: Coffee shop baker

Current wages: $8.25 an hour

Education: grade 12; on-the-job training with a senior baker

Career goal: store manager

Keyword search: Canada college chef culinary arts

This young woman is a student in the baking program at Vancouver Community College.

Notebook Assignment

1. Complete the following chart, which shows different ways to express a probability.

Fraction	Decimal	Percent	Words
			one in five
$\frac{1}{2}$			
	0.3		
		60%	

2. Complete the chart below. It shows the probability of randomly selecting a student with a particular hair colour from the population of a high school.

Colour	Decimal	Percent	Fraction	Words
Brown				five out of ten
Blonde			$\frac{1}{8}$	
Black	0.25			
Red		5%		
Other				Seventy-five out of 1000

3. When rolling a fair six-sided die, express the probability that:

   a) you will roll a 2; express this as a fraction

   b) you will roll a prime number; express this as a decimal

   c) you will roll a 3 or a 4; express as a percent

   d) you will roll a seven; express in words

Mental Math

1. Express 25% as a fraction.

2. Express $\frac{3}{10}$ as a decimal.

3. Express 0.35 as a percent.

Hints

1. A prime number is only divisible by 1 and itself. 1 is not considered a prime number.

2. In this chapter, assume that all dice are fair and six-sided.

4. You are rolling two dice and want to get a pair of threes. State the probability of this happening as a:

    a) decimal

    b) fraction

    c) percent

    d) word phrase

5. When drawing a card randomly from a standard deck of playing cards, what is the probability it will be a:

    a) heart

    b) red card

    c) 5

    d) face card (Jack, Queen, or King)

    e) black 6

6. When buying a box of 30 Christmas oranges, you can expect 10% of the oranges to be rotten. If you pick an orange at random, state the probability that you will pick:

    a) a rotten orange

    b) a good orange

7. If each month is equally likely, determine the probability of being born in a particular month. Express this probability as a fraction, a percent, and in words.

Extension

8. A car dealer is giving away a new SUV. Each day a person is chosen to try a key on a ring with 75 keys. The dealer states in the advertisements that "the probability of winning is one in seventy-five." Is this statement correct or incorrect? Explain.

Exploration 2

Making Predictions Using Probability

We can use probability to predict answers to questions. If our samples are random, or fairly chosen, we can use these probabilities to make predictions.

We use probabilities to make predictions in many areas of our lives. Consider the following conversation in the school cafeteria.

Jim: I am going to be in trouble in math class today.
Aimée: Why?
Jim: I didn't do my homework.
Aimée: So what! I didn't either.
Jim: Since the teacher asks half the class for answers each day, he will probably call on me today.
Aimée: The teacher called on me yesterday, so he probably won't catch me today.

In this dialogue, each student is making a judgement based on probability. Who is correct?

If you are selling ice cream cones, and you know that the probability of someone asking for vanilla is 3 in 4, then you can use this information to order enough vanilla ice cream to serve your customers.

If the weather forecast calls for an 80% chance of rain, would you prepare yourself for rain?

Goals

In this exploration, you will make predictions based on given probabilities.

Hints

Probability is always measured on a scale from 0 to 1 or 0% to 100%. Events which are impossible have a probability of 0 or 0%. Events that are certain to occur have a probability of 1 or 100%.

This farmer is applying fungicide to potato fields in Manitoba.

Example 1

If there is a probability that one person in seven has green eyes, how many in a group of 210 are likely to have green eyes?

Solution

$$\frac{\text{green eyes}}{\text{sample size}} = \frac{\text{green eyes in group}}{\text{total in group}}$$

$$\frac{1}{7} = \frac{x}{210}$$

where x is the number in the group with green eyes.

$$7x = 210$$

$$x = \frac{210}{7}$$

$$x = 30$$

Therefore, 30 people in the group are likely to have green eyes.

Example 2

In a pack of 20 wolves, 9 had frost damage to their ears, and 11 did not. If there are an estimated 610 wolves in the southern Yukon, how many do you predict will have frost-damaged ears?

Solution

$$\frac{\text{damaged ears}}{\text{sample size}} = \frac{\text{damaged ears}}{\text{total estimated population}}$$

Let x represent the number of wolves with damaged ears in southern Yukon.

$$\frac{9}{20} = \frac{x}{610}$$

$$20x = (9)(610)$$

$$x = \frac{(9)(610)}{20}$$

$$x = 274.5$$

You can predict that there are approximately 275 wolves with frost-bitten ears in the southern Yukon wolf population.

Example 3

You enter a store promising to award 10 door prizes per day. It is near closing time, and they have awarded 6 gifts so far. If there are 200 people in the store, what is the probability of you receiving a door prize?

Solution

If 6 prizes have been awarded, then there are 4 prizes for the remaining 200 customers.

The probability of receiving a door prize is:

$$\frac{4}{200} = \frac{1}{50}$$

The probability is one in fifty that you will receive a door prize.

Mental Math

1. If 6 T-shirts cost $42.00, what is the cost of 1 T-shirt?

2. Solve for "t" in the equation $6t = 42$.

Example 4

This bar graph indicates the number of hours a month that students in three grade 11 classes spend on the internet.

Determine the probability that a student chosen at random from these classes:

a) uses the internet for 12 to 16 hours a month.

b) uses the internet for 16 to 28 hours a month.

c) uses the internet more than 4 hours a month.

d) Will the probabilities determined from these three classes hold true for grade 11 students in your province? Explain.

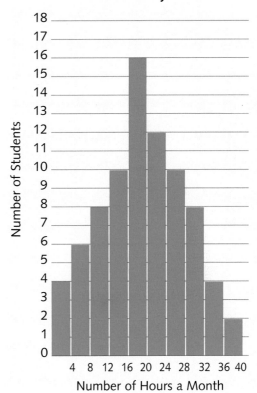

Internet Use by Students

Number of Students vs. Number of Hours a Month

Solution

a) The total number of students surveyed is:

$4 + 6 + 8 + 10 + 16 + 12 + 10 + 8 + 4 + 2 = 80$

The probability that a student in these classes uses between 12 to 16 hours a month on the internet is:

$\frac{10}{80} = \frac{1}{8}$

b) The number of students in these classes who spend between 16 and 28 hours a month on the internet is:

$16 + 12 + 10 = 38$

The probability that a student in these classes spends between 16 and 28 a month on the internet is:

$\frac{38}{80} = \frac{19}{40}$

continued on the next page

c) The number of students in these classes who spend between 0 and 4 hours a month on the internet is 4. The number of students in these classes who spend more than 4 hours a month on the internet is:

$80 - 4 = 76$

The probability that a student in these classes spends more than 4 hours a month on the internet is:

$$\frac{76}{80} = \frac{19}{20}$$

d) The probabilities determined from these three classes will not hold true for all grade 11 students in your province. The sample size from these three classes is not large enough to be representative of the entire province.

Project Activity

Select a charity you would like to support. Think about the type of game you will use to raise funds for your charity. Your game should be:

- fun
- easy to play
- relatively quick to play
- profitable

Design your game, and add the following information to your project file:

- how to play the game
- how to win the game
- a list of any materials needed

Notebook Assignment

1. The probability of experiencing a mechanical breakdown on the highway is one in seventy. If 3500 cars are travelling down the highway, how many do you predict will have a mechanical breakdown?

2. Harry's Chevrolet-Buick in Burnaby plans to sell 2400 vehicles this year, and 900 of them will have standard transmissions. Find the probability that the next car sold will have a standard transmission.

3. Danny's Disc Depot sold 1850 CDs over the holiday season. Thirty-seven were returned with defects. Using this data, what is the probability that any given customer purchased a defective CD? What must you assume to answer?

4. A video rental shop is holding a clearance sale on previously rented DVDs. The probability of a DVD being flawed is 3 in 100. The store has already sold 239 DVDs and none has been flawed. Based on probability, how many of these would you expect to be flawed?

5. Cruise Air offers its passengers a choice of two different types of meals on its dinner flights, vegetarian lasagna or meat lasagna. On its flights last year, approximately 18 000 out of 30 000 passengers chose the meat lasagna.

   a) What is the probability of a particular passenger choosing the meat lasagna?

   b) Based on this probability, how many vegetarian lasagna meals should Cruise Air order for a dinner flight on which there are 228 passengers booked? Explain your answer.

Hints

When making predictions using probability, remember to give answers as whole numbers. For example, if an answer works out to be 69.3 widgets, give the final answer as approximately 70 widgets.

6. The students in two grade 11 classes are asked to indicate the month in which they were born. The following graph shows these results.

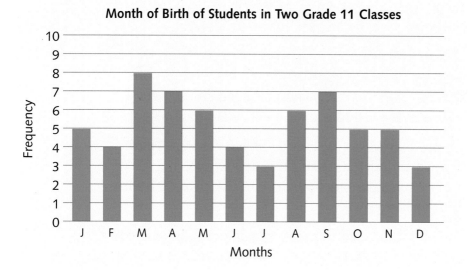

Month of Birth of Students in Two Grade 11 Classes

a) How many students in these classes were born in the month of August?

b) If a student in these classes is selected randomly, what is the probability the student was born in August? Express this probability as a percent.

c) If a student in these classes is randomly selected, what is the probability that the student was not born in April? Express this probability as a percent.

d) Are the probabilities determined from these two classes true for all grade 11 students in your province or territory?

7. The following chart indicates how often the 13th day of the month fell on each of the seven days of the week over the last 400 years.

Day of the week	S	M	T	W	T	F	S
How often the 13th day occurs	687	685	685	687	684	688	684

a) Find the probability that the 13th day of any month occurs on Friday. Express this probability as a percent.

b) Find the probability that the 13th day of any month does not occur on a Friday. Express this probability as a percent.

c) How does the probability of the 13th day of the month falling on a Friday compare to its falling on the other days of the week?

Extension

8. A coin is tossed 20 times.

a) If it were to land heads 11 times, would you believe it is a fair coin? Explain.

b) If it were to land heads 19 times, would you believe it is a fair coin? Explain.

c) If it were to land heads 15 times, would you believe it is a fair coin? Explain.

Exploration 3

Comparing Probability and Odds

People make decisions based on odds every day. If I don't study for a test, the chances in favour of my passing compared to the chance of my not passing are 5:7. Should I be sure to study? We want to make educated decisions in life, and so we need to know how to calculate odds for and against events happening.

The likelihood of an event occurring is not always expressed using probability. The likelihood of an event occurring can be expressed in terms of "odds in favour " or "odds against" it occurring. The odds of an event happening are found by comparing the number of desired outcomes to the number of undesired outcomes, which is different from finding probability.

Goals

In this exploration, you will calculate the odds in favour and odds against events occurring.

New Terms

odds in favour: the ratio of favourable to unfavourable outcomes.

odds against: the ratio of unfavourable to favourable outcomes.

Example 1

When rolling a six-sided die, determine the odds in favour of rolling a 4. How is this different from the probability of rolling a 4?

Solution

Odds in favour = favourable outcomes:unfavourable outcomes

= 1:5

Probability = $\dfrac{\text{number of desired outcomes}}{\text{total possible outcomes}}$

= $\dfrac{1}{6}$

The odds of rolling a 4 are 1:5 while the probability is $\frac{1}{6}$ or 17%. The probability is less since all possible outcomes are considered.

Example 2

When drawing a card from a well-shuffled deck of playing cards, determine the odds in favour of drawing a diamond.

Solution

Odds in favour = favourable outcomes:unfavourable outcomes

= 13:39

= 1:3

The odds of drawing a diamond are 1:3.

Example 3

A wallet contains three $5.00 bills, two $10.00 bills, and one $20.00 bill. What are the odds against drawing out a $10.00 bill?

Solution

The first step is to find the total number of bills:

3 + 2 + 1 = 6 bills

Odds against = unfavourable outcomes:favourable outcomes

= 4:2

= 2:1

The odds against drawing out a $10.00 bill are 2:1.

Example 4

A survey of 320 students in your school reveals that 240 of them listen to radio station CYYV. Find the odds against randomly selecting a student who listens to this station.

Solution

The unfavourable outcome is non-listeners, so that would be:

320 − 240 = 80.

The favourable outcome is the other 240 students who listen to the station.

Odds against = unfavourable outcomes:favourable outcomes

= 80:240

= 1:3

The odds against randomly selecting a student who listens to CYYV are 1:3.

Project Activity

For your game, calculate the probability of winning and the odds in favour of winning. Add this information to your project file.

Class Activity

Create two questions for the class, one using probability and the other using odds. Use examples from your immediate surroundings. Provide the solutions and try them out on your classmates.

Notebook Assignment

1. Complete the following chart.

Event	Odds in favour	Odds against	Probability
drawing a queen from a deck of cards			
rolling a sum of 9 using two dice			
drawing a 3 of diamonds from a deck of cards			
choosing the letter "a" from the word "aardvark"			
rolling a sum greater than 6 with 2 dice			
drawing a black 4, 6, or 8 from a deck of cards			
rolling a sum of 2 with two dice			

2. Explain the difference between probability and odds.

Mental Math

1. If the odds in favour are 4:7, what are the odds against?

2. If the odds in favour of an event are 3:1, what is the probability of the event occurring?

3. Each letter of the word "mathematical" is on a different card. All the cards are the same size. The cards are placed face down and shuffled.

   a) Determine the probability of drawing an M.

   b) Determine the odds in favour of drawing an M.

   c) Determine the probability of not drawing an M.

   d) Determine the odds against drawing an M.

4. Use the spinner shown here to answer the questions that follow:

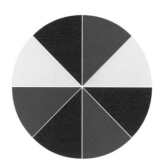

   a) What is the probability of spinning red?

   b) What are the odds in favour of spinning red?

   c) What is the probability of spinning yellow?

   d) What are the odds against spinning yellow?

5. There are 4 white, 14 blue, and 5 green marbles in a bag. A marble is selected from the bag without looking. Find the odds:

   a) against selecting a green marble.

   b) in favour of not selecting a green marble.

   c) in favour of the marble selected being either a white or blue marble.

   d) What do you notice about the odds in a), b), and c)? Explain.

6. In a class of 32 students, 18 students take art, 10 other students take drama, and the rest take music. One student is selected at random. Find the following:

   a) the odds in favour of the selected student taking drama.

   b) the odds against the selected student taking music.

   c) the odds in favour of the selected student taking either art or music.

7. Complete the following chart.

Probability of an event occurring (expressed as a decimal)	0.1	0.2	0.3	0.4	0.5	0.6	0.7	0.8	0.9
Odds in favour of the event occurring									

8. The probability of a soccer game in a particular league going into overtime is 0.125. Find the following:

   a) the odds in favour of a game going into overtime.

   b) the odds in favour of a game not going into overtime.

   c) If the teams in the league play 100 games in a season, about how many games would you expect to go into overtime?

9. Steve wants to flip a coin. He tells you that the odds in favour of him getting a head is 1:1. Do you agree? Why?

10. The odds in favour of purchasing jeans with a defect are 3:997.

   a) What are the odds in favour of purchasing jeans without a defect?

   b) What is the probability of purchasing jeans without a defect?

Extension

11. If the probability of an event is 0, what are the odds in favour of the event happening? Explain.

Exploration Four

Theoretical and Experimental Probability

Have you ever heard the expression "in theory"? Theoretically, the probability of having a girl is ½. So, in theory, a family with an even number of children should have an equal number of boys and girls. But some families have 4 girls, and no boys.

Theoretical probabilities can be calculated and then compared to the results from actual experiments. For example, a manufacturer may distribute enough prizes in cereal boxes so that, in theory, one in five cereal boxes has a prize. If we open 20 boxes in an experiment, we should theoretically find four prizes, but we may find only two prizes. The experimental probability is only one in ten. What do you think would happen if we opened 200 boxes?

Career Connection

Name: Stephen Howard
Job: sports fishing guide
Current wages: $150/day
Education: grade 12; on–the–job training
Career goals: fishing charter operater
Keyword search: Canada courses small business management

Goals

In this exploration, you will compare the results of experimental observations with theoretical predictions.

New Terms

theoretical probability: the chance of an event happening as determined by calculating the mathematical result that would occur.

experimental probability: the chance of an event happening based upon repeated testing or observation.

Activity 1

You and a partner will use 10 pennies and a cup in this activity. One partner will spill the pennies onto your desktop, and the other will record the number of heads that show.

Step 1

Using your knowledge of theoretical probability, how many heads should show when you toss 100 pennies? Write this as a probability statement.

Step 2

Use a table like the one below to record your data. Flip the 10 pennies and record the number of heads you see. Repeat this activity 10 times.

Number of pennies tossed	Number of heads observed
1	
2	
3	
4	

Step 3

Determine the number of heads when you tossed the 100 pennies. Write this as an experimental probability statement.

Step 4

Compare your experimental probability with the theoretical probability.

Activity 2

This activity is based on characteristics of huskies that are controlled by specific genes and can be modelled by the flip of a coin. Three characteristics are being considered: the length of hair (short or long), type of tail (straight or curly), and eye colour (brown or blue). All dogs have genes for each characteristic and so they must display one of each of the traits. Use the following letters to indicate each of the characteristics and set up a table that shows all of the possibilities for the traits a dog can display.

b   blue
B   brown
s   short
S   long
c   straight
C   curly

Complete the following table to show all the different possible combinations of characteristics that can occur in a dog:

Cbs		CBs	
	SAMPLE		CbS

a)   Count the possible number of combinations of dogs that have blue eyes and a curly tail.

b)   State the probability of a dog having blue eyes and a curly tail.

Based on the table you have completed, you can state that the theoretical probability of getting a blue-eyed, curly-tailed dog is $^2/_8$ or 25%. For every four dogs born, one should have blue eyes and a curly tail. If 20 dogs are born, how many blue-eyed, curly-tailed puppies should we expect?

Use three coins (each representing either eye colour, tail type, or hair length) to randomly determine the characteristics of 20 dogs. Use pieces of masking tape with the appropriate letters written on them to attach to the coins. Remember if one side of the coin has a "b" on it, the other should have a piece of tape with a "B." By tossing the three coins at once, you will then be able to record the characteristics of the husky that results.

Make a chart to record your data.

c)   What are the total number of blue-eyed, curly-tailed dogs?

d)   What is the experimental probability of a blue-eyed, curly-tailed pup being born?

e)   Compare this result with your theoretical probability. Are they the same? Are they close?

f)   Combine the results for your entire class. Now determine the experimental probability of a blue-eyed, curly-tailed pup being born. Is your answer closer to the theoretical probability? Why?

Activity 3

In this activity, you will determine the theoretical probability of rolling doubles with two dice. Then you will conduct an experiment and compare your experimental probability with the theoretical probability.

Use a chart such as the one below to record all possible outcomes for rolling a pair of dice.

Die 1

Die 2	1	2	3	4	5	6
1						
2						
3			SAMPLE			
4						
5						
6						

Circle all the combinations with doubles in your chart.

You should find a total possible number of doubles to be 6 out of a total of 36 possible combinations. So, the theoretical probability is $\frac{1}{6}$, or about 17%. This means, for every six rolls, we can expect one set of doubles.

Now, conduct an experiment to determine the experimental probability.

Step 1

Use a chart such as the one below to record your data. Roll the two dice a total of 20 times. Record "Yes" or "No" depending on whether you roll doubles or not.

Roll	Doubles?
1	
2	
3	
4	
5	
6	
7	
8	
9	
10	
11	
12	
13	
14	
15	
16	
17	
18	
19	
20	

Step 2

Count the total number of doubles rolled, and find the experimental probability of rolling doubles.

Step 3

Compare your results with the theoretical probability. Are they the same? Why? What might happen if you roll the dice 600 times?

Notebook Assignment

1. A deck of playing cards has an equal number of red and black cards. If you were to draw 20 cards randomly, how many red cards, theoretically, would you expect to draw? Perform an experiment to determine the experimental probability. Are the theoretical and experimental probabilities the same? Explain.

2. In an experiment rolling a die to get a 5, you and your partner rolled a five 13 times in 90 rolls. How does this result compare to the theoretical probability?

Extension

3. If the experiment in question 2 involved 15 pairs of students rolling a die 90 times each, how would you expect the results to compare to the theoretical probability? Explain.

Problem Analysis

Centennial Hockey League

The Centennial Hockey League has rented a rink from 8:00 a.m. to 5:00 p.m. each Saturday, and from 6:00 a.m. to noon each Sunday. How many teams can use the rink if each team shares the ice with another team (in a game or for practice) for one full hour each week? The ice must be cleaned each day before play begins and every two hours thereafter. It requires 15 minutes to clean the ice.

Games

Ovid's Game

One version of tic tac toe, sometimes called Ovid's Game, was found on the roof of the Temple of Kurna, built around 1400 BCE during the time of Ramses I in Egypt. Historians believe that Roman soldiers helped spread the popularity of the game as they conquered the known western world. This game is also called *luk tsut k'i* in China where it was played during the time of Confucius, about 500 BCE.

Players: Two

Materials
A standard tic tac toe board
six markers, three each of two different colours.

Objective: To be the first player to get any three markers in a row.

Rules

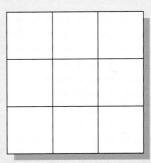

- Players take turns placing their markers on the board.
- If, after all six markers have been placed, no one has three in a row, players take turns moving the markers to any empty adjacent horizontal or vertical space. Note that players may not move diagonally after all the markers are on the board.
- The first player to obtain three in a row wins.

1. Describe in words your winning strategy for Ovid's Game.

2. Why do you think that diagonal moves are forbidden once all six markers are on the board?

Exploration 5
• • • • • • • • • • • • • • • • • • •

Finding Expected Values Using Probability

Expected value is an application of probability which involves the likelihood of a gain or a loss. It is relevant in business, insurance, and in many situations in our daily lives. You will learn how to use probabilities to calculate whether you can expect a gain or a loss in a mathematical situation.

The gain or loss associated with each event is known as its payout. In many games, you pay a given amount to play. If you win the game, you receive a payout. But is the game worth playing? Does the amount you could win sound too good to be true? Many charitable organizations hold fund-raising events using games of chance. You will learn to calculate the expected value of games of chance, and whether they are worth playing!

The payouts offered by lotteries attract many participants but are they worth playing when you consider the probability of winning?

Goals

In this exploration, you will learn to calculate expected value, gains, or losses using probabilities.

Pairs Activity: Expected Value

For this activity, you and your partner need 20 bingo chips and a 6-sided die. You can repeat this activity as many times as needed until a definite pattern emerges.

One person will act as the banker and will have 15 bingo chips. The other partner will have 5 bingo chips. The partner must pay the banker 1 chip each time the game is played. If the partner rolls a 5 on the die, the banker pays him or her 3 chips.

After a few rounds, switch roles. Are the results the same?

a)   What happened in each of the groups?

b)   Would you play this game with money? Why or why not?

c)   Does the player have much of an expectation of winning at this game? Why or why not?

The concept of expected value can be used to determine whether you should play games of chance. Expected value is an estimate of the average return or loss you have when playing a game of chance. Expected value can be found using the formula:

expected value = (probability of winning)(gain) − (probability of losing)(loss)

Example 1

A game has five cards, one of which is the winner. The game costs $1.00 to play. If you select the correct card, you win $4.00. Can you expect to make money if you play this game a few times?

Solution

Find the expected value of the game by determining the 4 basic components:

- the probability of winning: $\frac{1}{5}$ or 0.20
- the amount of gain if you win: $4.00 prize – $1.00 cost = $3.00
- the probability of losing: $\frac{4}{5}$ or 0.80
- the amount of loss: $1.00 (cost to play)

Substitute the values into the expected value formula:

$$
\begin{aligned}
EV &= \text{(prob. win)(gain)} - \text{(prob. lose)(loss)} \\
&= (\,0.20)(\,3) - (0.80)(1) \\
&= 0.60 - 0.80 \\
&= -0.20
\end{aligned}
$$

Every time you play this game, you can expect to lose 20 cents. If you play this game ten times, you can expect to lose $2.00.

Example 2

Based on past experience, a building contractor estimates that the probability of winning a contract is 0.30. The contract is worth $25,000 and she knows it will cost her $2,400 to prepare a contract proposal.

a) Find the expected value of the contract proposal.

b) Is it financially a good idea for her to bid on the contract?

c) What other factors might she consider before making a decision?

Solution

a) Find the expected value by determining:
- the probability of winning: 0.30
- the amount of gain if she wins the contract:
  $25,000 – $2,400 = $22,600
- the probability of losing: 0.70
- the amount of loss (cost to play): $2,400

EV = (prob. win)(gain) – (prob. lose)(loss)
= (0.30)($22,600) – (0.70)($2,400)
= $5,100

b) Since the expected value is positive, she should bid on the contract.

c) Other factors might include staff levels, time, and the reputation of the company offering the contract.

Hints

In general the following are true:

a) If you play any game with an expected value < 0, you can expect to lose money;

b) If you play any game with an expected value of 0, you can expect to break even;

c) If you play any game with an expected value > 0, you can expect to gain money.

Example 3

A farmer is deciding whether it is worthwhile to grow a mixed grain crop in one of his fields. He knows from experience that he will be able to harvest a crop 8 years out of 10. Seeding, fertilizing, and harvesting cost him $200 per acre. He estimates revenue from a good harvest to be $350 per acre.

   Should he continue growing crops in this field? How much money will he make or lose if he is farming a 160-acre field?

Solution

Establish the initial information:

- the probability of winning is $\frac{8}{10}$
- the amount of gain is $350 − $200 = $150
- the probability of losing is $\frac{2}{10}$
- the amount of loss is $200

EV = (prob. win)(gain) − (prob. lose)(loss)

$= (\frac{8}{10}) (\$150) − (\frac{2}{10}) (\$200)$

= $80 per acre

The farmer's gain on his 160-acre field is:
$80 per acre x 160 acres = $12,800

Project Activity

Answer the following questions and add the answers to your project file.

1. How much will you charge someone to play your game?

2. How much will you pay someone who wins your game?

3. What is the expected value of the game?

4. Will your game make a profit for the charity? If not, what changes could you make to ensure that the game is profitable?

Notebook Assignment

1. Based on past experience, a systems engineer sets the probability of winning a computer contract at 0.25. The contract is worth $10,000 and the engineer calculates it would cost her $1,800 to prepare a contract proposal.

    a) Find the expected value of the contract proposal.

    b) How much will the engineer gain if she wins the contract?

    c) How much will the engineer lose if she does not win the contract?

    d) Is it financially a good idea for the engineer to bid on the contract?

    e) Name some other factors she might consider in deciding whether or not to bid on the contract.

2. For each of the following games, determine:

    a) whether you would win, lose, or break even, if played many times.

    b) whether you are willing to play the game, and explain your decision.

        i)   Pay $1. Toss a coin. If it shows heads, you win $2.
        ii) Pay $1. Draw a card from a shuffled deck. If it is a heart, you get $5.
        iii) Pay $2. Draw a card from a shuffled deck. If it is a jack or an ace, you get $10.
        iv) Pay $1. Roll a die. If a 2 or a 3 shows, you get $4.
        v)   Pay $1. Toss two coins. If they are both heads, you win $3.

3. A carpet cleaning company uses flyers to promote its business. The company knows that on average 1 out of every 100 households receiving its flyer will use its service. On average, the company makes a profit of $50.00 on each household whose carpets it cleans. It costs the company $0.25 for each flyer.

   a) Find the expected value of each flyer.

   b) Find the expected value of 10 000 flyers.

   c) Is it financially a good idea for the company to send out flyers?

4. Maria pays $1 to pick a toy duck from a pond. If the duck has a red sticker on it she receives $10. If there are 260 ducks in the pond, and only 13 have a red sticker, what is Maria's expected value? If she played the game 10 times, how much would she probably gain or lose? Is this a good game to play? Why?

5. It costs $2 to play the game of "Pick the Marble." In this game, a bag contains four red marbles, one black marble, and five white marbles. You randomly pick a marble from the bag. If it is red, you win $5, and if it is black you win $10. If the marble is white, you win nothing. Determine the expected value of this game. If you played this game 20 times, what would your expected gain or loss be? Would this be a good game to play?

6. A community club raffles off a $1,500 big screen TV. The tickets each cost $5 and there are 2500 tickets sold. What is your expected value if you had bought only one of the tickets? How does the expected value change if you buy five of these tickets? Is it better to purchase more tickets?

7. A manufacturer builds and sells widgets. He knows that, on average, 13 widgets per 100 are defective. It costs him $12 to build each widget and he can sell them for $18 each. He plans on building 100 000 this year. Will the manufacturer make or lose money on widgets this year?

Chapter Review

1. If you have a one in eight chance of having green eyes, express this as a:

   a) fraction

   b) decimal

   c) percent

2. The probability of a pickerel fingerling living to be 5 years old is $\frac{1}{75}$. How many pickerel will live to be 5 years old from a batch of 1500 fingerlings?

3. Twelve Old English Sheepdogs are born deaf for every 24 000 births. Express this as a probability.

4. Winnipeg, Victoria, Whitehorse, Yellowknife, and Iqaluit are spelled out using letter tiles. These tiles are placed in a bag. If you pull out one tile, what is the probability that it is:

   a) a consonant

   b) the letter "a"

   c) not a consonant

   d) the letters "w" or "i"

5. You have a bag filled with bubble gum jaw breakers. You have 10 red, 34 white, 56 black, and 34 blue candies. Find the:

   a) probability of pulling out a red

   b) odds against pulling out a white

   c) odds in favour of pulling out a black or a blue

   d) probability of pulling out a white

6. You want to open a business near a high school. You know that 7 out of 20 students buy Slurpees every day. If the high school has 700 students, how many Slurpees can you expect to sell every week?

7. A baseball team sells 300 raffle tickets for a new DVD. If Sally buys 3 tickets, what is the probability that she will win the prize?

8. Determine the probability of the following events occurring if:

    a) the odds in favour of an event are 1:2

    b) the odds against an event are 4:1

    c) the odds in favour of an event are 99:1

    d) the odds against an event are 1:1

9. The probability of a soccer game going into overtime is 0.125. Find the following:

    a) the odds in favour of the game going into overtime

    b) the odds in favour of the game not going into overtime

    c) if the teams play 100 games in a season, how many games would you expect to go into overtime?

10. In a class of 36 students, 18 students take a woodworking option, 12 other students take a photography option, and the rest of the students take the metals option. One student is selected at random. Find the following:

    a) the odds in favour of the student taking photography

    b) the odds against the student taking metals

    c) the odds in favour of the student taking either woodworking or metals

11. Each letter of the word "probability" is printed on a different card. The cards are shuffled, and placed face down on a table. Determine:

    a) the probability of drawing a "b"

    b) the odds in favour of drawing a "b"

    c) the probability of not drawing a "b"

    d) the odds against drawing a "b"

12. A polling company conducted a poll prior to an election. A group of 400 people was selected at random from among the 475 000 voters. If 115 people indicated they would vote for candidate A, how many votes would you expect him to receive in the election?

13. The odds in favour of a person being left-handed are 1:11. In a group of 480 students, how many would you expect to be left-handed?

14. The graduation committee is holding a fund-raiser. 500 tickets at $10 each have been sold for a draw on a 54" colour television worth $2,700. Find the expected value of this raffle and calculate how much profit the graduation committee can expect to earn.

15. A card game costs $3.00 to play, and you could win $5.00. You must pick a card from a deck of playing cards, and it must be black, and a number lower than 8. An ace is considered a high card.

   a) Find the expected value.

   b) If you played this game 100 times, what would you expect to be your gain or loss?

16. You operate a construction business, and need to bid on a contract. The contract is worth $84,000, and you have a 1 in 12 chance of being selected. The cost of preparing the bid is $3,000. Using expected values, decide whether you should or should not bid on this contract, and justify your reasons.

17. Two hospitals in your city are holding fund-raising raffles. Hospital A is selling 20 000 tickets at $100 each, and the prize is $250,000. Hospital B is holding a raffle of 10 000 tickets at $100 each, and the prize is $100,000.

   a) Which raffle holds the better probability of winning?

   b) Find the expected value for each.

c) If you bought 2 tickets for the raffle for Hospital A, how would the expected value compare with the expected value for Hospital B?

d) If you decided to spend $100 to support the hospital's fund-raiser, which hospital would you choose, and why?

18. A person's eye colour is determined by the type of genes inherited from the parents. Brown eye colour, B, is dominant over blue eye colour, b. A brown-eyed individual may have BB or Bb genes. A blue-eyed person must have bb genes.

What is the probability that a brown-eyed father with Bb genes and a blue-eyed mother with bb genes will have a blue-eyed child?

Project Presentation

The charitable event is coming up! You must now prepare to put your game on display.

The more people you attract to your game, the more profit you stand to make. It is therefore important to have an attractive, appealing presentation.

You are required to set up and run your game for your classmates. In your presentation, you need to explain and demonstrate your game and its rules clearly. Explain the mathematics involved in your game. Be sure to indicate your game's profitability. Use items from your project file to set up your display.

Creativity is an important part of your presentation. You might consider using the following:

- an attractive background for your game—a colourful poster, for example
- a video of players winning at your game
- a convincing oral sales pitch inviting players to your game
- an indication of the charity you are supporting

Case Study

● ● ● ● ● ● ● ● ● ● ● ● ● ● ● ●

In this case study, you will use your skills in working with probability in a business setting.

You are thinking of opening a business selling health food supplements. As Canada's population ages, you believe that more and more people will turn towards these supplements to maintain good health.

Statistically, 1 in 5 Canadians will be retired within 10 years. You live in a city of 600 000 people. If 30% of those who are retired purchase health food supplements, how many customers can you expect, assuming you have no competition?

You project that the odds of a retired person shopping in your store are 1:8. Given these odds, calculate how many customers you can reasonably expect.

You have the option of purchasing flyers to be distributed in your city at a cost of $3,000. You believe that you have a 90% chance of increasing your customer base by 400 customers through this flyer distribution. Knowing that each customer spends an average of $75, and that your profit is 15% of these sales, justify whether or not you should go ahead with the advertising promotion. State any assumptions you use to help you make the decision. Explain any additional costs you may incur to accommodate your new customers.

The selection of health food supplements on the market is increasing as Canada's population ages.

Chapter 7

Personal Income Tax

Preparing an Income Tax Return

Canadian residents pay a tax on their income to the Canadian government. The amount depends on the amount of money they earn. Employed residents usually have a percentage of their pay deducted each pay period for this tax. Their employers pay this tax monthly to the government.

Each year, by the end of April, residents complete an income tax return to determine whether they have paid the correct amount of income tax the preceding year. If they have paid too much money, they receive a refund from the Canadian government. If they have paid too little money, they owe money instead.

Understanding income tax is important because you are legally required to fill in a tax return and you can minimize the amount of tax you have to pay if you are familiar with tax requirements. An understanding of tax may also help you with your overall financial planning.

Goals	Technology
In this chapter, you will learn how to prepare a simple income tax return for a single, employed person with no dependents.	There are several software programs available to help people prepare their income tax returns. Examples include CANTAX and QuickTax.

The Purpose of Taxation

Taxes have been part of Canadian life since 1650, when Louis XIV of France introduced an export tax on beaver and moose pelts. When the British North America (BNA) Act was passed in 1867, the government of Canada obtained the right to raise money by any system of taxation it thought necessary. For the next 50 years, the government of Canada raised funds through indirect taxation methods such as sales taxes, customs duties, and excise taxes. In 1917, to help pay the costs of taking part in World War I, the federal government introduced personal income tax.

Although the federal government collects all income tax, a portion of that tax is transferred to the province or territory in which an individual lives. Each province and territory has its own income tax system, and rates vary among them.

Personal income tax supplies the federal government with a large portion of its revenue. In addition to supporting the administration of government, personal taxes pay for health and welfare, education, research, defense, transportation, culture and recreation, foreign aid, and economic development and support. Taxes also finance many other programs that governments offer to Canadians.

New Terms

excise tax: a tax charged on non-essential goods produced and distributed within the country in which they were made.

Chapter Project

The project for this chapter will be to imagine your own life at two points in the future and to calculate how much income tax you might pay or receive as a refund in each situation. When you have completed the project, you will have the following items in your project file:

1. Two profiles, one of a college student who works part-time in the school year and full-time during the summer, and the other of a recent graduate who works full-time.
2. Mock-ups of T4 slips for each person profiled.
3. A completed tax form for each person profiled.

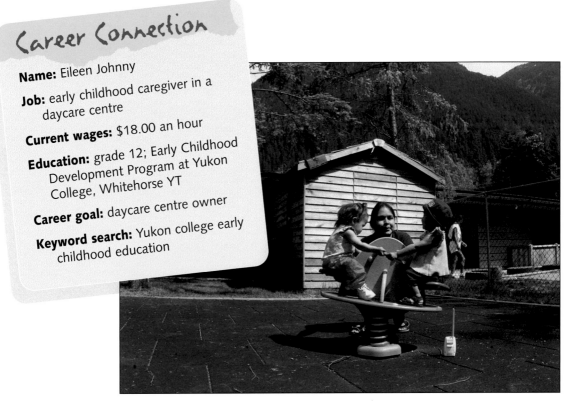

Career Connection

Name: Eileen Johnny

Job: early childhood caregiver in a daycare centre

Current wages: $18.00 an hour

Education: grade 12; Early Childhood Development Program at Yukon College, Whitehorse YT

Career goal: daycare centre owner

Keyword search: Yukon college early childhood education

At the Tesplin child care center on the Mount Currie reserve near Pemberton, BC.

Exploration 1

Income Tax Rates

The amount of income tax you pay depends on the amount of money you earn. Earnings are divided into a series of tax brackets. The money you earn is taxed according to the tax bracket in which it falls. The table below shows the taxation rates for money earned in the Canadian provinces and territories in 2001. Each value in the table represents the percent of your salary in the given range that is owed in taxes before deductions. The rates in the table can be used to estimate the amount of tax you owe on any money you earn.

Your marginal tax rate refers to the highest tax rate that is applied to your earnings. It can also help you estimate the amount of tax you will owe if you earn extra income such as overtime pay. For example, if you receive a $2,000 bonus, you could use your marginal tax rate to estimate the amount of tax you would pay on the bonus. You could also compare the tax rates for different provinces and territories if you are considering moving.

Canadian Tax Rates—2001

First, calculate the amount of federal tax by using the federal tax rates. Then use the rates from the province or territory in which you live to calculate the amount of provincial or territorial tax. Finally, add the two amounts together to find the total amount of tax.

FEDERAL TAX RATES 2001

Annual Taxable Income	Tax Rate
$0 – $30,754	16%
$30,755 – $61,509	22%
$61,510 – $100,000	26%
$100,001 and over	29%

Goals

In this exploration, you will consider the effect of marginal tax rates on the amount of income tax paid.

PROVINCIAL AND TERRITORIAL TAX RATES 2001

Province/Territory	Annual Taxable Income	Tax Rate
British Columbia	$0 – $30,484	7.3%
	$30,485 – $60,969	10.5%
	$61,970 – $70,000	13.7%
	$70,001 – $85,000	15.7%
	$85,001 and over	16.7%
Alberta	All taxable income	10%
Saskatchewan	$0 – $30,000	11.5%
	$30,001 – $60,000	13.5%
	$60,001 and over	16%
Manitoba	$0 – $30,544	10.9%
	$30,545 – $61,089	16.2%
	$61,090 and over	17.4%
Ontario	$0 – $30,814	6.16%
	$30,815 – $61,629	9.22%
	$61,630 and over	11.16%
Quebec	$0 – $26,000	17%
	$26,001 – $52,000	21.25%
	$52,001 and over	24.5%
New Brunswick	$0 – $30,754	9.68%
	$30,755 – $61,509	14.82%
	$61,510 – $100,000	16.52%
	$100,001 and over	17.84%
Nova Scotia	$0 – $29,590	9.77%
	$29,591 – $59,180	14.95%
	$59,181 and over	16.67%
Prince Edward Island	$0 – $30,574	9.8%
	$30,755 – $61,509	13.8%
	$61,510 and over	16.7%
Newfoundland	$0 – $29,590	10.57%
	$29,591 – $59,180	16.16%
	$59,181 and over	18.02%
Yukon	$0 – $30,754	7.36%
	$30,755 – $61,509	10.12%
	$61,510 – $100,000	11.96%
	$100,001 and over	13.34%
Northwest Territories and Nunavut	$0 – $30,754	7.2%
	$30,755 – $61,509	9.9%
	$61,510 – $100,000	11.7%
	$100,001 and over	13.05%

Example 1

George Maracle earns $28,000 a year working for a logging company on Vancouver Island, BC. How much additional tax will he owe if he earns an additional $1,000 by working overtime?

Solution

George will use the federal and BC tax rates to estimate the amount of tax he will pay on his overtime earnings.

George's regular salary falls into the lowest federal and provincial tax brackets. To find the rate at which his regular earnings are taxed, add the two rates:

16% + 7.3% = 23.3%

George's overtime of $1,000 falls into the same tax bracket so he will pay tax at the same rate on his overtime earnings:

$1,000 × 0.233 = $233.00

George will owe $233.00 in income tax on his overtime earnings.

Hints

To find the decimal fraction equivalent of a tax rate, divide the tax rate by one hundred.

Example 2

Melissa is a resident of Yellowknife, NWT, and earns $36,900 a year. In 2001, she receives a raise of $3,000. How much additional income tax will she owe on the raise?

Solution

Use the federal and Northwest Territories tax rates to calculate the income tax Melissa owes on her raise. First, check to see what her marginal tax rate is. Her income falls into the second tax bracket in both the federal and the territorial tables. Her marginal tax rate is the sum of the federal and territorial rates:

22% + 9.9% = 31.9%

Next, see whether the raise falls into the same tax bracket by adding the raise to Melissa's current salary and comparing the total to the federal and territorial tax rates:

$36,900 + $3,000 = $39,900

A salary of $39,900 still falls into the second tax bracket for both federal and territorial taxes. To calculate the tax on her raise, multiply the amount of the raise by 31.9%:

$3,000 × 0.319 = $957.00

Melissa will owe an additional $957.00 in income tax on her raise.

Notebook Assignment

Work in pairs to complete the following assignment. Use the tables of marginal tax rates on pp. 364–365 to answer the questions.

1. If you live in Manitoba, what percent of any salary you earn between $39,001 and $47,900 would you pay in income tax? Justify your answer.

2. If you live in Saskatchewan, what percent of any salary you earn between $49,181 and $53,440 would you pay in income tax? Justify your answer.

3. A welder working in Nunavut earned $70,000 in regular pay. She states, "I don't work any overtime because the government takes it all in taxes." Is she correct? Justify your answer by calculating the amount of tax she would pay if she earned $2,500 in overtime.

4. How much would you pay in income tax on a bonus of $3,000 if you earned $40,000 in 2001 and live in Northwest Territories?

5. A person earning $40,000 is due to receive a $1,000 raise. In which province would this person pay more income tax on the raise, Ontario or Alberta? Explain your answer.

6. In general, what happens to the taxation rate as salary increases?

7. Which two provinces or territories have the lowest taxation rate? Justify your answer.

8. Which two provinces or territories have the highest taxation rate? Justify your answer.

Extension

9. How much would you pay in income tax on a raise of $5,000 if you earned $60,000 in 2001, and live in BC?

10. How much would you pay in additional income tax if you earned $100,000 in 2001, live in BC, and received an unexpected $10,000 bonus? In which province or territory would you pay the least additional tax if your salary is $100,000 and you received the same bonus? Is it possible to answer this question without calculating the exact tax for each province and territory? Explain your reasoning.

Mental Math

Alistair pays about 25% of his salary in income tax. How much tax does he pay if his income is $44,000?

Exploration 2

Completing an Income Tax Return

An income tax return is a form you use to calculate the amount of tax you owe. The Canadian tax return form is called a T1 General form. In printed form, it is part of a booklet called *T1 General Income Tax Forms*. This booklet contains the T1 General form and a variety of specialized forms for specific tax calculations. Each taxpayer fills in only those forms that apply to him or her. The *T1 General Income Tax Forms* booklet is accompanied by a guide to filling in the forms, called the *General Income Tax and Benefit Guide*. Both these booklets are available on-line as well as in printed form. Printed copies are available at any branch of Canada Post in the spring or at any Regional Tax Services office.

Goals

In this exploration, you will become familiar with the documents needed to file an income tax return and you will complete a simple income tax return.

Technology

All tax forms are available on-line at the Canada Customs and Revenue Agency web site at www.ccra-adrc.gc.ca. The T1 General can be found at:
www.ccra-adrc.gc.ca/tax/individuals/t1general

To complete a tax return, you need information slips from your employer and other institutions such as your bank. The information on these slips is transferred to your tax return form and used to calculate the amount of tax you owe.

The most important information slip for most taxpayers is the T4 slip. Employers are required to provide their employees with a T4 slip showing their earnings and deductions each year by February 28. The T4 slip shows a person's total employment income as well as the amounts deducted by the employer for the Canada Pension Plan (CPP), Employment Insurance (EI), and income tax. It may also show other amounts, such as union dues or the amount contributed to the employee's registered pension plan.

The T1 General return accommodates most tax situations an individual may encounter. Although this form looks complex, an individual usually needs to fill in only a small percentage of the lines. Any lines that do not apply to you can be left blank.

Once you complete your first return, the government will send you an income tax package each year.

Hints

a) It is sound practice to collect any documents you need to complete your annual tax return on an ongoing basis.

b) The annual basic CPP exemption is $3,500.

Mental Math

a) Eric received two T4 slips. One showed that he earned $1,500 and the other that he had earned $475. What is the total employment income he will report on his tax return?

b) A server in a café must declare tips as income. If she estimates that her tips for a day average 15% of the value of the meals she serves, what would she expect to earn in tips if her bills totalled $300?

Example 1

Profile of a High School Student

Name: Maxine Morrison

Date of birth: September 4, 1985

Home address: R.R. #1 Williams Lake, BC

Employment biography: Maxine is a single high school student. She lives at home with her parents in Williams Lake, BC. During the summer of 2001, Maxine worked part-time as a server at Ali Baba's Diner. In addition to her salary, she received $380 in tips from customers at the diner.

In February 2002, Ali Baba's Diner sends Maxine the T4 slip shown below. Based on the information given, complete a 2001 tax return for Maxine.

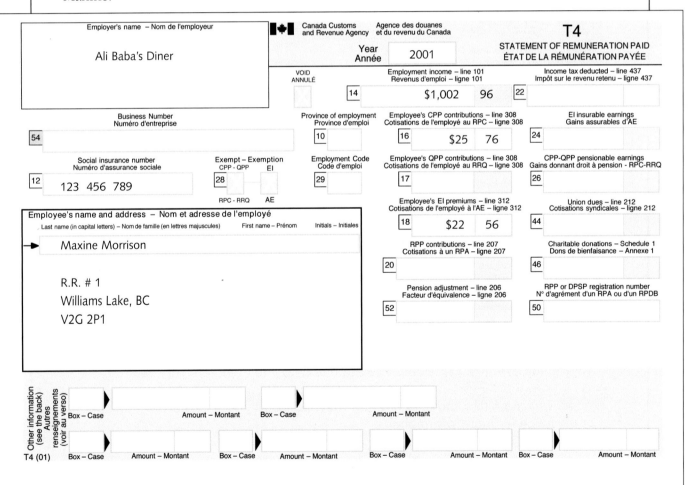

Solution

| Canada Customs and Revenue Agency | Agence des douanes et du revenu du Canada | **T1 GENERAL 2001** |

Income Tax and Benefit Return

Identification

8

Attach your personal label here. Correct any wrong information.
If you are not attaching a label, print your name and address below.

First name and initial   *Maxine*

Last name   *Morrison*

Mailing address: Apt. No. – Street No. Street name

P.O. Box, R.R.   *RR #1*

City   *Williams Lake*   Prov./Terr.   Postal code
    BC   *V 2 G 2 A 1*

Information about you

Enter your social insurance number (SIN) if it is not on the label, or if you are not attaching a label: *1 2 3 4 5 6 7 8 9*

Enter your date of birth:

	Year	Month	Day
	1 9 8 5	*0 9*	*0 4*

Your language of correspondence:
Votre langue de correspondance :   English ✓   Français

Check the box that applies to your marital status on December 31, 2001:
(see the "Marital status" section in the guide for details)

1 ☐ Married   2 ☐ Living common law   3 ☐ Widowed
4 ☐ Divorced   5 ☐ Separated   6 ✓ Single

Information about your spouse or common-law partner (if you checked box 1 or 2 above)

Enter his or her SIN if it is not on the label, or if you are not attaching a label:

Enter his or her first name:

Enter his or her net income for 2001 to claim certain credits: (see the guide for details)

Check this box if he or she was self-employed in 2001:   1

Information about your residence

Enter your province or territory of residence on December 31, 2001:

Enter the province or territory where you currently reside if it is not the same as that shown above for your mailing address:

If you were self-employed in 2001, enter the province or territory of self-employment:

If you became or ceased to be a resident of Canada in 2001, give the date of:

	Month	Day		Month	Day
entry			or departure		

If this return is for a deceased person, enter the date of death:

	Year	Month	Day

Do not use this area

Elections Canada (Canadian citizens only; see the guide for details)

Do you authorize the Canada Customs and Revenue Agency to provide your name, address, and date of birth to Elections Canada for the National Register of Electors? ....   Yes ✓ 1   No ☐ 2
Your authorization is needed each year. This information will be used for electoral purposes only.

Goods and services tax / Harmonized sales tax (GST/HST) credit application

Are you applying for the GST/HST credit? (see the guide for details).........................   Yes ✓ 1   No ☐ 2

If yes, we will now get the number of children for purposes of this credit from the Canada Child Tax Benefit information we have on file.

Your guide contains valuable information to help you complete your return.

When you come to a line on the return that applies to you, look up the line number in the guide for more information.

Do not use this area	172			171			

Solution

2

Please answer the following question

Did you own or hold foreign property at any time in 2001 with a total cost of more than CAN$100,000? (read the "Foreign income" section in the guide for details) .... 266 Yes ☐ 1 No ☑ 2

If yes, complete Form T1135.

If you had certain dealings with a non-resident trust or corporation in 2001, see the "Foreign income" section in the guide.

As a Canadian resident, you have to report your income from all sources both inside and outside Canada.

Total income

Employment income (box 14 on all T4 slips)		101	1,002 96
Commissions included on line 101 (box 42 on all T4 slips)	102		
Other employment income		104+	380 00
Old Age Security pension (box 18 on the T4A(OAS) slip)		113+	
CPP or QPP benefits (box 20 on the T4A(P) slip)		114+	
Disability benefits included on line 114 (box 16 on the T4A(P) slip)	152		
Other pensions or superannuation		115+	
Employment Insurance benefits (box 14 on the T4E slip)		119+	
Taxable amount of dividends from taxable Canadian corporations (see the guide)		120+	
Interest and other investment income (complete Schedule 4)		121+	
Net partnership income: limited or non-active partners only (complete Schedule 4)		122+	
Rental income Gross 160		Net 126+	
Taxable capital gains (complete Schedule 3)		127+	
Support payments received Total 156	Taxable amount	128+	
RRSP income (from all T4RSP slips)		129+	
Other income Specify:		130+	
Self-employment income (see lines 135 to 143 in the guide)			
Business income Gross 162		Net 135+	
Professional income Gross 164		Net 137+	
Commission income Gross 166		Net 139+	
Farming income Gross 168		Net 141+	
Fishing income Gross 170		Net 143+	
Workers' compensation benefits (box 10 on the T5007 slip)	144		
Social assistance payments	145+		
Net federal supplements (box 21 on the T4A(OAS) slip)	146+		
Add lines 144, 145, and 146 =	▶ 147+		
Add lines 101, 104 to 143, and 147 This is your total income. 150=			1,382 96

Solution

 Attach here all of the schedules, information slips, forms, receipts, and other
documents that you need to attach to your return.

3

Net income

Enter your total income from line 150   150   1,382 |96

Pension adjustment
(box 52 on all T4 slips and box 34 on all T4A slips)   206

Registered pension plan deduction (box 20 on all T4 slips and box 32 on all T4A slips)	207
RRSP deduction (see Schedule 7; attach receipts)	208+
Saskatchewan Pension Plan deduction (maximum $600)	209+

Annual union, professional, or like dues (box 44 on all T4 slips, or from receipts)	212+
Child care expenses (complete Form T778)	214+
Attendant care expenses	215+

Business investment loss Gross 228	Allowable deduction 217+
Moving expenses	219+

Support payments made Total 230	Allowable deduction 220+
Carrying charges and interest expenses (complete Schedule 4)	221+
Deduction for CPP or QPP contributions on self-employment and other earnings (complete Schedule 8)	222+
Exploration and development expenses (complete Schedule 4)	224+
Other employment expenses	229+
Clergy residence deduction (complete Form T1223)	231+
Other deductions Specify:	232+

Add lines 207 to 224, 229, 231, and 232. 233=   ▶ _

Line 150 minus line 233 (if negative, enter "0"). This is your net income before adjustments. 234=   1,382 96

Social benefits repayment (if you reported income on line 113, 119, or 146, see line 235 in the guide)   235– ●

Line 234 minus line 235 (if negative, enter "0"). If you have a spouse or common-law partner, see line 236 in the guide.
This is your net income. 236=   1,382 96

Taxable income

Employee home relocation loan deduction (box 37 on all T4 slips)	248
Stock option and shares deductions	249+

Other payments deduction (if you reported income on line 147, see line 250 in the guide)	250+
Limited partnership losses of other years	251+
Non-capital losses of other years	252+
Net capital losses of other years	253+
Capital gains deduction	254+
Northern residents deductions (complete Form T2222)	255+
Additional deductions Specify:	256+

Add lines 248 to 256. 257=   ▶ _

Line 236 minus line 257 (if negative, enter "0")
This is your taxable income. 260=   1,382 96

Use your taxable income to calculate your federal tax on Schedule 1.

Starting this year you will also use Schedule 1 to claim your federal non-refundable tax credits.

Solution

Refund or Balance owing

4

Net federal tax: Complete Schedule 1 and enter the amount from line 19 of that schedule	420	∅	
CPP contributions payable on self-employment and other earnings (from Schedule 8)	421+		
Social benefits repayment (enter the amount from line 235)	422+		
Provincial or territorial tax (complete Form 428)	428+	∅	

Add lines 420 to 428
This is your total payable. 435= ∅ •

Total income tax deducted (from all information slips)	437		•
Refundable Quebec abatement	440+		•
CPP overpayment (enter your excess contributions)	448+	25.76	•
Employment Insurance overpayment (enter your excess contributions)	450+	22.56	•
Refundable medical expense supplement (see the guide)	452+		•
Refund of investment tax credit (complete Form T2038(IND))	454+		•
Part XII.2 trust tax credit (box 38 on all T3 slips)	456+		•
Employee and partner GST/HST rebate (complete Form GST370)	457+		•
Tax paid by instalments	476+		•
Provincial or territorial credits (complete Form 479 if it applies)	479+		•

Add lines 437 to 479
These are your total credits. 482= 48.32 ▶ − 48 | 32

Line 435 minus line 482 = −48 | 32

If the result is negative, you have a refund.
If the result is positive, you have a balance owing.
Enter the amount below on whichever line applies.

We do not charge or refund a difference of less than $2.

Refund 484   48 | 32 •

Balance owing 485   •

Amount enclosed 486   •

Attach to page 1, a cheque or money order payable to the Receiver General. Your payment is due no later than April 30, 2002.

Direct deposit – Start or change (see line 484 in the guide)

You do not have to complete this area every year. Do not complete it this year if your direct deposit information for your refund has not changed.

Refund and GST/HST credit – To start direct deposit or to change account information only, attach a "void" cheque or complete lines 460, 461, and 462.

Note: To deposit your CCTB payments (including certain related provincial or territorial payments) into the same account, also check box 463.

Branch number	Institution number	Account number	CCTB
460 _____	461 _____	462 _____	463 ☐
(5 digits)	(3 digits)	(maximum 12 digits)	

I certify that the information given on this return and in any documents attached is correct, complete, and fully discloses all my income.

Sign here   *Maxine Morrison*
It is a serious offence to make a false return.
Telephone (250) 123-4567 - Date *April 15, 2002*

490
For professional tax preparers only.

Name:
Address:

Telephone: ( )

Do not use this area	487 ☐	488 ☐			

Solution

T1-2001   Federal Tax   **Schedule 1**

Use this schedule to claim your federal non-refundable tax credits and to calculate your net federal tax.
Be sure to attach a copy of this schedule to your return.

Enter your taxable income from line 260 of your return   *1,382.96* 1

Use the amount on line 1 to determine which ONE
of the following columns you have to complete.

If the amount on line 1 is:	$30,754 or less	more than $30,754, but not more than $61,509	more than $61,509 but not more than $100,000	more than $100,000
Enter the amount from line 1 above	*1,382* 96 2	2	2	2
Base amount	− 0 00 3	− 30,754 00 3	− 61,509 00 3	− 100,000 00 3
Line 2 minus line 3 (this amount cannot be negative)	= *1,382* 96 4	= 4	= 4	= 4
Rate	× 16% 5	× 22% 5	× 26% 5	× 29% 5
Multiply the amount on line 4 by the rate on line 5	= *221* 27 6	= 6	= 6	= 6
Tax on base amount	+ 0 00 7	+ 4,921 00 7	+ 11,687 00 7	+ 21,694 00 7
Add lines 6 and 7	= *221* 27 8	= 8	= 8	= 8

Federal non-refundable tax credits (Read the guide for details about these credits.)

Basic personal amount	claim $7,412 **300**	*7,412* 00
Age amount (if you were born in 1936 or earlier)	**301** +	
Spouse or common-law partner amount:		
Base amount	6,923 00	
Minus: His or her net income (from page 1 of your return)	−	
Result: (if negative, enter "0") (maximum $6,293) =	▶ **303** +	
Amount for an eligible dependant	(maximum $6,293) **305** +	
Amount for infirm dependants age 18 or older	**306** +	
CPP or QPP contributions:		
through employment from box 16 and box 17 on all T4 slips	(maximum $1,496.40) **308** +	•
on self-employment and other earnings (from Schedule 8)	**310** +	•
Employment Insurance premiums from box 18 on all T4 slips	(maximum $877.50) **312** +	•
Pension income amount	(maximum $1,000) **314** +	
Caregiver amount	**315** +	
Disability amount	**316** +	
Disability amount transferred from a dependant	**318** +	
Interest paid on your student loans	**319** +	
Tuition and education amounts (complete Schedule 11)	**323** +	
Tuition and education amounts transferred from a child	**324** +	
Amounts transferred from your spouse or common-law partner (complete Schedule 2)	**326** +	

Medical expenses (attach receipts)	**330**	
Minus: $1,678, or 3% of line 236, whichever is less	−	
Subtotal =		
Minus: Medical expenses adjustment	**331** −	
Allowable portion of medical expenses (if negative, enter "0") =	▶ **332** +	

Add lines 300, 301, 303 to 326, and 332. **335** = *7,412.00*

Multiply the amount on line 335 by 16% = **338** *1,185* 92
Donations and gifts (complete Schedule 9)   **349** +

Total federal non-refundable tax credits: Add lines 338 and 349. **350** = *1,185* 92

continue on the back

Solution

Enter the amount from line 8 on the other side		*221* *27*	9
Federal tax on split income (from line 4 of Form T1206)	424 +		• 10
	Add lines 9 and 10 =	*221* *27*	11

Enter your total federal non-refundable tax credits from line 350 on the other side   350   *1,185.92*

Federal dividend tax credit (13.3333% of the amount on line 120 of your return)	425 +	•	
Overseas employment tax credit (complete Form T626)	426 +		
Minimum tax carry-over	427 +	•	
Add lines 350, 425, 426, and 427 =	*1,185.92* ▶ −	*1,185* *92*	12

Basic federal tax: Line 11 minus line 12 (if negative, enter "0") 429 =			13

Federal foreign tax credit: Complete the federal foreign tax credit calculation below and enter the amount from line (i) or line (ii), whichever is less   −   14

Federal tax: Line 13 minus line 14 (if negative, enter "0") 406 =		*∅*	15

Total federal political contributions
(attach receipts)   409

Federal political contribution tax credit (see the guide)	410	•	
Investment tax credit (complete Form T2038(IND))	412 +	•	
Labour-sponsored funds tax credit			
Net cost 413 Allowable credit 414 +		•	
Add lines 410, 412, and 414. 416 =		▶ −	16
Line 15 minus line 16 (if negative, enter "0") (if you have an amount on line 424 above, see Form T1206) 417 =			17
Additional tax on RESP accumulated income payments (complete Form T1172)	418 +		18
Net federal tax: Add lines 17 and 18			
Enter this amount on line 420 of your return. 420 =		*∅*	19

Federal foreign tax credit: (see lines 431 and 433 in the guide)

Make a separate calculation for each foreign country.

Non-business-income tax paid to a foreign country   431   • (i)

Net foreign non-business income * 433
Net income **   **X**   Basic federal tax ***   =   (ii)

*   Reduce this amount by any income from that foreign country for which you claimed a capital gains deduction, and by any income from that country that was, under a tax treaty, either exempt from tax in that country or deductible as exempt income in Canada (included on line 256). Also reduce this amount by the lesser of lines E and F on Form T626.

**   Line 236 plus the amount on line 3 of Form T1206, minus the total of the amounts on lines 248, 249, 250, 253, 254, and minus any foreign income deductible as exempt income under a tax treaty or any income deductible as net employment income from a prescribed international organization (included on line 256). If the result is less than the amount on line 433, enter your Basic federal tax*** on line (ii).

***   Line 429 plus the amount on lines 425 and 426, and minus any refundable Quebec abatement (line 440) and any federal refundable First Nations abatement (line 441 on the return for residents of Yukon).

British Columbia Tax

BRITISH COLUMBIA

BC428
T1 General – 2001

Complete this form and attach a copy of it to your return. For details, see pages 1 to 4 in the forms book.

Step 1 – British Columbia tax on taxable income

Enter your taxable income from line 260 of your return _____ *1,382 |96* 1

Use the amount on line 1 to determine which ONE of the following columns you have to complete. Then, enter the amount from line 1 in the applicable column.	If line 1 is $30,484 or less	If line 1 is more than $30,484, but not more than $60,969	If line 1 is more than $60,969, but not more than $70,000	If line 1 is more than $70,000, but not more than $85,000	If line 1 is more than $85,000	
	1,382 96					2
Line 2 minus line 3 (cannot be negative)	– 0 00	– 30,484 00	– 60,969 00	– 70,000 00	– 85,000 00	3
	= *1,382 96* =	=	=	=	=	4
	× 7.3%	× 10.5%	× 13.7%	× 15.7%	× 16.7%	5
Multiply line 4 by line 5	= *100 96*	=	=	=	=	6
	+ 0 00	+ 2,225 00	+ 5,426 00	+ 6,663 00	+ 9,018 00	7
Add lines 6 and 7 Go to Step 2	= *100 96*	=	=	=	=	8

Step 2 – British Columbia non-refundable tax credits

Important: Provincial non-refundable tax credits may be different from the federal amounts claimed on Schedule 1. For details, see the *Provincial Worksheet* and pages 1 to 3 in the forms book.

For internal use only 5609

Basic personal amount	claim $8,000	5804	*8,000 00*		9
Age amount (if born in 1936 or earlier)	(use provincial worksheet)	5808 +			10
Spouse or common-law partner amount					
Basic amount	7,535 00				
Minus his or her net income from page 1 of your return	–				
(if negative, enter "0") (maximum $6,850)	=	▶ 5812 +			11
Amount for an eligible dependant	(use provincial worksheet)	5816 +			12
Amount for infirm dependants age 18 or older	(use provincial worksheet)	5820 +			13
Canada Pension Plan or Quebec Pension Plan contributions:					
Amount from line 308 of your federal Schedule 1		5824 +		●	14
Amount from line 310 of your federal Schedule 1		5828 +		●	15
Employment Insurance premiums (from line 312 of your federal Schedule 1)		5832 +		●	16
Pension income amount	(maximum $1,000)	5836 +			17
Caregiver amount	(use provincial worksheet)	5840 +			18
Disability amount	(if you were under age 18, use provincial worksheet)	5844 +			19
Disability amount transferred from a dependant	(use provincial worksheet)	5848 +			20
Interest paid on your student loans (from line 319 of your federal Schedule 1)		5852 +			21
Tuition and education amounts [attach Schedule BC(S11)]		5856 +			22
Tuition and education amounts transferred from a child		5860 +			23
Amounts transferred from your spouse or common-law partner [attach Schedule BC(S2)]	5864 +				24
Medical expenses	5868		25		
Enter $1,663 or 3% of line 236, whichever is less	–		26		
Line 25 minus line 26 (if negative, enter "0")	=		27		
Medical expenses adjustment (use provincial worksheet)	5872 –		28		
Line 27 minus line 28 (if negative, enter "0")	5876 =	▶ +	29		
Add lines 9 through 24, and line 29	5880 =	*8,000 00* ▶	*8,000 00*		30
Non-refundable tax credit rate			× 7.3%		31
Multiply the amount on line 30 by 7.3%	5884 =		*584 00*		32
Donations and gifts:					
Amount from line 345 of your federal Schedule 9	× 7.3% =		33		
Amount from line 347 of your federal Schedule 9	× 16.7% =	+	34		
Add lines 33 and 34	5896 =	▶ +	35		
Add lines 32 and 35	British Columbia non-refundable tax credits 6150 =		*584 00*		36

Go to Step 3 on the back

Solution

Step 3 – British Columbia tax

Enter the amount from line 8			*100 96* 37
Enter your British Columbia tax on split income, if applicable, from Form T1206	6151 +		• 38
Add lines 37 and 38		=	*100 96* 39
Enter your British Columbia non-refundable tax credits from line 36		*584 00* 40	
British Columbia dividend tax credit:			
Amount from line 120 of your return	× 5.9% =	6152 +	• 41
British Columbia overseas employment tax credit:			
Amount from line 426 on federal Schedule 1	× 49.5% =	6153 +	• 42
British Columbia minimum tax carry-over:			
Amount from line 427 on federal Schedule 1	× 49.5% =	6154 +	• 43
Add lines 40 through 43	=	*584 00* ▶	− *584 00* 44
Line 39 minus line 44 (if negative, enter "0")		=	*0* 45
British Columbia additional tax for minimum tax purposes, if applicable, from Form T1219		+	46
Add lines 45 and 46		=	47
Enter the provincial foreign tax credit, if applicable, from Form T2036		−	48
Line 47 minus line 48		=	49

British Columbia logging tax credit

Enter the provincial logging tax credit, if any, from Form BCFIN 542		−	50
Line 49 minus line 50 (if negative, enter "0")		=	51

British Columbia political contribution tax credit

Enter British Columbia political contributions made in 2001	6040		52
Credit you calculated on the *Provincial Worksheet*	(maximum $500)	−	53
Line 51 minus line 53 (if negative, enter "0")		=	54

British Columbia employee investment tax credits

Enter your employee share ownership plan tax credit from Form ESOP 20	6045		• 55
Enter your employee venture capital tax credit from Form EVCC 30	6047 +		• 56
Add lines 55 and 56	(maximum $2,000) =	▶ −	57
Line 54 minus line 57 (if negative, enter "0")		=	58

British Columbia mining flow-through share tax credit

Enter the tax credit amount calculated on Form T1231		−	59
Line 58 minus line 59 (if negative, enter "0") Enter this amount on line 428 of your return.	British Columbia tax	= *0*	60

Workers in service industries such as waitressing must report tips as income for purposes of income tax.

Solution

◼️◼◼	Canada Customs and Revenue Agency	Agence des douanes et du revenu du Canada	EMPLOYEE OVERPAYMENT OF 2001 CANADA PENSION PLAN CONTRIBUTIONS AND 2001 EMPLOYMENT INSURANCE PREMIUMS

Complete Part 1 to determine any overpayment of Canada Pension Plan (CPP) or Quebec Pension Plan (QPP) contributions made through employment if you had no self-employment earnings and you were not a resident of Quebec on December 31, 2001. If you were a resident of Quebec on December 31, 2001, and you made CPP or QPP contributions, see your Quebec provincial tax guide.

Complete Part 2 to determine any overpayment of Employment Insurance (EI) premiums.

Part 1 – Calculating your Canada Pension Plan overpayment

If any of the following situations apply to you, use the "Monthly Proration Table for 2001" below to find the amounts for lines 1, 2, 3, and 5.

- If you turned 18 in 2001, use the number of months in the year after the month you turned 18.
- If you turned 70 in 2001, use the number of months in the year up to and including the month you turned 70.
- If you received, or were entitled to receive, a CPP or QPP retirement or disability pension for part of 2001, use the number of months in the year you did not or were not entitled to receive the pension.
- If the individual died in 2001, use the number of months in the year up to and including the month the individual died.

Total CPP pensionable earnings (box 26 or, if blank, box 14 of your T4 slips) .... (maximum $ 38,300)   **1002 | 96** 1
Basic CPP exemption .... (maximum $ 3,500)   −   **3500 | 00** 2
Earnings subject to contribution (if negative, enter "0") .... (maximum $ 34,800)   =   **0 | 00** 3

Total CPP and QPP contributions deducted (from boxes 16 and 17 of your T4 slips) ....   **25 | 76** 4
Required contribution: Multiply line 3 by 4.3% .... (maximum $1,496.40)   −   5
Line 4 minus line 5 (if negative, enter "0") .... Canada Pension Plan overpayment =   **25 | 76** 6

If the amount from line 6 is positive, enter it on line 448 of your return.
Enter the amount from line 4 or 5, whichever is less, on line 308 of Schedule 1 and, if it applies, on line 5824 of Form 428.

Monthly Proration Table for 2001

Applicable number of months	Line 1 Maximum amount of total CPP pensionable earnings	Line 2 Maximum amount of basic CPP exemption	Line 3 Maximum amount of earnings subject to contribution	Line 5 Maximum amount of required contribution
1	$ 3,191.66	$ 291.66	$ 2,900.00	$ 124.70
2	$ 6,383.33	$ 583.33	$ 5,800.00	$ 249.40
3	$ 9,575.00	$ 875.00	$ 8,700.00	$ 374.10
4	$ 12,766.66	$ 1,166.66	$ 11,600.00	$ 498.80
5	$ 15,958.33	$ 1,458.33	$ 14,500.00	$ 623.50
6	$ 19,150.00	$ 1,750.00	$ 17,400.00	$ 748.20
7	$ 22,341.66	$ 2,041.66	$ 20,300.00	$ 872.90
8	$ 25,533.33	$ 2,333.33	$ 23,200.00	$ 997.60
9	$ 28,725.00	$ 2,625.00	$ 26,100.00	$ 1,122.30
10	$ 31,916.66	$ 2,916.66	$ 29,000.00	$ 1,247.00
11	$ 35,108.33	$ 3,208.33	$ 31,900.00	$ 1,371.70
12	$ 38,300.00	$ 3,500.00	$ 34,800.00	$ 1,496.40

Part 2 – Calculating your Employment Insurance overpayment

Total EI insurable earnings (box 24 or, if blank, box 14 of your T4 slips and box 16 of your T4F slips)
(maximum $39,000. If $2,000 or less, enter "0")   **1,002 | 96** 1

Total premiums deducted (box 18 of your T4 and T4F slips) ....   **22 | 56** 2
Line 1 minus $2,000 (if negative, enter "0") .... =   3
Line 2 minus line 3 (if negative, enter "0") .... =   **22 | 56** 4

Total premiums deducted (box 18 of your T4 and T4F slips) ....   **22 | 56** 5
Required premium: Multiply line 1 by 2.25% .... (maximum $877.50)   −   **22 | 56** 6
Line 5 minus line 6 (if negative, enter "0") .... =   7

Enter the amount from line 4 or line 7, whichever is greater .... Employment Insurance overpayment   **22 | 56** 8

Enter the amount from line 8 on line 450 of your return.
Enter the amount from line 3, 5, or 6, whichever is least, on line 312 of Schedule 1 and, if it applies, on line 5832 of Form 428.

T2204 (01)
Printed in Canada   (Français au verso)   **Canadä**

Notebook Assignment

1. Complete a T1 General income tax return using the information in the profile, the T4 slip shown below, and a blank tax return form.

Profile of a High School Student

Name: David McLeod

Date of birth: January 24, 1984

Home address: Grand Forks, BC

Employment biography: David is a single high school student who lives with his parents. He works part-time in the spring and fall and full-time during the summer as a golf caddy at a local golf course. David earned $960 in tips in 2001.

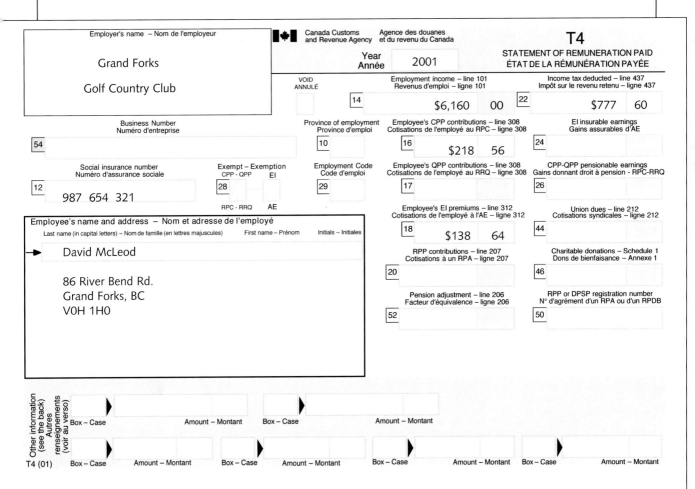

Problem Analysis

Hockey Salaries

Two National Hockey League (NHL) rookies choose different types of contracts. Moe Fortier negotiates a salary that pays him $100,000.00 in his first year and doubles for each season that he plays. John Zwiernecky's contract pays $2,000,000.00 in his first year and gives him a $100,000.00 increment in each subsequent year that he plays.

Henrik Sedin (#33) and Daniel Sedin (#22) celebrating a win with the Vancouver Canucks.

1. Graph these data either by hand or using a spreadsheet.
2. Who has negotiated the better contract?
3. Under what conditions is it a better contract?
4. Gordie Howe played in the NHL for 26 years. During his career, salaries were not as high as they have since become. What would his final salary have been if he had been able to play under Moe Fortier's contract? Under John Zwiernecky's contract?
5. Many NHL players' careers last only a few years. Find out the average number of years of an NHL career.
6. What assumptions or factors should you consider when negotiating a contract?
7. If you were a player's agent, what would you recommend?

Games

Mission Impossible

The following puzzle is not an easy one. It could swallow up a considerable amount of time. However, if you organize the information, the mission is certainly possible. Good luck!

The following 15 facts are all you need to solve it:

1. There are five hunting cabins on a lake. Each cabin is a different colour, and is inhabited by a man of a different nationality, each drinking a different kind of soft drink, firing a different brand of shotgun shell, and shooting a different duck.
2. The Englishman lives in the red cabin.
3. The Canadian shoots only bluebill ducks.
4. Pepsi is drunk in the green cabin.
5. The American drinks Coke.
6. The green cabin is immediately to the right (your right) of the brown cabin.
7. The hunter who uses Winchester shells shoots mallard ducks.
8. Remington shells are shot by the man in the yellow cabin.
9. Dr. Pepper is drunk in the middle cabin.

10. The Norwegian lives in the first cabin on the left.
11. The man who buys Federal shells lives in the cabin next to the cabin of the man who shoots redhead ducks.
12. Remington shells are used in the cabin next to the cabin where the man lives who shoots canvasback ducks.
13. The hunter who fires Western shells drinks 7-Up.
14. The Irishman loads up with Peters shells.
15. The Norwegian lives next to the blue cabin.

Who drinks the Orange Crush and who shoots the teal ducks?

Exploration 3

Tax Implications

At various times during a person's life, different tax situations occur. A high school student who works on Saturdays, holidays, and full-time during the summer may have to pay income tax because he or she has no deductions to claim. If you take a new job and earn more money, your tax rate may increase. As your personal circumstances change, perhaps by marrying, you may also become eligible for particular deductions.

Canadians who live in the northern territories and some northern communities in the provinces can claim the Northern residents deductions to reduce the amount of tax they must pay. To claim this deduction, eligible residents fill in Form T2222 and enter the amount on p. 3 of the tax return form. Northern residents receive this deduction because the costs of living in the north are much higher than they are for Canadians who live in the south.

Project Activity

Create a profile for a recent graduate who has just started his or her first full-time job. Select a job and estimate annual earnings. Make a mock T4 for the graduate. Use deduction tables from the Canada Customs & Revenue Agency in print form or on the internet to find amounts for income tax, CPP, and EI deductions. Assume that the claim code is 1. Complete a T1 General return for the graduate. Does the graduate receive a refund or does he or she owe tax?

Goals

In this exploration, you will consider the tax implications of careers and lifestyle choices.

Notebook Assignment

Use the T1 General tax return form and guide as a resource to answer the following questions.

1. What are the two pieces of information needed to apply for the GST/HST credit?

2. What line is used to record income from commissions?

3. Does a person have to claim Employment Insurance benefits as income? How do you know? What line is used?

4. What line is used to record income from self-employment?

5. What line is used to record union dues?

6. On what line do residents of northern Canada claim the Northern residents deduction?

7. On what line are moving expenses claimed? In what circumstances is a person allowed to claim moving expenses?

8. On what line are tuition expenses claimed?

Extension

9. Imagine that you have one of the careers listed below. Research the salary you would be paid, and create a T1 General form showing the amount of tax you would pay.

   a) a full-time high-school student who worked as a lifeguard over the summer.

   b) an NHL hockey player

   c) a firefighter

   d) an artist

   e) a small business owner

   f) a child care worker

   g) a fisherman

   h) another person of your choice

Chapter Review

●●●●●●●●●●●●●●●●●●●●●●●●●●●

1. Why is it important to supply complete identification information on tax forms? Give 2 reasons.

2. What page of the T1 General form is used to determine total income? Net income?

3. Where can you find explanations for each line?

4. Why is it important to keep moving expense receipts?

5. What is the difference between a refund and a balance owing?

6. Consider the two individuals whose T4 information slips are shown below. Complete tax returns for each person, assuming that they are single and have no dependents. If each owes a different amount of tax, explain why.

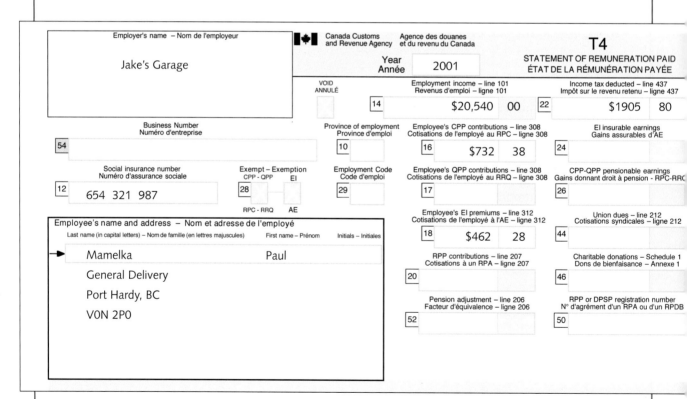

Employer's name – Nom de l'employeur		Canada Customs and Revenue Agency	Agence des douanes et du revenu du Canada	T4

Friendship Community

Year
Année   2001

STATEMENT OF REMUNERATION PAID
ÉTAT DE LA RÉMUNÉRATION PAYÉE

VOID ANNULÉ	Employment income – line 101 Revenus d'emploi – ligne 101	Income tax deducted – line 437 Impôt sur le revenu retenu – ligne 437
14	$20,592 00	22 $1910 75

Business Number Numéro d'entreprise	Province of employment Province d'emploi	Employee's CPP contributions – line 308 Cotisations de l'employé au RPC – ligne 308	EI insurable earnings Gains assurables d'AE
54	10	16 $734 76	24

Social insurance number Numéro d'assurance sociale	Exempt – Exemption CPP - QPP EI	Employment Code Code d'emploi	Employee's QPP contributions – line 308 Cotisations de l'employé au RRQ – ligne 308	CPP-QPP pensionable earnings Gains donnant droit à pension - RPC-RRQ
12 996 172 413	28	29	17	26

RPC - RRQ   AE

Employee's EI premiums – line 312 Cotisations de l'employé à l'AE – ligne 312	Union dues – line 212 Cotisations syndicales – ligne 212
18 $463 32	44

Employee's name and address – Nom et adresse de l'employé

Last name (in capital letters) – Nom de famille (en lettres majuscules)   First name – Prénom   Initials – Initiales

Cristall   Ferne

9731–4th St.

New Westminster, BC

V3L 2W4

RPP contributions – line 207 Cotisations à un RPA – ligne 207	Charitable donations – Schedule 1 Dons de bienfaisance – Annexe 1
20	46 $300

Pension adjustment – line 206 Facteur d'équivalence – ligne 206	RPP or DPSP registration number N° d'agrément d'un RPA ou d'un RPDB
52	50

Project Presentation

Use the tax returns in your project file to create a poster presentation. Attach the returns to a poster board and include information boxes that explain how you made each calculation.

Select a tax return from the ones you have created for your project file. Attach pages 1 to 4 of the T1 General form to poster board and add information boxes that explain the contents of the lines you filled in for that form and an explanation of any calculations that you made. Identify the source of the amounts you transferred from information slips. Create a poster that will help a viewer understand how to complete their own tax return.

Case Study

●●●●●●●●●●●●●

The Tax Return of Joseph Strong

In this case, you will complete the tax form for Joseph Strong, who works full-time in 2001 as a clerk in Atlin, BC. Joseph is single and has no dependents. He is eligible for a Northern residents deduction of $2,737.50.

   The following T4 was sent by his employer.

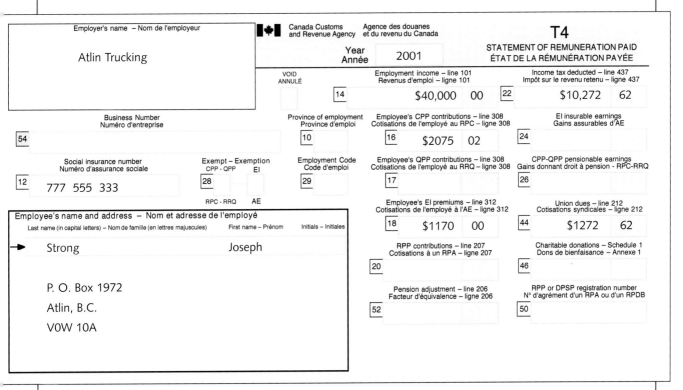

Complete a T1 General for Joseph, given the information provided.

Chapter 8
Preparing a Business Plan

Planning a Business of Your Own

As an adult, you will need to earn a living. Many Canadians earn a living by owning and operating a business of their own. In this chapter, you will explore the idea of starting your own business by developing a business plan.

A business is an enterprise that sells goods, manufactures products, or provides a service to customers. A business plan is a document that outlines the idea for a business, and specifies strategies the owner will use for marketing and financing his or her business.

Goals	New Terms
In this chapter, you will prepare a business plan.	**business:** a company, corporation, or other commercial enterprise.

Chapter Project

In this project, you will develop a business plan for a business idea you choose to investigate. As you work through the project activities, you will develop the components of a business plan. In your project presentation, you will role-play a business owner presenting his or her business plan to a group of potential investors in your business.

When you have completed the project, you will have the following items in your project file:

1. A name, a mission statement, and a logo for your business.

2. A description of the product or service you will offer.

3. A description of your own interests and skills.

4. A plan for the space your business will occupy, including a floor plan and an estimate of space costs.

5. An assessment of possible competitors.

6. A marketing plan, including a sample advertisement or brochure.

7. A staffing plan, including a work schedule and an estimate of payroll costs.

8. A financial plan, including a statement of revenues and expenses and a calculation of profit or loss.

New Terms

mission statement: a statement of a company's primary goals and operating principles.

Career Connection

Name: Larry Shultz

Job: assistant manager of a camera store

Current wages: $38,000 a year

Education: grade 12; diploma in business administration

Career goal: to own his own camera store

Keyword search: Canada college business administration

Exploration 1

What Is a Business Plan?

A business plan describes a business and the way in which it plans to operate. A business plan usually contains a description of the business and its products or service, a marketing plan, a staffing plan, and a financial plan.

The first step in planning a business is to decide on the kind of business you wish to operate. Before you decide, you need to evaluate your skills and interests as well as your ability to manage a business. Do you have the skills you need to run your business successfully? If you do not, could you obtain the necessary training? Once you have decided on the business that interests you, it is a wise idea to develop a mission statement that describes your overall business goal and your operating principles.

You need to describe the business and the product or service you will offer. Businesses often fall into one of three broad categories. They may be a retail business, selling goods to the public, often in a store. They may be part of the service industry and provide services to customers. They may be manufacturing businesses that make a product.

Financial institutions usually require a business plan from business owners who wish to borrow money or arrange a line of credit. Government departments may require a business plan if you plan to participate in a government program aimed at assisting businesses. A business plan is also an important tool for the business owner, helping him or her develop a list of goals and a plan of activity to achieve them.

Goals	Technology	New Terms
In this exploration, you will learn what a business plan is and why business owners need to prepare them.	There are a number of web sites with excellent business planning information on them. One place to begin is the government of Canada web site at: http://businessgateway.ca/en/hi/	**manufacture:** to make a product, often in a factory setting. **retail:** sales of goods to the general public. **service industry:** businesses that provide services to customers rather than goods.

Example 1

Prepare a business plan for a retail computer bookstore.

Solution

DIGITAL BOOKS

Mission Statement

To stock the most comprehensive selection of computer books in Langley, BC, in order to serve retail customers effectively.

Business Description

To operate a retail bookstore selling computer-related books to the general public.

Space Plan

The store will be located in a shopping mall in Langley, BC.

Marketing Plan

To advertise the store and its products, the company will advertise in the local newspaper and on the local cable channel. There will be a summer sale and a Christmas sale annually. The store will hold product demonstrations for customers.

Staffing Plan

The owner will work full-time in the store. Two part-time sales clerks will work evening hours and weekends. Occasional help will be hired to stock shelves and perform inventory counts.

Financial Plan

Revenue		
Total Annual Sales		**$156,000**
Expenses		
• Annual Store Rental	$12,000	
• Annual Utilities, Telephone, and Insurance	$1,200	
• Annual Cost of Wages	$39,984	
• Annual Cost of Inventory	$93,600	
• Annual Cost of Advertising	$6,000	
Total Annual Expenses		**$152,784**
Profit		**$3,216**

New Terms

inventory: the items a business stocks for resale or as part of a product that they make.

Example 2

Prepare a business plan for a small manufacturing company in which CD racks and stereo speaker boxes are built.

Solution

BOOMING SOUND MANUFACTURING

Mission Statement

To produce technically sound, well-designed stereo speaker boxes and CD racks.

Business Description

To operate a manufacturing business that sells its stereo-related products on a wholesale basis to retail stereo shops and department stores.

Space Plan

The business will operate in a small industrial mall located in Kelowna, BC. There will be a shop space for building products and offices for managing the company.

Marketing Plan

To sell its products, the company will advertise in trade newspapers, mail a promotional brochure to retail stereo stores annually, and have a salesman visit potential and existing customers twice a year.

Staffing Plan

The owner will work full-time in the plant and will design the company's products. Six employees will work building products and there will be an office manager. A part-time salesperson will handle promotions and sales calls as needed.

Financial Plan

Revenue		
Total Annual Sales		**$880,000**
Expenses		
• Annual Space Rental	$74,000	
• Annual Utilities, Telephone, and Insurance	$5,000	
• Annual Cost of Wages	$280,000	
• Annual Cost of Raw Materials	$178,000	
• Annual Cost of Advertising	$60,000	
• Annual Loan Payments	$20,000	
Total Annual Expenses		**$617,000**
Profit		**$263,000**

New Terms

wholesale: sale of large quantities of goods to customers who will retail them to the general public.

trade newspapers: newspapers of special interest to a particular type of business.

Example 3

Prepare a business plan for an errand-running "gopher" service.

Solution

Go4It Services

Mission Statement
To provide customers with a service that performs tasks that many busy people do not have time for but need to have done.

Business Description
To provide errand-running and shopping services to customers throughout the community of Whitehorse, YT.

Space Plan
The business will operate from an office in the owner's home.

Marketing Plan
To advertise this service, the business will advertise in the local newspapers and send promotional cards to potential customers.

Staffing Plan
The owner will work part-time in this business, spending 20 hours a week serving customers and 5 hours on administrative tasks.

Financial Plan

	Year 1	Year 2
Revenue		
Total Annual Sales	**$10,000**	**$15,000**
Expenses		
• Office Supplies	$600	$600
• Vehicle Costs	$1,000	$1,400
• Telephone and Insurance	$1,020	$1,300
• Annual Cost of Wages	$10,000	$10,000
• Annual Cost of Advertising	$600	$675
Total Annual Expenses	**$13,220**	**$13,975**
Profit/Loss	**($3,220)**	**$1,025**

Class Discussion

Brainstorm reasons why a business plan could be helpful to a business owner.

Project Activity

Select a business idea that interests you, and consider the following questions:

- What will the business make, do, or sell?
- What need will the business fill that is not being met in your community?
- What kind of customers would the business attract?
- Do you have the skills, education, and interests needed to operate this business?

Complete the following items and add them to your project file.

1. Select a name for your business.

2. Write a vision statement that describes your business goal, and design a company logo. If possible, think of a catchy slogan that will become associated with your business.

3. Write a description of the product or service you will offer.

4. List those qualities and skills that you have that will help you own and operate your business successfully. If you need further training, identify how and where you will get the training.

Mental Math

Alistair pays about 30% of his salary in income tax. How much tax does he pay if his income is $45,000?

Notebook Assignment

1. What is a business?

2. Describe two reasons to prepare a business plan.

3. What is a retail business? List two examples from your own community.

4. What is a service business? List two examples from your own community.

5. What is a manufacturing business? List two examples from your own community.

Extension

6. You are planning to operate a bicycle courier business that will pick up and deliver documents and small packages for local businesses and individuals. Make a list of the equipment and supplies you will need to operate your business for a year. Estimate the operating costs for one year.

7. A carpentry student found that he enjoyed making wooden toys. Create a business plan for this student, assuming that he could use his father's tools and equipment for free.

New Terms

operating costs: the cost of equipment, space, supplies, and other items needed to run a business.

Exploration 2

Planning the Space for Your Business

Any business needs space. A retail space needs a store. A manufacturing business may need a warehouse or a plant. Many service businesses are operated from office spaces or shops. Even services such as lawn and garden care, where the service is provided at the customer's home or office, need to have space that will serve as an office.

Many owners rent or lease the space they need to operate their businesses. Space costs are one important expense that is added to the business plan. You may also need to plan for other costs related to space, such as insurance, property taxes, and utilities. Minimum estimates for these costs are listed in the table on the next page, but they vary widely from place to place.

Planning the space to effectively serve your business's needs is another important aspect of business planning. For example, if you are planning a store, you need to consider where to arrange the goods for sale and how to display them and where to situate the cash register. For a manufacturing business, you may need a shop space with equipment, along with a showroom to display your products, and an office where the office work is carried out. Service businesses may operate from an office space or they may simply use some space in the owner's home if most of the work is performed at the customer's site.

Goals

In this exploration, you will consider the space needs of businesses and calculate the cost of leasing space.

New Terms

utilities: heating and electricity for a building.

Minimum Annual Estimates for Space-Related Costs*

Lease of Space	$12.00/square foot
Property Taxes	$2.25/square foot
Insurance	$1.00/square foot
Utilities	$2.25/square foot
Janitorial Services	$1.00/square foot

* These costs vary greatly from community to community and may also depend on the condition of the leased space.

Example 1

Marcia Braundy is planning to open a store where she sells knitting supplies. She is considering leasing a store that costs $108/m^2$ per year. The dimensions of the store are 12 m × 18 m. What will her monthly leasing cost be?

Solution

First calculate the area of the store:
12 m × 18 m = 216 m^2

Next, multiply the area in square metres by the cost per year:
216 m^2 × $108 = $23,328

Finally, divide by 12 to find the monthly cost:
$23,328 ÷ 12 = $1,944

Marcia's monthly leasing cost will be $1,944.

Hints

1 You may find cost estimates for insurance, property taxes, and utilities from realtors, chambers of commerce, the newspaper, or government offices in your community.

2. $12.00/sq ft per year equals $1.00/sq ft per month.

Example 2

Klaus is considering leasing a 2000 square foot office space. It costs $12.00 a square foot plus $6.50 a square foot for insurance, taxes, and utilities a year. Calculate how much this office will cost Klaus per month.

Solution

Total annual expenses per square foot are:
$12.00 + $6.50 = $18.50/square foot per year

Total annual expenses are:
$18.50/ft^2 × 2000 ft^2 = $37,000 a year

Divide by 12 to find the monthly expenses:
$37,000 ÷ 12 = $3,083.33 (rounded)

The office space will cost Klaus about $3,083.33 a month.

Small Group Activity

In a small group, make a floor plan for a retail clothing store in a shopping mall. Assume that the store has the same area as your classroom. On the plan, show where you would place the clothing, where the change rooms would be located, and where you would place the sales counter and cash register. Also consider the need for a space to store goods not yet on display and office supplies.

What items might a retail clothing store place near the cash register? Why might they place such items in this spot? List the items you would place by the cash register.

Project Activity

Develop a space plan for the business you are planning.

1. First, decide on the kind and amount of space your business will need. What is the best location in your community for it? It may be best in a retail store in a mall, an office in an office tower or at home, or a shop space in an industrial mall.

2. Once you have decided on the kind of space, research the costs of this type of space in your local newspaper and estimate your monthly and annual leasing costs.

3. Plan how your space will be arranged and develop a floor plan drawn to scale that indicates the overall size and shape as well as the location of equipment, furnishings, and work spaces your business may need.

Notebook Assignment

1. Calculate the area of a store that is 15 feet wide and 20 feet long.

2. Calculate the area of an office that is 5 metres wide and 11 metres long.

3. Find the yearly cost of leasing an office that is 18 feet wide by 17 feet long. The lease costs are $12/sq ft per year.

4. Ramon is looking for a small shop to lease for his auto mechanic business. He is considering one in an industrial mall that measures 20 ft by 31 ft and rents for $12/sq ft a year. How much will the monthly leasing costs be? The lease on the shop is a two-year lease. How much will Ramon pay in total for the lease?

5. The Soup Cup restaurant is considering opening a second location. The owners look first at a space on a busy downtown street that costs $135/m^2 a year. They also look at a space of the same size on a side street nearby that costs $108/m^2 a year. List some factors the owners could consider as they make a decision about which space to lease.

6. A sporting goods store wants to compare its store leasing costs to its average yearly, weekly, and daily sales. Its lease costs are $12/sq ft per year and the store measures 20 feet by 35 feet. Its average daily sales are $640. Calculate the store's weekly and yearly sales and its yearly, weekly, and daily leasing costs. Are the store's sales covering its lease costs?

7. An office supplies business wants to rent additional storage space in the basement of the office building. If the lease for this space costs $6.00 a square foot per year and the business estimates that it needs a 20 by 20 foot area, what will the monthly lease costs be?

8. A clothing boutique wants to lease retail space on the ground floor of an expensive building. The costs are double those listed in the table on p. 401. If the store space measures 25 feet by 50 feet, what will the monthly costs be?

Extension

9. An auto mechanic is planning to open a repair shop. She finds an empty shop on a side street and meets with the owner. The owner wants to charge $1,500/month for the lease of the space and says that additional charges will add up to about $700/month.

   Another shop located on the main highway that passes through the town is 2000 square feet and costs $10.00/square foot per year plus maintenance, insurance, taxes, and utility costs that add up to $8.50/square foot per year.

   Which of these options is less expensive? Explain your answer. What other factors should the mechanic consider before she makes a choice of shop?

Exploration 3

Assessing Your Competitors

Researching the demand for your product or service and assessing the competition that exists in the marketplace are essential parts of planning your business. As you develop a business plan, it is wise to consider the following questions:

- Is there a need in your community that is not being filled?
- Who has a need for your product or service?
- Who already offers a similar service or product?
- Who might be starting up a business offering the same product or service in the future?
- Is there enough demand for your product or service to support your business?
- Will people be able to afford your product or service?

Once you have researched your competitors, you need to assess whether you can capture enough market share for your business to be successful. Market share refers to that portion of the total possible sales that a business can attract. For example, if one ice cream stand in a park sells ice cream cones to 50% of the visitors to the park who buy ice cream, it has captured 50% of the market share. Different types of businesses need different minimum amounts of market share to be successful.

Goals

In this exploration, you will learn how businesses research competing businesses in the marketplace.

New Terms

market share: one company's proportion of the total sales of a particular product or service.

Example 1

A welder at a local shop is planning to set up his own welding business. Many of the shop's customers have asked for him personally to do specialty welding jobs on stainless steel and aluminum and he thinks there may be a special market niche for a business that provides specialty welding. He researches the specialty welding market in his community and finds that such welding earns about $400,000 in all and earnings are growing at a rate of 5% a year.

How much would his welding business earn a year for the first three years if he was able to acquire 25% of the market share?

If his old shop hired a new specialty welder and won back half of his business, how much would he earn in the first three years?

Solution

In Year 1, the welder would expect to earn 25% of the total market:
$0.25 \times \$400,000 = \$100,000$

In Year 2, the total business will have grown 5%:
$\$400,000 \times 1.05 = \$420,000$

The welder's earnings will be:
$\$420,000 \times 0.25 = \$105,000$

In Year 3, the total business will have grown another 5%:
$\$420,000 \times 1.05 = \$441,000$

The welder's earnings will be:
$\$441,000 \times 0.25 = \$110,250$

If his old shop won back half the market share, his earnings would be half these amounts:
Year 1 $\$100,000 \times 0.5 = \$50,000$
Year 2 $\$105,000 \times 0.5 = \$52,500$
Year 3 $\$110,250 \times 0.5 = \$55,125$

New Terms

market niche: a small, specialized segment of the total market.

Career Connection

Name: Janet Rothman

Job: pet groomer at a veterinarian's office

Current wages: $18.75/h

Education: grade 12; 3-month college course in pet grooming

Career goal: veterinarian technician

Keyword search: Canada college veterinarian technician programs

Classroom Discussion

1. Consider fast food restaurants in your community. Are there many of them? If yes, why do you think that is so? Who are the customers for these restaurants? Are the outlets located close to each other? How are they similar to each other? How do they differ?

2. Can you think of any businesses that could exist in your community that are not there now?

3. Are there any products or services that could occupy a specialized market niche? Could you target a special segment of the market, such as students? Are there enough customers to support a specialized business?

Project Activity

Evaluate the competition that will exist for your business.

1. Identify the customers for your business.

2. Investigate whether businesses already exist in your community that will compete with you for customers. List any you discover.

3. Prepare a collage that illustrates the existing competition for your business. Your collage may include flyers or business ads from the local newspaper or the yellow pages. You may include information about the products offered to customers and the prices charged.

4. If there are competitors for your business, assess whether another business could survive and what might set it apart from the existing competitors and allow it to attract customers.

Notebook Assignment

1. How can you investigate what competitors there are if you are planning a new business?

2. A pizza parlour chain is planning to open a new outlet. How can the owners research what other pizza parlours they will be competing against?

3. A fast food outlet is opening in a neighbourhood in a large city. To assess the competitors, create a tally chart in which you will record the number of fast food ads that appear on a local television station. Complete the tally chart while you watch that station over the dinner hour. How many advertisements for fast food restaurants appear in that hour?

4. The Vanderheide family is considering opening a specialty delicatessen. They want to produce all the delicatessen meats they sell themselves and to

stock marinated and spiced meats, both fresh and frozen. They visit the Statistics Canada web site and find that their potential customer base is 15,000 people, with predicted growth of 4% a year. They also find that average meat consumption per person is 1.75 kg per week. The Vanderheides survey 500 people in their town and find 40 people who are likely to purchase their products.

How many kilograms of meat could the Vanderheides expect to sell in their first, second, and third years of operation? If the average selling price of their products is $7.00/kg, what would their weekly sales be?

5. A high school with 1500 students is considering opening a coffee shop as part of their chef's training program and as a way to earn money to fund their graduation dance. One-third of the students buy coffee regularly. If the coffee shop could capture 50% of the market share, how many students would become customers? If each customer bought a cup of coffee a day for $1.45, what would the shop's weekly sales be? If each cup of coffee costs the shop 45 cents and the rest is profit, how much would the shop earn each week towards the graduation dance?

What other products could the coffee shop offer to increase its earnings? Describe how you could find out what products competitors offer.

Extension

6. Jean-Pierre is planning to open a DVD rental store in his town. He needs to find the following information:

- the average distance people travel to rent DVDs
- the population in his target area
- whether customers are satisfied with their current service
- how much customers will pay to rent a DVD

For each item above, describe how Jean-Pierre could find a valid numerical estimate or graph that gives him the information he needs.

Exploration 4

....

Marketing Your Business

While you assessed your competitors, you determined who your customers are likely to be. If you have found there is a need for your business and that there are not an overwhelming number of competing businesses already, you need to develop a marketing plan.

A marketing plan is a strategy that a business creates to attract and maintain customers. Your marketing plan outlines how you plan to make your business and its products or services known to potential customers. It also outlines how you will keep your established customers familiar with your company on an ongoing basis. The costs of marketing are added to the overall budget for the business.

There are many effective techniques used in marketing. For example, advertising in the local newspaper can be an excellent way for a retail store to attract and keep customers. Many retail businesses also have special events such as sales to attract customers. Mailing a flyer out to homes in a community may be the best way to promote a home or garden service business. Having a salesperson who can call on new and old customers to show products may be effective for a manufacturing company. Many businesses offer their customers a discounted price in slow sales periods of the year.

A marketing campaign may take many forms and businesses need to be creative in their campaigns so that their business stands out from their competitors.

Goals	Technology	New Terms
In this exploration, you will develop a marketing plan for your business. You will identify your customers and consider the best way to promote your business to them.	The internet provides an important way for businesses to advertise their services or goods.	**marketing campaign:** a specific activity that is part of an overall marketing plan, such as a mailing campaign.

Example 1

Bill Johnson, who owns Bill's Shoebox, wants to advertise a shoe sale at his store by mailing out printed flyers to his established customers. He has 400 customers on his customer list. He will need to print the flyers and pay the cost of mailing them out. He needs to calculate the cost of this flyer mailing campaign so he can add the amount to his budget.

Bill has obtained two price quotations for printing the flyers. He can buy 100 flyers for $4.95 or 200 for $10.00. What is the per-flyer cost in each of these quotations? Which quotation should Bill choose?

If it costs Bill 48 cents to mail each flyer, how much will it cost to print and mail flyers to Bill's customer list?

Solution

First, find the per-flyer cost in the first quotation Bill receives:
$4.95 ÷ 100 = $0.0495 or a little less than 5 cents per flyer

Find the per-flyer cost in the second quotation:
$10.00 ÷ 200 = $0.05 or 5 cents per flyer

Bill should select the first quotation because:
$4.95 × 4 = $19.80

To mail 400 flyers will cost:
400 × $0.48 = $192.00

The total mailing campaign will cost:
$19.80 + $192.00 = $211.80

New Terms

quotation: an estimate of the cost of something obtained in advance of making a purchase.

Example 2

A sporting goods store is having a sale day. The store usually doubles its wholesale prices to arrive at the retail prices. The store usually sells 100 items a day at an average price of $20.00 per item.

For the sale day, the store marked all items in the store off by 10%. On the day of the sale, the store sold 10% more items than it normally would.

Did the store benefit financially from holding the sale? Did it achieve more or less profit than usual?

Solution

The sporting goods store makes an average profit of $10.00 per item sold since it doubles its wholesale prices to arrive at its retail price.
100 items/day × $10.00 = $1,000.00

On the sale day, the store sells 10% more items:
100 items × 1.10 = 110 items

The average price of the items is 10% less than usual:
$20.00 × 0.90 = $18.00

The profit on the sale items is calculated by subtracting the wholesale price from the sale price:
$18.00 − $10.00 = $8.00

Since the store sells 110 items, the total profit on sale day is:
$8.00 × 110 = $880.00

Therefore, the store makes less profit on the sale day.

New Terms

retail price: the price a retail store charges its customers.

wholesale price: the price a retail store pays to a supplier such as a manufacturer for items to sell.

Example 3

A salmon distribution company hires a sales representative to sell its salmon to restaurants. The company pays the representative a monthly $1,500 base salary plus a 50 cents/pound commission on sales. The representative sells an average of 3500 pounds of salmon each month.

The company wishes to calculate the amount the representative costs per pound of salmon she sells each month. Calculate the average monthly per-pound cost to the company.

Solution

The sales representative's average monthly commission is:
3500 lbs × 0.50 = $1,750.00/month

Find her salary plus commission:
$1,500 + $1,750 = $3,250/month

Find the amount the representative costs per pound of salmon she sells:
$3,250 ÷ 3500 lb = .92857142857 or $0.93 (rounded)

The cost is approximately 93 cents per pound of salmon sold.

Example 4

An accounting firm is planning an ad campaign. The firm is considering running a series of ads on the local television station. The station will charge $3,000 for 10 thirty-second ads, and the ad will be seen by 198,000 viewers.

If 1% of these viewers are potential customers of the accounting firm, how many potential customers could be reached by the ads? What would the cost per potential customer be?

Solution

The firm realizes that most people who see the ads will not become customers. If 1% of the viewers are potential customers, the ads would reach:

198,000 × 0.01 = 1980 potential customers

The cost per potential customer would be:
$3,000 ÷ 1980 = $1.52 (rounded)

The ads would reach about 1980 potential customers at a cost to the accounting firm of $1.52 each.

Classroom Discussion

Consider grocery stores in your community. What form does their advertising take? Do they advertise on television or radio? In the newspaper? In other media?

Why do many advertisers repeat their broadcast advertisements many times? Discuss the elements that make an effective advertisement. Do advertisements always contain prices? Why might they vary?

Small Group Activity

In small groups, examine newspaper ads or printed flyers from competing businesses. Discuss what features they have in common and how they are different. Is it possible to compare prices charged by competing businesses? Are many products listed or only a few? What features mentioned in the advertising might cause a buyer to prefer one business over another. What features other than prices are mentioned?

 ## Project Activity

1. List the marketing activities you will use to promote your business.

2. Develop a media advertisement or a product brochure for your business, selecting the type that will best promote your products or services to your potential customers.

3. Describe where you will advertise or how you will distribute your brochure.

Notebook Assignment

1. List three ways that a new business can attract customers.

2. A restaurant that specializes in steak dinners finds that Mondays are very slow and their earnings are low. The restaurant usually makes a profit of 50% of the price of the meals it serves. If the restaurant creates a "Monday Madness" sale in which they offer two meals for the price of one, would the restaurant earn more profit if four times the usual number of customers ate at the restaurant? What might the possible effect of such a sale be on Tuesday's earnings?

3. A gardening service is planning to use flyers to advertise the service it offers. The Apex Printing Company provides the following quotation: 20 cents each for the first 5000 flyers and 10 cents each for the next 5000. Premium Printers quotes a price of 15 cents each for the first 5000 flyers, 10 cents each for the next 2500 flyers, and 5 cents each for the next 5000. If the gardening service needs 8000 flyers, which printer should it select?

4. A coffee store in a mall wants to create a marketing plan to increase the sales of their products during the summer months when coffee is not as popular as it is in the winter. The owner is considering adding some new products to the menu that may sell better in hot weather. With a partner, develop a list of two or three new products the coffee shop could sell and write a marketing plan to promote these new products.

5. A company that manufactures picnic tables hires a door-to-door salesperson. The salesperson sells an average of two tables a day at a commission of $50.00 per table. He also receives a $1,000 bonus if he meets a quota of 60 tables a month, which he does. What does the salesperson's commission and bonus cost the company?

6. A small business that specializes in sales, installation, and servicing of fireplaces and furnaces wants to open a new store in a town of 15 000 inhabitants. The business manager wants to develop a marketing plan to introduce the business to the community and to advertise its presence and its products. Create a marketing plan for this business.

Extension

7. Investigate the marketing practices of internet-based businesses. Select two on-line businesses with the same product or service, such as bookstores, and compare their prices. If possible, select Canadian websites.

8. A fitness club begins a marketing campaign that includes incentives for current members to sign up new members. The club offers an extra month's registration to a member for every new member they sign up for one year. The club also offers a chance to win two mountain bikes as prizes to those members who sign up new members. The mountain bikes cost the club $500 each and the winners' names will be drawn from a prize bin. If a year's membership costs $250 and a month's registration costs $25.00, what is the net effect to the club if 20 new yearly memberships are signed up due to the incentives?

Exploration 5

• • • • • • • • • • • • • • • • • • • •

Staffing a Business

An important part of planning a business is to consider whether you will need to hire staff and, if the answer is yes, how much your payroll would cost.

As you plan your business, consider the following questions:

- Will you be the only employee of the business or will you need to hire other staff people to work for you?
- If yes, how many staff people would your business need?
- When would they work?
- What is the average wage paid to such staff?
- Will they be paid an hourly wage, an annual salary, a commission, or will their pay be calculated on another basis?

In addition to the amounts you pay your employees, you need to budget a salary for yourself. There are also payroll amounts that must be paid to the federal government for each employee you have, such as Employment Insurance and Canada Pension Plan contributions.

Goals

In this exploration, you will consider the staffing needs of a business, prepare a staffing schedule, and calculate the cost of wages.

New Terms

payroll: the total costs to a company of its staff.

Example 1

Joan is calculating the weekly cost of wages for the staff of her novelty decoration store. She has three employees. One works 32 hours a week and earns $9.75/hour. Another works 24 hours a week and earns $11.60/hour. The third employee works for 16 hours a week and earns $12.90/hour. Find the weekly cost of wages for this store.

Solution

First, find the wages for each of the three employees:

Employee 1   32 h × $9.75   = $312.00
Employee 2   24 h × $11.60   = $278.40
Employee 3   16 h × $12.90   = $206.40

Then add these amounts together to find the weekly total:
$312.00 + $278.40 + $206.40 = $796.80

The total wages for one week are $796.80.

Mental Math

1. A store hires a student at $10.00 an hour for 12 hours a week. What is the weekly cost of the student's wages?

2. A student earns $8.50 an hour and works four hours a day. How much do the student's wages cost her employer?

Example 2

Jane Nelson needs to set a staff schedule and calculate the weekly cost of wages for her travel agency. Her agency is open from 9 am to 5 pm daily except Sundays, and staff work 8-hour shifts. Jane needs two staff working from Mondays to Thursdays and three staff on Fridays and Saturdays. Jane's employees Susan and Jill work 40 hours a week and Bob works when needed. All Jane's employees earn $14.00 an hour.

How many hours would Bob need to work? Create a sample schedule for one week that meets the agency's staff needs, and calculate the weekly staff costs.

Solution

The staff schedule will be as follows:

Monday	Tuesday	Wednesday	Thursday	Friday	Saturday
Susan	Bob	Susan	Susan	Susan	Susan
Bob	Jill	Jill	Jill	Jill	Jill
				Bob	Bob

Other weekly schedules are possible but all three staff need to work on Fridays and Saturdays and Bob needs to work 32 hours a week.

The cost of wages per employee will be:

Susan	40 hours × $14.00	= $560.00
Jill	40 hours × $14.00	= $560.00
Bob	32 hours × $14.00	= $448.00

The total will be:
$560.00 + $560.00 + $448.00 = $1,568.00

Technology

A spreadsheet can be a very helpful tool when calculating the cost of wages for a number of employees that work different hours at different rates of pay, and for creating staff schedules.

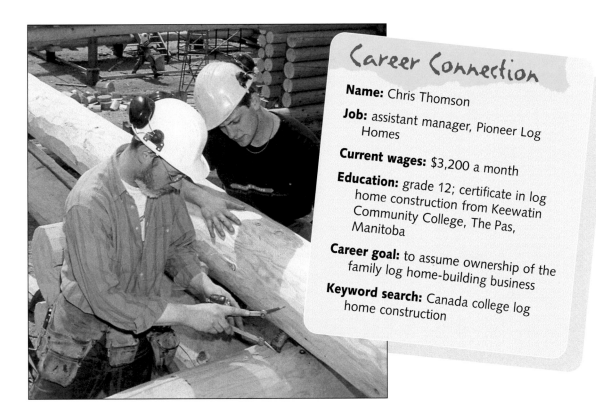

Career Connection

Name: Chris Thomson

Job: assistant manager, Pioneer Log Homes

Current wages: $3,200 a month

Education: grade 12; certificate in log home construction from Keewatin Community College, The Pas, Manitoba

Career goal: to assume ownership of the family log home-building business

Keyword search: Canada college log home construction

Project Activity

Develop a staffing plan for your business.

1. Decide how many staff people you will need and what their jobs will be. Prepare a staff shift schedule that shows your hours of operation and which staff people will work when. Don't forget to include yourself!

2. Research the average wages paid for these jobs and use this information to estimate the annual payroll cost of your business. Prepare a statement of the annual cost of wages.

3. Add the amount you would like to pay yourself to the annual cost of wages. Later you will compare your estimates with the revenues you expect to earn to see if your projected payroll costs are feasible. You could choose to display your schedule and staff costs on a spreadsheet and add it to your project file.

Notebook Assignment

1. Tiffany works for a shoe store and is in charge of staffing. Find the weekly wages of the shoe store if Tiffany works 40 hours a week and is paid $13.50 an hour and two sales assistants are each paid $9.50 an hour and work 25 hours a week.

2. Jerry prepares the staff schedule for a small grocery store. The total cost of the regular full-time staff is $3,300 a week. Jerry hires two students to work from 4 pm to 9 pm on weekdays and two more students to work 8 hour shifts on Saturday. The students are paid $9.50 an hour. Find the total cost of weekly wages for Jerry's store.

3. Paco completes the following staffing schedule for a courier business. Each employee makes $18.50 an hour. Find the total cost of staffing for a week.

Monday	Abe and Heather, 8 hours each
Tuesday	Abe and Heather, 8 hours each, John 4.5 hours
Wednesday	Abe, Heather, John, and Trish, 8 hours each
Thursday	Abe, 8 hours
Friday	Abe, Heather, and John, 8 hours each; Trish 5.5 hours

4. A store manager needs to find sales staffing for a weekend. She needs 5 employees on Friday, 8 employees on Saturday, and 5 employees on Sunday. The employees work 8 hour shifts, and the store is open from 9 am to 9 pm Friday and Saturday, and from 10 am to 6 pm Sunday. Create a possible staffing schedule she could use and find the cost of staffing for each day if each employee makes $15.50 an hour.

5. Consider a gas station in your community. Estimate the annual cost of wages by making a list of staff members and the hours they likely work in an average week. Calculate the costs of staff for a year if they earn $9.75/hour each.

Extension

6. A sawmill pays students to do clean-up on Saturdays. They pay $19.50 an hour and time and a half to individuals that work more than 8 hours. A foreman estimates that they need 20 hours of work done one Saturday. How can the foreman arrange to have the work completed at the least cost to the company? Explain your reasoning.

Problem Analysis

Designing a Work Schedule

A new power house is being built at the Blackshell Industrial Complex. Operation of the power house will require a charge engineer and an assistant engineer on duty 24 hours per day. As director of the physical plant, you have been given the task of scheduling the engineers' work rotations. In (b), additional conditions will require you to decide how many engineers must be hired. You must also design a work schedule for them. What is the minimum number of days for a complete rotation?

a) You must schedule four charge engineers and four assistant engineers.
- The charge engineer must hold at least a 2nd class ticket.
- The assistant engineer must hold at least a 3rd class ticket.
- Different pairings of charge and assistant engineers are required each work rotation.
- The engineers will work 12-hour shifts.
- No more than 48 hours may be worked without at least two days off.

b) It was later decided in the plant that, in addition to the above conditions . . .
- Each engineer should work no more than 48 hours in a given week and no more than 80 hours in a two-week stretch.
- Shifts must be fairly distributed among all the employees. Nobody wants to work all night shifts and nobody wants to work all weekends.
- A complete rotation may run less than, but no more than, 13 weeks. You may find it helpful to use the chart below to get started. You may need to extend it either to the right or down to accommodate more weeks and/or employees. As an alternative, you may design your own chart or use a spreadsheet to record your information.

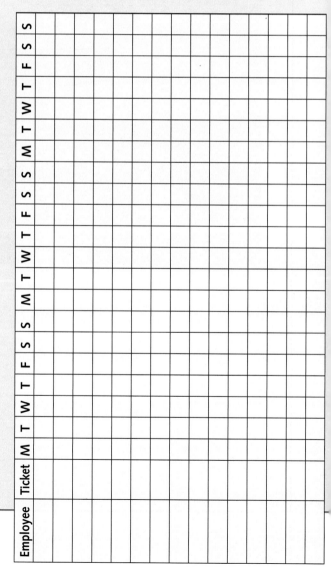

Games

Happy Numbers and Their Friends

Number theory is a fascinating branch of mathematics which studies the characteristics of the counting numbers. Here are several simple examples.

Happy Numbers

A happy number is a counting number for which the sum of the squares of the digits eventually results in 1.

Is 19 a happy number?

Compute the sum of the squares of the digits:

$$1^2 + 9^2 = 1 + 81 = 82$$

Stop if the result is 1, otherwise repeat the process.

Find the sum of the squares of the digits of 82:

$$8^2 + 2^2 = 64 + 4 = 68$$
$$6^2 + 8^2 = 36 + 64 = 100$$
$$1^2 + 0^2 + 0^2 = 1$$

Stop; the result is 1. Therefore 19 is a happy number!

1. Determine whether 11 is a happy number.

2. Twenty of the first 100 counting numbers are happy. Find them. Use any short cuts you discover.

3. It turns out that every number which is not happy enters a repeating cycle of eight numbers. You may have discovered this in working on the previous activity. The cycle never ends because it repeats itself and never becomes 1.

   Determine this cycle of eight numbers.

4. Is the sum of two happy numbers always a happy number?

5. Is the product of two happy numbers always a happy number?

6. Is 1998 a happy number year? What about 2000?

Exploration 6

Financial Plan

Among the most important parts of a business plan is the financial plan. In the financial plan, you estimate your total revenues and expenses, and calculate whether your business will be profitable or not.

You need to incorporate the financial portions of your space, marketing, and staffing plans into your overall financial plan. Added to this information are estimates of your revenues and any other operating expenses you may have. A statement of revenues and expenses is then used to prepare a profit and loss statement.

Estimating Sales

Most businesses earn their revenue from sales of their products or services. In a business plan, sales are estimated or predicted, usually on an annual basis. Annual sales projections are often based on past business records and may be calculated by working out average daily or weekly sales and multiplying to estimate annual sales.

Goals

In this exploration, you will prepare a financial plan for your business and determine whether or not it is profitable.

Example 1

A grocery store sells an average of $125,000 worth of groceries each week. What are the store's annual sales? The store marks up its prices 25%. What is its annual gross profit?

Solution

Calculate the annual sales:
$125,000/week × 52 weeks = $6,500,000
The store's annual sales are $6,500,000.

Calculate the gross profit:
$6,500,000 × 0.25 = $1,625,000
The store's annual gross profits are $1,625,000.

Estimating Expenses

Part of a business plan is estimating the expenses of operating the business. There are several types of expenses that businesses incur.

Operating expenses refer to expenses that the business will have regardless of its sales. Such expenses include space leasing costs, insurance, and wages paid to staff. These expenses are sometimes referred to as overhead costs.

Some expenses are incurred to make and market the company's products or services. In retail stores, this type of expense covers the cost of inventory or stock. In manufacturing companies, expenses may include raw materials for the products they make. Service companies may need to buy supplies that they use when they provide services. These costs often vary depending on the level of sales a company has.

Another type of expense is called a capital expense. Capital expenses are long-term purchases of buildings, tools, and equipment that the business needs.

A business may also pay financial charges if it needs to borrow money to cover its expenses. If a company borrows money from a financial institution, loan payments become a regular expense for that company.

Advertising a company's services can be as simple as displaying a sandwich board in a parking lot.

New Terms

overhead costs: general operating costs of a business

Example 2

Claire opens an ice cream stand for the summer to earn money for college. She borrows $3,000 to buy a $2,500 ice cream stand and $500 for one week's worth of supplies, such as ice cream, cones, and chocolate sprinkles. Her loan payments are $1,066.66/month. She must pay the city $50.00/month for three months for a business licence and electrical power to operate the stand in a city park. Her insurance costs are $50.00/month and she spends $200 on decorating her stand to attract customers. Claire works five days a week for 8 hours a day and hires another student to work on weekends. Estimate her expenses for the three months she operates her ice cream stand.

Solution

Cost of ice cream stand		$2,500.00
Cost of supplies	$500/week × 12 weeks	$6,000.00
Cost of licence and power	$50/month × 3	$150.00
Cost of decorating the stand		$200.00
Cost of loan payments	$1,066.66 × 3	$3,199.98
Cost of insurance	$50/month x 3	$150.00
Total expenses for the summer		**$12,199.98**

Example 3

Roger offers a pedicab service for tourists visiting downtown Victoria. The cabs cost $3,500 each and will last for 3 years. Maintenance costs are $50.00/month. Insurance and licensing cost $400/month. Roger hires students at $8.00 an hour plus a commission of $2.00 a ride. If the pedicab operates 16 hours a day and averages 3 rides an hour, calculate Roger's costs for one year.

Solution

Cab purchase	($3,500 ÷ 3 years)	$1,166.67
Maintenance	($50 × 12)	$600.00
Insurance and licensing	($400 × 12)	$4,800.00
Wages	(16 h/day × 365 days × $8.00/h)	$46,720.00
Commissions	(3 rides/h × 16 h/day × 365 days × $2.00	$35,040.00
	Total annual costs	**$88,326.67**

Profit and Loss

One of the final steps in preparing a business plan is to calculate whether a business will earn more than it spends. If it does, the business is said to earn a profit when expenses are deducted from revenues. If it does not, the business is losing money and expenses are greater than revenues.

Gross profit is the difference between what a business pays for the products or services it sells to its customers and what it charges.

Net profit is the profit remaining after the operating costs of the business have been deducted from the gross profit. Operating costs are also called overhead costs and refer to costs the business has whether it sells anything or not. Costs such as leases, insurance, wages, and office supplies are operating costs.

Example 4

A boat-builder charges $85,000 for a sailboat. The materials and labour needed to build the boat cost $62,000. Find the gross profit. List expenses the builder might deduct to find the net profit made by his boat-building company.

Solution

The gross profit is:
$85,000 − $62,000 = $23,000

To find his net profit, the builder might deduct the costs of rent for a shop, tools, and insurance.

Project Activity

Develop a financial plan for your business.

1. Prepare a statement of revenues and expenses. Gather information from your space, staffing, and marketing plans. Estimate your operating costs and the cost of providing your company's goods or service. Prepare a listing of all the different expenses and revenues you estimate you will have in one year.

2. Compare the revenues and expenses and calculate and add a statement showing the profit or loss you expect to earn.

Notebook Assignment

1. Complete the following table to find the estimated daily gross profit at a jewellery store.

Item	Wholesale cost	Retail price	Profit per item	Number sold	Gross profit
Ring	$58	$150		4	
Watch	$150	$350		1	
Bracelet	$20	$50		5	
Earrings	$70	$140		2 pairs	
				Daily Profit:	$

2. Complete the following table to find the estimated weekly gross profit at a jeans store.

Item	Wholesale cost	Retail price	Profit per item	Number sold	Gross profit
Bell-bottoms	$25	$50		24	
Flares	$30		$30	30	
Belts	$15			6	$90
Overalls	$55	$100		18	
				Weekly Profit:	$

3. A student acts as a fishing guide. He works 6 days a week and earns $150 a day. He averages $50 in tips each day. Find his earnings over the summer. He works for 8 weeks in all.

4. A candy store has revenues of $3,251.18 and expenses of $2,242.29. How much profit does the store earn?

5. A fishing and sporting goods store has revenues of $15,852 and expenses of $18,527.18. Is the store profitable? By how much?

6. A sewing shop has staffing costs of $3,500 a month, lease costs of $600 a month, and other costs that add up to $429 a month. The revenues one month are $2,422.18 from the sale of fabrics and patterns, and $552 from providing sewing lessons. Is the business profitable that month? By how much?

7. A machinist's shop that serves the forestry industry has revenues of $50,842.17 and expenses of $51,642.95. One month, the weather is so poor that the forestry companies that are the shop's customers are unable to operate. Should the machinist's shop consider shutting down? Explain your reasoning.

Extension

8. A gourmet foods store has a high level of sales just before Christmas and other holidays throughout the year. However, there are several months each year in which sales are so low that the store loses money. What can the owner do if she wants to decide whether to keep her business open or not? How can she determine whether her business is viable?

Chapter Review

● ●

1. Suggest two reasons for developing a business plan.

2. A shoe store sells the following stock over a one-month period:

    - 20 pairs of dress shoes with an average wholesale cost of $55.00 a pair
    - 62 pairs of sports shoes with an average wholesale cost of $60 a pair
    - 23 pairs of sandals with an average wholesale cost of $25 a pair
    - 15 pairs of work books with an average wholesale cost of $55 a pair

    Find the cost of replacing the inventory that is sold.

3. A card and gift shop measures 15 feet by 18 feet. The shop pays $1.25/square foot per month for its lease and $0.75/square foot for other space costs such as insurance and utilities. What is the total cost of the space each month?

4. A restaurant leases a space that measures 10 m by 5 m. The cost of the leased space is $108 per square metre per year. How much does it cost annually to lease this space? How much is it on a monthly basis?

5. A music store offers music lessons. The two teachers, Tim and Josh, are paid $25.00/hour. Tim works from 3:30 pm to 9:00 pm Monday to Friday and Josh works on Saturdays from 10:00 am to 4:30 pm. What is the cost of wages for the teachers each week? What is the annual cost of their wages?

6. A sewing store sells three brands of patterns. They buy Brand A at a wholesale cost of $6.00, Brand B at $9.50, and Brand C at $12.00. The store marks up the wholesale prices 50% to arrive at the retail prices. How much does the store charge for each brand of pattern? How much profit do they make on each brand?

7. A custom golf club manufacturer is working on a financial plan for his business. He estimates that he will pay $1.25/square foot a year for insurance on his 400 square foot factory space. He plans to spend $1,200 on advertising his clubs at the local golf courses over the year. He also makes $327/month payments on a business loan. What is the total monthly cost of these expenses?

8. A hamburger stand sells on average 125 cheeseburger meals for $5.00 and 100 hamburger meals for $4.50 during their lunch-hour rush between 11:00 am and 1:00 pm. The stand costs $20.00/hour to rent and operate. The hamburger meals cost $2.00 each to make and the cheeseburger meals cost an additional $0.10. Find the following:

   a) total average sales during the lunch-hour rush
   b) total costs to make the meals sold during the lunch-hour rush
   c) the gross profit per hour during the lunch-hour rush
   d) the net profit per hour during the lunch-hour rush

9. A snowboard sales and repair shop opens in Whistler, BC. The shop occupies a space that is 12 feet wide and 16 feet deep. The owner estimates that he needs 25 square feet for the till area, 60 square feet for a repair space, and space for a display rack that measures 2 feet by 8 feet. Create a scale floor plan for this store.

10. A baby-sitting service at a large resort hotel needs to plan weekend evening staffing from 5:00 pm Friday to 1:00 am Saturday and 5:00 pm Saturday to 1:00 am Sunday. The service needs to have two babysitters working at all times, and three from 7:00 pm to midnight. Create a staffing schedule that uses the minimum number of babysitters. Explain your reasoning.

11. The manager of an office services business is creating a financial plan. She estimates the company's wages for one week to be $1,000, the lease of the office to be $100/week, and gross profit after they have bought new equipment to be $1,600/week. Create a statement of revenues and expenses that shows whether or not the store makes a profit or incurs a loss during the week in question.

Project Presentation

As you have worked through this chapter, you have created the components of a business plan for a business of your choice.

In this presentation, you will present your plan to your classmates, who will role-play a group of potential investors in your business idea.

Assemble the materials in your project file into a business plan document. Include the following items:

1. a title page with a name for your business, a mission statement, and a logo

2. a description of the product or service you will offer

3. a description of the skills, interests, and abilities that will help you create and run the business

4. a space plan for your business premises

5. a description of your competitors

6. a marketing plan

7. a staffing plan

8. a financial plan

Case Study

Planning a Summer Business

Jan and Daniel decide to open a photography business called Arctic Images to serve tourists who travel to a fly-in wilderness lodge near Yellowknife, NWT during the summer months.

Jan and Daniel plan to offer their customers CDs that contain photographic images of their adventures in the north. The CDs will contain still photographs or videotaped images, or a mixture of both.

They will accompany their customers on day trips from the lodge. The lodge has agreed to rent them a cabin at a discounted rate and to allow them to approach their customers. Arctic Images will operate during July and August.

Revenues

This table lists the revenues the students expect to earn during their first summer.

Package	Price	Projected Number Sold
#1 Still Photographs	$100	20
#2 Videotape	$200	20
#3 Photographs and Videotape	$400	10

Expenses

The following table lists the operating expenses the students expect to have. They already own their cameras.

Item	Cost
computer rental	$115/month
cabin rental and meals	$400/month
photography supplies	$250/month

1. Prepare a cash flow statement for Arctic Images using the information above.

2. Are there any additional expenses that you think the students should have considered? If so, list them.

3. Describe how the students might evaluate the competitors that might exist for this type of business.

4. Describe how the students could advertise Arctic Images to potential customers.

5. Would the two students be able to staff their business or might they need to consider hiring additional staff?

6. Write a memo to the students advising them how to prepare a business plan for Arctic Images.

Answer Key

Chapter 1

INCOME & DEBT

Exploration 1

Performance-Based Income: Commission

Notebook Assignment (p. 18)

1.

Item	Commission
hair spray	$13.51
razor blades	$16.77
shaving foam	$4.19
shower gel	$4.79

2. $960

3. gross pay $170
net pay $119

4.

Week	Commission	Total Weekly Earnings
1	$312.03	$462.03
2	$375.00	$525.00
3	$495.00	$645.00
4	$293.67	$443.67
	Total	$2,075.70

5.

Employee	Commission	Total Gross Income
89551	$384.42	$584.42
89553	$622.21	$752.21
89554	$185.65	$335.65
89556	$183.75	$383.75

6. $295

7. Monthly salary:

Weekly Sales	$\leq$ $2,500	$2,501 – $4,000	>$4,000	Weekly Commission
	15%	$17\frac{1}{2}$%	20%	
Week 1: $3,750	$375	$218.75		$593.75
Week 2: $2,880	$375	$66.50		$441.50
Week 3: $4,400	$375	$262.50	$80	$717.50
Week 4: $3,900	$375	$245.00		$620.00
Total Commission	$1,500	$792.75	$80	$2,372.75

8. $1,800

9. **a)** Commission: $450; net pay: $301.50

b) Commission: $800; net pay: $520

c) Commission: $1,900; net pay: $1,102

10. a) Commission: $201; salary plus commission: $268

b) Commission: $402; salary plus commission: $335

c) Answers may vary.

11. a) $1,900
   b) No

Extension

12. $55,756.24

Exploration 2
Performance-Based Income: Piecework
Notebook Assignment (p. 25)

1. Answers may vary.

2. Answers may vary.

3. Weekly earnings: $277.68

4. $752

5. $336

6. $150

7. $437.04

8. $3,750

9. $322.50

10. $496.65

11. $1,005

Extension

12. a) $786.75
   b) Skirts
   c) Skirts

Exploration 3
Simple Interest
Notebook Assignment (p. 32)

1.

Principal Paid	Rate of Interest	Term	Interest
$530	4%	2 years	$42.40
$1,600	5.2%	3 years	$249.60
$1,200	3.6%	8 months	$28.80
$840	2.5%	80 days	$4.60
$1,860	3.8%	10 months	$58.90
$4,000	6.6%	7 years	$1,848.00
$3,600	4.8%	200 days	$94.68

2. a) $183.33
   b) 164.25 days
   c) 3.38%
   d) $5,500
   e) 351.18 days

3. 7%

4. 2.5 years

5. $3,000

6. 10.92%

7. $2,179.49

Exploration 4
Compound Interest
Notebook Assignment (p. 38)

1.

Year	Principal (P)	Interest Earned (I = Prt)
1	$5,000	$250.00
2	$5,250	$262.50
3	$5,512.50	$275.63
4	$5,788.13	$289.41
5	$6,077.54	$303.88
6	$6,381.42	$319.07

2. **a)** $1,150.26
   b) $1,153.08

3. **a)** $424.73
   b) $749.34
   c) $1,990.74

4. $536.48

5. Quarterly, because you begin to accumulate interest on interest sooner.

6. Answers may vary.

7. Dividing 72 by a given interest rate gives you a quick estimate of the length of time it takes an investment to double.

8. **a)** 7.2 years
   b) 96 years
   c) 16.94 years
   d) 12 years
   e) 9 years
   f) 25.04 years
   g) 6 years
   h) 24 years

9. Answers may vary.

10. After 10 years: $2,593.74; after 30 years: $17,449.40

Exploration 5
Shopping with a Credit Card
Notebook Assignment (p. 44)

1. See table below.

Month	Previous Balance	Payment	Unpaid Balance	Interest on Unpaid Balance	Purchases	New Balance	Payment Due
Jan.	$1,000.00	$95.00	$905.00	$18.10	$900.00	$1,823.10	$91.16
Feb.	$1,823.00	$95.00	$1,728.00	$34.56	$400.00	$2,162.56	$108.13
Mar.	$2,162.56	$108.13	$2,054.43	$41.09	$0.00	$2,095.52	$104.78
Apr.	$2,095.52	$104.78	$1,990.74	$39.82	$200.00	$2,230.56	$111.53

2. **a)** 3
    b) $62.50
    c) March 8
    d) $3,958.46
    e) $1,556.58
    f) $197.92
    g) No
    h) April 28, 1997

3. **a)** 0.0384%
    b) 0.0466%
    c) 0.0603%

4. **a)** 10.04%
    b) 4.38%
    c) 1.28%

5. **a)** $10.71
    b) $16.67
    c) $33.77

6. **a)** $0
    b) $0
    c) $658.12
    d) $658.12
    e) $32.91
    f) $5,141.88

7. $25.59

Extension

8. $10.45

9. Answers may vary.

Exploration 6
In-Store Promotions
Notebook Assignment (p. 56)

1. **a)** $192.60
    b) 12%

2. **a)** $458
    b) $510
    c) $52

3. **a)** $853.86
    b) i) $930.71
        ii) $933.96
        iii) $934.26

4. **a)** $70.20
    b) 8.2%

Exploration 7
Personal Loans
Notebook Assignment (p. 62)

1. **a)** $181.70
    b) $353.30

2. **a)** $232.01
    b) $2,073.48

3. **a)** $233.36
    b) $843.96

4. **a)** $399.17
    b) $5,049.95

5. **a)** $79.86
    b) $124.39

Exploration 8
Exchange Rates
Notebook Assignment (p. 69)

1. **a)** 1.4748
    b) 0.2173
    c) 0.9970

2. **a)** 0.1646
    b) 2.2580
    c) 1.5752

3. **a)** $736.80
    b) $19,832.50
    c) $3,162.83
    d) $7,992.14

4. 813.67 euro

5. **a)** 440.74 euro
    b) 275.24 pounds
    c) 4,034.76 krone

6. **a)** 2,092.05 pesos
    b) $344.35
    c) Answers may vary.

7.

United States	$8,065.00
Scotland	$20,156.90
Canada	$3,000.00
Singapore	$13,711.50
Austria	$5,899.20
Total amount in Canadian dollars:	$50,832.60

Chapter Review (p. 71)

1. $468

2. **a)** $316.50
    b) $202.56

3. $1,103

4. **a)** $1,254
    b) $764.94

5. $360

6. **a)** $10
    b) $8.02
    c) $42.41

7. **a)** $240.19
    b) 8.7%
    c) 9.16 months

8. **a)** $169.11
    b) $87.96
    c) $137.55

9. $206.64

10. $26.34

11. **a)** $444.60
    b) $680.00

12. **a)** $594.26
    b) $755.65
    c) $161.39
    d) 27.16%

13. **a)** $248.04
    b) $1,129.44

14. $589.92

15. 210.85 Scottish pounds

16. $1,770.75

17. $88.55 Cdn

18. **a)** $433.97 US
    b) $683.59 Cdn
    c) The bank earns money by charging a service charge when it handles foreign currency.

Chapter 2

DATA ANALYSIS

Exploration 1
Line Plots
Notebook Assignment (p. 86)

1. See Figure 1 below.
    a) 34, 35
    b) 31
    c) 4–8, 11–12, 16–17
    d) 10
    e) Nine of the countries listed.
    f) 2
    g) 6
    h) Answers may vary.

2. See Figure 2 below.
    a) 26 million (Michael Jackson, *Thriller*); 27 million (Eagles, *Greatest Hits*)
    b) 23–26 million
    c) There is one cluster between 14 and 16.
    d) 13 million
    e) 10
    f) 5
    g) Answers may vary.
    h) The Beatles
    i) 48 million

Extension

3. **a)** Answers may vary.
    b) Answers may vary.

Figure 1

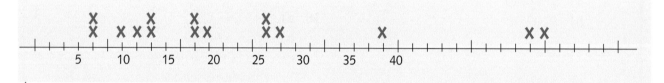

Figure 2

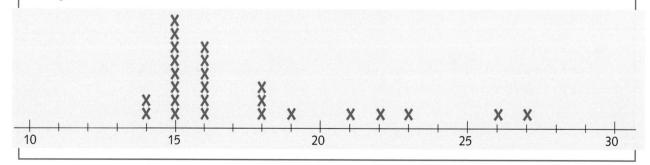

Exploration 2

Determining Measures of Central Tendency

Notebook Assignment (p. 93)

1. **a)** mean: 14.2; median: 11; mode: 4, 8, 11, 16
   b) Answers may vary.

2. **a)** mean: 17.4 million; median: 16 million; mode: 15 million
   b) Answers may vary.

3. Answers may vary.

4. **a)** mean
   b) mode
   c) mean
   d) median
   e) mode
   Answers may vary depending upon explanation.

5. **a)** See Figure 3 below. Mean: 7.5; median: 7; mode: 6; range: 6.
   b) See Figure 4 below. Mean: 15; median: 14; mode: 12; range: 12.
   c) It doubles all of them.

6. **a)** See Figure 5 below. Mean: 12.5; median: 12; mode: 11; range: 6.
   b) Mean, median, and mode increase by 5. Range remains the same.

7. No, because 50 is weighted by 3 scores and 70 is weighted by 1 score.

Extension

8. 55 points

Figure 3

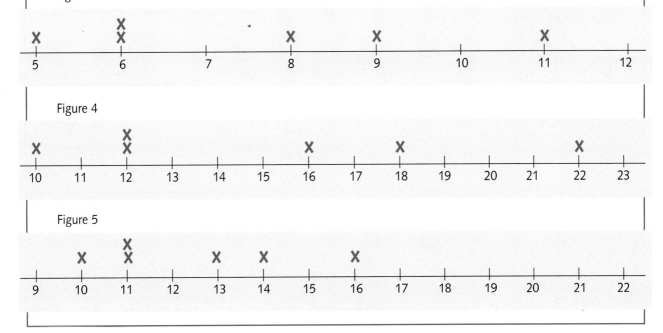

Exploration 3

Adjusting Measures of Central Tendency

Notebook Assignment (p.100)

1. Mean: $3.74; median: $3.75; mode: $3.75

2. **a)** Mean: 23; median; 23; mode: 23
   b) They are all the same.

3. Answers may vary.

4. Answers may vary.

5. **a)** 77%
   b) Yes, it is realistic considering her other marks.

Extension

6. Answers may vary.

7. **Scenario A**
   a) See Figures 6, 7, and 8 below.

b) Olga Pavlova: 7.5; Nadia Ionescu: 7.5

c) Olga Pavlova—mean: 8.7; median: 8.8; mode: 8.6 and 8.8
Nadia Ionescu—mean: 9.1; median: 9.3; mode: 9.4
Rita O'Brien—mean: 9.2; median: 9.3; mode: 9.3

d) Mean: Rita O'Brien; median: a tie—Rita O'Brien and Nadia Ionescu; mode: Nadia Ionescu

e) Olga Pavlova—mean: 8.8; median: 8.8; mode: 8.6, 8.8
Nadia Ionescu—mean: 9.3; median: 9.3; mode: 9.4
Rita O'Brien—mean: 9.2; median: 9.3; mode: 9.3

f) Nadia Ionescu

g) Low outlier: mean decreases; high outlier: mean increases.

h) If they are equidistant from the mean, it will not be affected.

Figure 6: Olga Pavlova

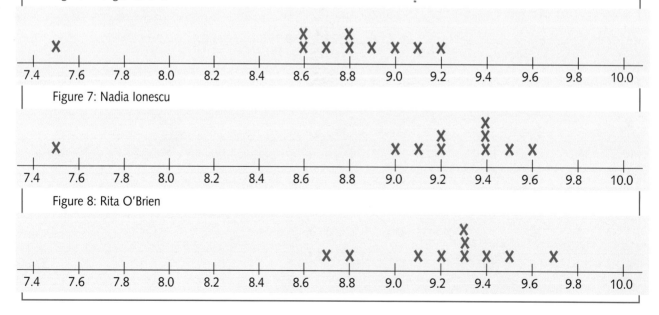

Figure 7: Nadia Ionescu

Figure 8: Rita O'Brien

Scenario B
   a) See the spreadsheet below
      i)   Mean: $45,211; median:
           $40,000; mode: $40,000
      ii) Mean: $38,636; median:
           $40,000; mode: $40,000
   b) She considered all 71 employees.
   c) More than $45,000: 17; less than
      $45,000: 54
   d) Mode

   e) Mode; mode; because most
      employees earn $40,000.
   f) i)   Mean: $48,169; median:
           $40,000: mode: $40,000
      ii) Mean increases; mode and
           median remain unchanged.
      iii) The mode and the mean.
   g) The mean of all 71 employees.
   h) Answers may vary.

Payroll Information for Greenwood Manufacturing Ltd.

Type of Job Position	Number of Employees	Salary	Total Salary	Union Member
President	1	$250,000	$250,000	No
Vice-President	2	$130,000	$260,000	No
Plant Manager	2	$75,000	$150,000	No
Supervisor	12	$50,000	$600,000	Yes
Labourer	30	$40,000	$1,200,000	Yes
Payroll Clerk	3	$37,000	$111,000	Yes
Custodian	5	$35,000	$175,000	Yes
Sales Clerk	10	$32,000	$320,000	Yes
Secretary	6	$24,000	$144,000	Yes
Total:	71		Total: $3,210,000	

Exploration 4
Using Bar Graphs to Represent Data
Notebook Assignment (p. 110)

1.

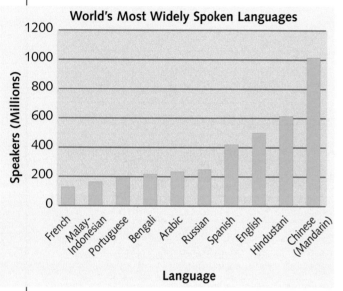

2.

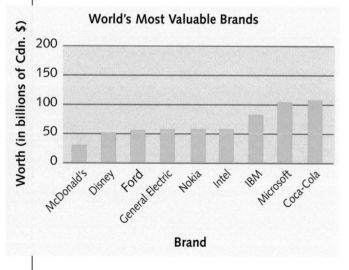

3.

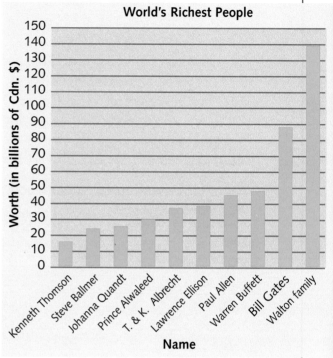

Extension

4. Answers may vary.

Exploration 5
Using Circle Graphs to Represent Data
Notebook Assignment (p. 120)

1.

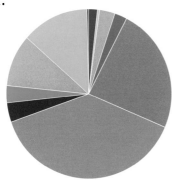

Population of Canada's Provinces/Territories

- Newfoundland and Labrador (1.71%) 6°
- Prince Edward Island (0.44%) 2°
- Nova Scotia (3.13%) 11°
- New Brunswick (2.43%) 9°
- Québec (23.80%) 86°
- Ontario (38.13%) 137°
- Manitoba (3.69%) 13°
- Saskatchewan (3.26%) 12°
- Alberta (9.84%) 35°
- British Columbia (13.15%) 47°
- Northern Territories (0.32%) 1°

2. He sold many more TVs in 2001. His sales actually increased by 68.9%.

Extension

3. No, because you would have to divide 1° into 3 parts and each would be too small to see.

Chapter Review (p. 123)

1. a) See Figure 9 below.
  b) 1531–1624 points
  c) 1326 points
  d) 2857
  e) Between 1850 and 2857.
  f)

Wayne Gretzky	1.9	Steve Yzerman	1.2
Gordie Howe	1.0	Phil Esposito	1.2
Mark Messier	1.1	Ray Bourque	1.0
Marcel Dionne	1.3	Mario Lemieux	2.0
Ron Francis	1.1	Paul Coffey	1.1

There seems to be no relationship between a player's per-game mean and his standing in the Top 10.
  g) There appears to be no relationship.
  h) Answers may vary.

2. a) See Figure 10 below.

Figure 9

Figure 10

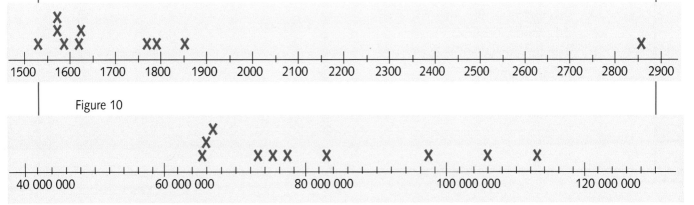

b) $97,500,000; $106,000,000; $112,500,000

c) $82,500,000–$97,500,000

d) Between $65,000,000 and $68,000,000

e) $47,000,000

f) Pablo Picasso's paintings, which sold for $351,500,000.

g) Answers may vary.

3. a) Mean: 179.3 cm; median: 178.5 cm; mode: 174 cm

b) Mean: 185.9 cm; median: 183 cm; mode: 174 cm

c) The mean is most affected, since it changes by 6.6 cm

4. a) 55 is the mode; 72 is the median; 67 is the mean.

b) Answers may vary.

5. Mean: 7.1; median: 7; mode: 6. The largest group of students obtained 6–8 on the quiz.

6. Answers may vary.

7. a) 94%

b) It does not seem realistic.

8. Mean: $102,500; median: $82,500; mode: $90,000 or $60,000. The median best represents the average.

9. a) Mean: 494.8 mL; median: 398 mL; mode: 680 mL

b) The mode, since this is the size most people buy.

10. a)

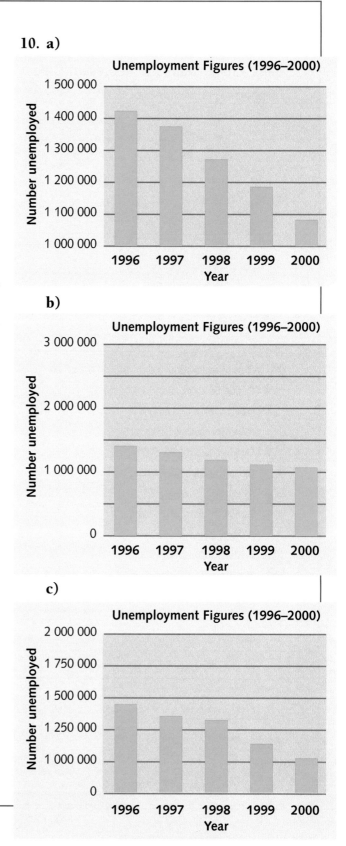

11. a)

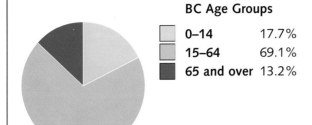

BC Age Groups

☐	0–14	17.7%
☐	15–64	69.1%
■	65 and over	13.2%

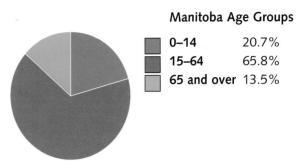

Manitoba Age Groups

■	0–14	20.7%
■	15–64	65.8%
☐	65 and over	13.5%

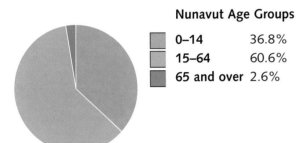

Nunavut Age Groups

☐	0–14	36.8%
☐	15–64	60.6%
■	65 and over	2.6%

Northwest Territories Age Groups

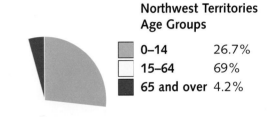

☐	0–14	26.7%
☐	15–64	69%
■	65 and over	4.2%

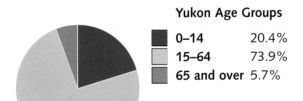

Yukon Age Groups

■	0–14	20.4%
☐	15–64	73.9%
■	65 and over	5.7%

b) Its percentage of children aged 0–14 compared to the rest of its population is twice that of BC.

c) Answers may vary.

Chapter 3

OWNING AND OPERATING A VEHICLE

Exploration 1
Choosing a Vehicle
Notebook Assignment (p. 139)

1. Answers may vary.

2. Answers may vary.

3. **a)** $500
   b) $820
   c) $1,300
   d) $1,800
   e) $392

4. **a)** $875
   b) $1,300
   c) $1,700
   d) $2,125
   e) $3,000

5. Taxes: $3,984.60; total cost: $31,464.60

6. Taxes: $595; total cost: $9,095

7. Taxes: $1,785; total cost: $27,285

8. Taxes: $0; total cost: $8,300

9. Taxes: $4,550; total cost: $37,050

Extension

10. $1,715 compared to Manitoba; $1,837.50 compared to BC. Explanations may vary.

Exploration 2
Operating a Vehicle: Fuel Economy
Notebook Assignment (p. 146)

1. Answers may vary.

2. Answers may vary.

3. **a)** $50.13
   b) $8.32
   c) $24.32
   d) $39.50
   e) $63.01

4. **a)** 1036.7
   b) 413.5
   c) 174.5
   d) 3491.9
   e) 806.8

5.

	Distance	Fuel Economy (L/100 km)
a)	323 km	17.83
b)	556.7 km	9.84
c)	873.3 km	11.13
d)	709.7 km	5.24
e)	313.5 km	14.00

6. **a)** 10.87 L/100 km
   b) 12.82 L/100 km

7. **a)** 11.92 L/100 km
   b) 9.35 L/100 km

8. **a)** 12.13 L/100 km
   b) $27.01

9. 149.5 litres; $89.70

10. 197.2 litres; $128.57

Extension

11. a) 291.9 L
   b) $164.08
   c) 17.33 L
   d) $9.74
   e) Answers may vary.
   f) Answers may vary.

Exploration 3
Maintaining a Vehicle
Notebook Assignment (p. 152)

1. Answers will vary, depending on PST.

2. Answers will vary, depending on PST.

3. Total cost: $798.76

4. $378.42

5. $156.70

Extension

6. $854.76

Exploration 4
Insuring and Registering Your Vehicle
Notebook Assignment (p. 158)

Note that answers to this assignment are based on the Western Insurance Company tables included in the teacher's resource. If other tables are used to complete the assignment, answers may vary.

1. Answers may vary.

2. Answers may vary.

3. $100 deductible. Explanations may vary.

4. In a city, there are more drivers and more chances for an accident.

5. It costs less for pleasure use because you will drive less than if you were going to work every day so there is less chance of an accident occurring.

6. If you are a safe driver, you will make fewer claims, so you will cost the insurance company less money, and so you will get a safe driving discount.

7. Insurance: $728; total: $763

8. Insurance: $980; total: $1,025

9. Insurance: $756.70; total: $791.70

Exploration 5
Buying a New Vehicle
Notebook Assignment (p. 163)

1. Answers may vary.

2. $18,830

3. Answers may vary.

4. See Figure 1 below.

5. $24,285.42

6. $27,911.67

7. $23,925.84

Extension

8. Answers may vary.

Exploration 6
Vehicle Depreciation
Notebook Assignment (p. 168)

1. **a)** $9,826
 b) $10,460.10
 c) $13,874.15
 d) $19,748.10

2. **a)** $7,174
 b) $5,947.90
 c) $12,558.85
 d) $18,950.90

3. **a)** $4,374
 b) $2,528.75
 c) $6,429.78
 d) $9,518.94

Extension

4. **a)** $4,827.51
 b) $17,517.87

Exploration 7
Buying a Used Vehicle
Notebook Assignment (p. 175)

1. Answers may vary.

2. Answers may vary.

3. $14,170.20

4. $8,530.25

5. $2,935.76

6. $4,606.25

7. $5,180.30

8. $10,423.88

9. $5,606.25

10. $5,231

11. **a)** $8,668.75 (does not includes sales tax on the book value)
 b) $9,897.50
 c) The private purchase is less expensive by $1,228.75
 d) Answers may vary.

Figure 1

Vehicle	Base Price	Options & Freight	Sticker Price	Documen-tation Fee	Cost of Vehicle	Trade-in	PST	GST	Total Price
1	$19,400	$2,230	$21,630	$150	$21,780	$5,700	$1,206.00	$1,125.60	$18,411.60
2	$27,960	$2,760	$30,720	$185	$30,905	$9,000	$1,642.88	$1,533.35	$25,081.23
3	$15,275	$975	$16,250	$125	$16,375	$7,200	$688.13	$642.25	$10,505.38
4	$22,740	$1,525	$24,265	$155	$24,420	$10,000	$1,081.50	$1,009.40	$16,510.90

Exploration 8
Taking Out a Loan to Purchase a Vehicle
Notebook Assignment (p. 182)

1. Answers may vary.

2. Answers may vary.

3. Total paid: $9,096; finance charge: $596

4. Total paid: $28,800; finance charge: $3,264.12

5. Total paid: $14,716.80; finance charge: $2,036.55

6. a) $11,500
   b) $260.59
   c) $12,508.32
   d) $1,008.32
   e) $15,508.32

7. a) $29,265.40
   b) $860.70
   c) $30,985.20
   d) $1,719.80
   e) $36,985.20

8. a) $81.73
   b) $2,942.28
   c) $142.28
   d) $2,942.28

Extension

9. Option 1: $32,525; option 2: $34,893.00; option 3: $35,720.16. Choices may vary.

Exploration 9
Leasing a Vehicle
Notebook Assignment (p. 187)

1. a) $285.00
   b) $9,840
   c) $3,785

2. a) $208.65
   b) $10,011.40
   c) $3,208.65

3. $28,329

4. $24,732

5. $46,097.92

6. Total lease payment: $21,373.28; total paid: $39,056.10

7. a) $352.03
   b) $14,060.90
   c) $24,115.13
   d) $38,176.03
   e) $6,022.53

Extension

8. a) Total lease payment: $17,089.60; total cost: $34,953.89
   b) $31,869.44
   c) Answers may vary.
   d) Answers may vary.

Chapter Review (p. 189)

Note that the answer to question 5 is based on the Western Insurance Company tables included in the teacher resource. If other tables are used, answers may vary.

1. $1,450

2. Fuel economy: 8.33 L/100 km; cost per 100 km: $5.46

3. 12 litres; $6.58

4. $137.29

5. Insurance: $723.80; total price: $758.80

6. Sticker price: $81,830; total price: $93,695.35

7. Value after 4 years: $15,426.82; total depreciation: $15,973.18

8. The private sale vehicle is $346.75 less expensive in BC.

9. Assume that prices include appropriate taxes. New Subaru: $32,783.88; used Subaru: $26,732.28. Choices may vary.

10. a) $15,258.60
    b) $30,773.60

Chapter 4

MEASUREMENT TECHNOLOGY

Exploration 1
The History of Measurement
Notebook Assignment (p. 198)

1. **a)** Answers may vary.
   b) Answers may vary.
   c) Answers may vary.

2. **a)** Answers may vary.
   b) Answers may vary.

3. **a)** Answers may vary.
   b) Answers may vary.
   c) Answers may vary.
   d) Answers may vary.

4. **a)** Answers may vary.
   b) Answers may vary.
   c) Answers may vary.

5. **a)** Answers may vary.
   b) Answers may vary.
   c) Answers may vary.

6. **a)** Answers may vary.
   b) Answers may vary.
   c) Answers may vary.

7. **a)** metres or centimetres; feet and inches
   b) centimetres; inches
   c) millimetres; inches
   d) kilometres; miles
   e) centimetres; inches
   f) metres; feet or yards

Extension

8. Two fathoms: 12 feet; less than 12 feet

Exploration 2
Measurement in the Metric and Imperial Systems
Notebook Assignment (p. 205)

1. **a)** $\frac{5}{8}$
   b) $\frac{5}{8}$
   c) $3\frac{1}{16}$
   d) $\frac{9}{32}$
   e) $1\frac{11}{16}$

2. **a)** A: 3 cm. $1''$
   B: 7 cm. $3''$
   C: 9 cm. $3\frac{1}{2}''$
   b) A: 31 mm
   B: 75 mm
   C: 94 mm
   c) A: $1\frac{4}{16}''$
   B: $3''$
   C: $3\frac{11}{16}''$

3. $7\frac{9}{16}''$

4. 252 mm

5. 1396 mm^2

6. $1\frac{244}{256}$ in^2

7. 1426 mm^2

8. **a)** Answers may vary.
   b) 446 mm
   c) 6082 mm^2

Extension

9. Answers may vary.

Exploration 3
Conversions within Systems
Notebook Assignment (p. 213)

1. **a)** $\dfrac{1000 \text{ m}}{1 \text{ km}}$

   b) $\dfrac{1 \text{ yd}}{36 \text{ in}}$

   c) $\dfrac{1 \text{ mi}}{5280 \text{ ft}}$

   d) $\dfrac{10 \text{ mm}}{1 \text{ cm}}$

   e) $\dfrac{1 \text{ mi}}{1760 \text{ yd}}$

   f) $\dfrac{1000 \text{ mm}}{1 \text{ m}}$

2. **a)** 2000 mm
   b) 36 in
   c) 7.5 km
   d) 10 560 ft
   e) 47 mm
   f) 76.50 m
   g) 2 mi
   h) 7.2 km

3. **a)** 35 mm
   b) 122 in
   c) 5580 ft
   d) 312 in
   e) 532 cm
   f) 5320 mm
   g) 26 ft
   h) 312 in

4. **a)** 2.6 m or 260 cm
   b) 5.008 km or 5008 m
   c) 2.5 cm or 25 mm
   d) 0.91 m or 91 cm
   e) 1.9 km or 1900 m
   f) 6.8 cm or 68 mm

5. **a)** 11 ft, 8 in or 140 in
   b) 12 yd or 36 ft
   c) 3 mi, 1720 ft or 17 560 ft
   d) 23 ft, 3 in or 279 in
   e) 4 yds, 2 ft or 14 ft
   f) 2 ft, 5 in or 29 in
   g) 1 mi, 4280 ft or 9560 ft
   h) 8 ft, 2 in or 98 in

6. 18 bouquets

7. The airline will not accept the package because the box's dimensions add up to more than 62 inches.

8. 2 yds, 10 in or 82 in

Extension

9. 4 hours, 11 minutes, 3 seconds

Exploration 4

Conversions Between Systems

Notebook Assignment (p. 218)

1. **a)** 7.09 ft
   b) 22.86 m
   c) 182.88 cm
   d) 257.49 km
   e) 1367.08 mi

2. **a)** 5.98 yd^2
   b) 5.02 m^2
   c) 27 ft^3
   d) 22.95 m^3
   e) 10.46 yd^3
   f) 156.84 yd^3

3. 1662.41 km; answers may vary.

4. 762.46 mile; answers may vary.

5. No; 1.4 cm over.

6. 1828 $1.00 coins

7. 45 litres; 99 pounds

Exploration 5

Measuring with Vernier Calipers

Notebook Assignment (p. 227)

1. **a)** 3.72 cm
   b) 3.40 cm
   c) 4.92 cm
   d) 1.84 cm
   e) 2.11 cm
   f) 3.42 cm

2. **a)** 0.63 cm
   b) 1.62 cm
   c) 2.23 cm
   d) 1.42 cm
   e) 1.31 cm
   f) 3.62 cm

3. Answers may vary.

4. Answers may vary.

5. Answers may vary.

Exploration 6

Measuring with Micrometers

Notebook Assignment (p. 235)

1. **a)** 7.18 mm
   b) 12.43 mm
   c) 21.87 mm
   d) 13.62 mm
   e) 4.15 mm
   f) 7.44 mm
   g) 16.03 mm
   h) 18.97 mm

2. **a)** 15.55 mm
   b) 9.68 mm
   c) 22.22 mm
   d) 0.83 mm
   e) 11.41 mm
   f) 19.42 mm
   g) 5.27 mm
   h) 19.49 mm

3. Answers may vary.

4. The micrometer measurements are more precise.

5. Answers may vary.

Extension

6. They are used to measure the diameter or width of small objects.

Chapter Review (p. 238)

1. a) 10 mm; $\frac{12}{16}''$

  b) 17 mm; $\frac{10}{16}''$

  c) 25 mm; $1''$

  d) 47 mm; $1\frac{13}{16}''$

  e) 129 mm; $\frac{1}{16}''$

  f) 162 mm; $6\frac{6}{16}''$

  g) 7 mm; $\frac{5}{16}''$

  h) 50 mm; $1\frac{15}{16}''$

  i) 11 mm; $\frac{7}{16}''$

  j) 18 mm; $\frac{11}{16}''$

  k) 43 mm; $1\frac{10}{16}''$

  l) 106 mm; $4\frac{4}{16}''$

2. Using base 10 makes conversions easier.

3. a) Answers may vary.
  b) Answers may vary.
  c) Answers may vary.
  d) Answers may vary.

4. a)

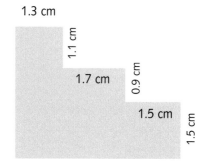

  b) 10.5 cm^2 or 10.8 cm^2

5. a) 615 cm
  b) 54 in
  c) 7 ft
  d) 12.5 cm
  e) 16 590 ft
  f) 1080 mm

6. a) 3.45 m or 345 cm
  b) 11 ft, 1 in or 133 in
  c) 15 836 ft, 2 in

7. 2.01 cm

8. 3.25 cm

9. 16.63 mm

10. 5.68 mm

Chapter 5

RELATIONS AND FORMULAS

Exploration 1
Linear Relations between Quantities
Notebook Assignment (p. 254)

1. **a)** Independent variable: the time spent at the keyboard; dependent variable: the number of words typed
   b) Independent variable: the quantity of stamps purchased; dependent variable: the cost of the stamps
   c) Independent variable: the value of sales; dependent variable: the commission income earned
   d) Independent variable: the number of paper clips; dependent variable: the mass of paper clips

2. **a)**

	Mon	Tues	Wed	Thurs	Fri
Hours worked	2	0	3	6	5
Gross pay ($)	16	0	24	48	40

b)

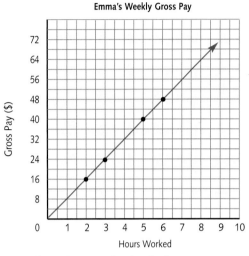

Emma's Weekly Gross Pay

c) The graphs look the same.
d) Answers may vary.

3. **a)** The distance travelled in kilometres is equal to eight times the volume of gasoline in litres.

b)

Amount of gasoline (L)	30	45	10	35
Distance travelled (km)	240	360	80	280

c) Let d = distance in km and g = volume of gasoline in litres.
$d = 8g$

4. a) Independent variable: the volume of gasoline in litres
   b) Dependent variable: the distance travelled in kilometres
   c)

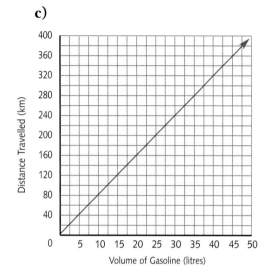

5. a) The cost of distilled water is equal to three dollars times the volume of water in litres.
   b) Answers may vary.
   c) Let v = volume of water and c = cost of water in dollars
   $c = 3v$

6. a) Independent variable: the volume of the water in litres
   b) Dependent variable: the cost of the water in dollars

c)

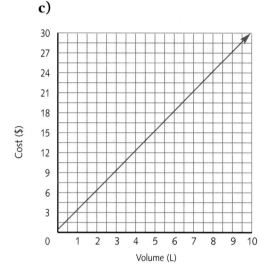

7.

Volume of water (litres)	Cost of water ($)
2.5	$7.50
8	$24.00
4.5	$13.50
7.5	$22.50

Extension

8. Answers will vary.

Exploration 2
Slope of a Line
Notebook Assignment (p. 262)

1. a) Points may vary; slope is 40 words/minute.
   b) Points may vary; slope is 40 words/minute.
   c) No. Answers may vary.

2. **a)** Graph A is steeper.
   b) Slope A is $\frac{3}{2}$; slope B is 1; slope A is steeper than slope B.
   c) The mass per paper clip.
   d) In graph A, each paper clip has a mass of 1.5 gm; in graph B, each has a mass of 1 gm.

3. **a)** Independent variable: the time in seconds; dependent variable: the speed in metres per second
   b)

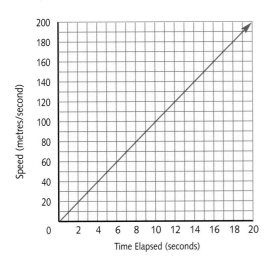

   c) Slope is 10
   d) The slope of the line graph represents the change in speed over a certain time.

4. **a)** Independent variable: the number of boxes of chocolates sold; dependent variable: the profit in dollars.
   b) Slope is $\frac{3}{4}$ or 0.75
   c) The slope of the line represents the profit from 1 box of chocolates.

5.

Boxes of chocolates	3	6	12	14
Profit ($)	$2.25	$4.50	$9.00	$10.50

Extension

6. Answers may vary.

Exploration 3
Determining the Equation of a Line Through the Origin
Notebook Assignment (p. 273)

1. **a)** Independent variable: the time in hours; dependent variable: the distance walked in kilometres
   b) Slope is 4
   c) The slope indicates the number of kilometres walked per hour (4 km/h).
   d) Let t = time (hours) and d = distance walked (km)
   $d = 4t$

2. **a)** Independent variable: the number of bottles; dependent variable: the volume in mL.

b)

Number of bottles	2	4	8	9
Volume (mL)	200	400	800	900

    c) Slope is 100

    d) The slope is the volume of one
           bottle in mL.

    e) Answers may vary.

3. a)

Number of bottles	2.5	5	6	7
Volume (mL)	250	500	600	700

    b) Answers may vary.

    c) Answers may vary.

4. a) Independent variable: the value of
the property sold in dollars;
dependent variable: the
commission in dollars

    b)

Sales ($)	$0	$20,000	$40,000	$60,000	$80,000	$100,000
Salary ($)	$0	$1,000	$2,000	$3,000	$4,000	$5,000

5. a)

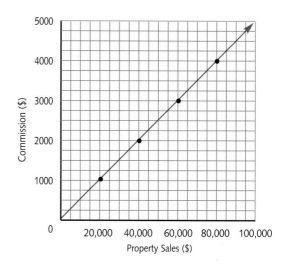

    b) Slope is 0.05

    c) The slope represents the rate of
commission.

    d) Let s = sales in dollars and
c = commission in dollars
$c = 0.05s$

Extension

6. a) Answers may vary.

    b) Answers may vary.

    c) The slope of the steeper line is
larger than for the other line.

Exploration 4
Linear Relations with a Fixed Value
Notebook Assignment (p. 282)

1. Answers may vary.

2. **a)** Independent variable: the number of guests
   b) Dependent variable: the rental fee in dollars
   c) Answers may vary.

3. **a)** No; explanations may vary.
   b) The slope is 5 for both lines.
   c) The slopes of the lines are the same. The steepness of the lines is the same.

4. Answers may vary.

5. **a)** Independent variable: sales
   b) Dependent variable: gross pay
   c) The slope of each line represents the rate of commission based on sales.
   d) No.
   e) Slope is 0.1
   f) The slopes of the lines are the same.

6. **a)** The fixed value for the line in Graph B is 80.
   b) The fixed value for the line in Graph B represents a beginning salary of $80.
   c) Let s = sales in dollars and g = gross pay in dollars
   $g = 0.1s$
   $g = 80 + 0.1s$

7. **a)** In words: The cost of membership is equal to $35 times the number of months plus $50. Tables of values, graphs, and formulas may vary.
   b) Answers will vary.

Extension

8. Answers will vary.

Exploration 5

Applications of Linear Relations

Notebook Assignment (p. 290)

1. **a)** Independent variable: time in hours; dependent variable: the cost of parking a vehicle in dollars

    b) Graph 1: slope is 3/2; Graph 2: slope is 2/5; Graph 3: slope is 1; Graph 4: slope is 0.

    c) Each slope represents the cost of parking vehicles for one hour.

    d) Answers may vary.

    e) Cost is always increasing in Graph 3 and is constant in Graph 4.

2. **a)** Independent variable: number of students; dependent variable: the cost of the trip in dollars

    b) $C = 45n + 200$

    c) $C = 40n + 250$

3. **a)**

b) Travel Agency A has the lower cost.

c) Travel Agency B has the lower cost.

d) The lines cross when there are 10 students. This is the point at which both agencies charge the same price ($650).

4. **a)** Independent variable: number of months; dependent variable: the cost of the jacket in dollars

    b) Slope is –25

    c) This slope represents the amount the jacket is discounted each month.

    d) If C represents the cost of the jacket and n represents the number of months, then

    $$C = -25\,n + 200$$

Extension

5. a) Independent variable: time in hours; dependent variable: the altitude in metres

b)

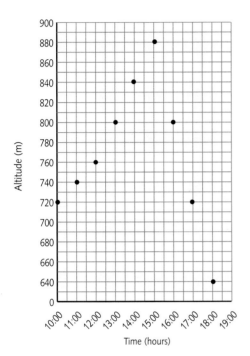

c) The balloon rises 20 metres each hour from 10:00 to 12:00, 40 metres each hour from 12:00 to 15:00 and then begins its descent of 80 metres per hour.

d) (i) Slope is 20 m/h

(ii) Slope is 40 m/h

(iii) Slope is – 80 m/h

Exploration 6

Interpreting Graphs

Notebook Assignment (p. 299)

1. Graph D

2. a) The driver bought gasoline twice during the trip.

b) After a distance of 100 km.

c) 45 litres

d) 35 litres

e) At about 135 km.

f) At the beginning of the journey and at 200 km.

3. a) Monday and Thursday

b) Monday

c) About 40 cm

d) Wednesday

e) About 10 cm

f) About 20 cm

4. a) (iii)

b) (ii)

c) (ii)

d) (iv)

e) (iii)

5. a) Answers may vary.

b) Answers may vary.

c) Answers may vary.

d) Answers may vary.

6. **a)** Answers may vary.
    b) Answers may vary.
    c) Answers may vary.

Extension

7. Answers may vary.

Exploration 7
Formulas
Notebook Assignment (p. 307)

1. $P = 70$ cm

2. **a)** 190.5 beats/minute
    b) 180 beats/minute
    c) As a person ages, the maximum heart rate decreases.

3. **a)** 9.24 m
    b) Answers may vary.
    c) 28.56 m
    d) Answers may vary.

4. **a)** 7 771 537 890
    b) 6 497 140 234
    c) Answers may vary.

5. 9 diagonals

6. 32 000 lemmings

7. $\frac{20}{3}$ or 6.67 ohms

8. 13

9. 4877.5 m

Extension

10. 199

11. $1,194.05

Chapter Review (p. 311)

1. **a)** graph vi
    b) graph iv
    c) graph ix
    d) graph vii
    e) graph viii
    f) graph ii
    g) graph i

2. **a)** The discount is 0.2 times the marked price.
    b) Answers may vary.
    c) Answers will vary.
    d) $d = 0.2\,p$

3.

Marked price	$30	$25	$110	$130
Discount	$6	$5	$22	$26

4. a) Independent variable: time in seconds

b) Dependent variable: the speed in metres per second

c)

Time (sec)	5	10	12	14
Speed (m/s)	50	100	120	140

5. a) The slope represents the change in speed compared to time, or the acceleration.

b) Slope is 10.

c) $s = 10t$

d)

Time (sec)	9	18	60
Speed (m/s)	90	180	600

6. a) The cost of repairs is equal to $20 times the number of half-hours plus $50.

b) Answers may vary.

c) Answers may vary.

d) $C = 20t + 50$, where t is the number of half-hours

7. a) Slope is 20

b) The fixed value is $50.

c) The slope of $20 per half-hour and the fixed value of $50 are the same as the values in the formula $C = 20t + 50$.

8. a) 25 km

b) 15 km

c) 9:45

d) 1 hour

e) (i) 5 km/h
(ii) 30 km/h
(iii) 40 km/h

9. See Figure 1 below.

10. Graph c is most realistic. Student graphs may vary. Graph f is impossible.

11. 339.6 m/s

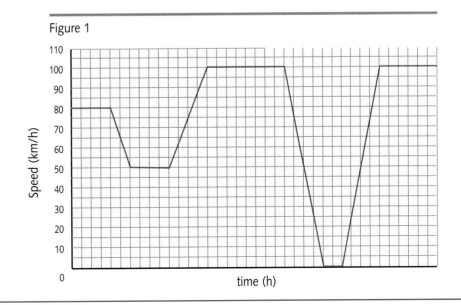

Figure 1

Chapter 6

APPLICATIONS OF PROBABILITY

Exploration 1
Expressing Probabilities
Notebook Assignment (p. 324)

1. See Figure 1 below.

2. See Figure 2 below.

3. **a)** $\frac{1}{6}$

    b) $\frac{3}{6}$ or 0.5

    c) 33.3%

    d) 0 chances out of 6

4. **a)** 0.03 (rounded)

    b) $\frac{1}{36}$

    c) 2.8% or 3% rounded

    d) one out of thirty-six

5. **a)** $\frac{1}{4}$

    b) $\frac{1}{2}$

    c) $\frac{1}{13}$

    d) $\frac{3}{13}$

    e) $\frac{1}{26}$

6. **a)** $\frac{1}{10}$

    b) $\frac{9}{10}$

Figure 1

Fraction	Decimal	Percent	Words
1/5	0.2	20%	one in five
$\frac{1}{2}$	0.5	50%	one in two
3/10	0.3	30%	three in ten
3/5	0.6	60%	three in five

Figure 2

Colour	Decimal	Percent	Fraction	Words
Brown	0.5	50%	1/2	five out of ten
Blonde	0.125	12.5%	$\frac{1}{8}$	one out of eight
Black	0.25	25%	1/4	one out of four
Red	0.05	5%	1/20	one out of twenty
Other	0.075	7.5%	3/40	seventy-five out of one thousand

7. $\frac{1}{12}$, 8.3%, one chance in twelve

8. Answers may vary.

Exploration 2
Making Predictions Using Probability
Notebook Assignment (p. 331)

1. 50

2. $\frac{3}{8}$ or 37.5%

3. 2% or $\frac{1}{50}$

4. 7 or 8 DVDs

5. **a)** $\frac{3}{5}$

   b) 92

6. **a)** 6

   b) 9.5%

c) 88.9%

d) Answers may vary.

7. **a)** 14.3%

   b) 85.7%

   c) Answers may vary.

8. **a)** Answers may vary.

   b) Answers may vary.

   c) Answers may vary.

Exploration 3
Comparing Probability and Odds
Notebook Assignment (p. 337)

1. See Figure 3 below.

2. Probability is desired outcomes compared to total outcomes. Odds in favour is desired outcomes compared to undesired outcomes.

Figure 3

Event	Odds in favour	Odds against	Probability
drawing a queen from a deck of cards	1:12	12:1	$\frac{1}{13}$
rolling a sum of 9 using two dice	1:8	8:1	$\frac{1}{9}$
drawing a 3 of diamonds from a deck of cards	1:51	51:1	$\frac{1}{52}$
choosing the letter "a" from the word "aardvark"	3:5	5:3	$\frac{3}{8}$
rolling a sum greater than 6 with 2 dice	7:5	5:7	$\frac{7}{12}$
drawing a black 4, 6, or 8 from a deck of cards	3:23	23:3	$\frac{3}{26}$
rolling a sum of 2 with two dice	1:35	35:1	$\frac{1}{36}$

3. **a)** $\frac{1}{6}$ or 16.6%

b) 2:10 or 1:5

c) $\frac{5}{6}$ or 83.3%

d) 10:2 or 5:1

4. **a)** $\frac{3}{8}$

b) 3:5

c) $\frac{2}{8}$ or $\frac{1}{4}$

d) 3:1

5. **a)** 18:5
b) 18:5
c) 18:5
d) They are all the same.

6. **a)** 10:22 or 5:11
b) 28:4 or 7:1
c) 22:10 or 11:5

7. See Figure 4 below.

8. **a)** 1:7
b) 7:1
c) 12 or 13 games

9. Yes. Explanations may vary.

10. a) 997:3

b) $\frac{997}{1000}$ or 99.7%

11. There is no chance of it happening.

Exploration 4
Theoretical and Experimental Probability
Notebook Assignment (p. 345)

1. 10 red cards

2. Theoretical probability: $\frac{1}{6}$

Experimental probability: $\frac{13}{90}$

Experimental probability is less than theoretical probability.

Extension

3. The results likely would get closer.

Figure 4

Probability of an event occurring	0.1	0.2	0.3	0.4	0.5	0.6	0.7	0.8	0.9
Odds in favour of event occurring	1:9	2.8 or 1:4	3:7	4:6 or 2:3	5:5 or 1:1	6:4 or 3:2	7:3	8:2 or 4:1	9:1

Exploration 5
Finding Expected Values Using Probability
Notebook Assignment (p. 353)

1. **a)** $700
   b) $8,200
   c) $1,800
   d) Yes
   e) Answers may vary.

2. **a)**
   - i) Break even
   - ii) Win
   - iii) Lose
   - iv) Win
   - v) Lose

   b) Answers may vary.

3. **a)** 0.25
   b) $2,500
   c) Yes

4. -0.5; lose $5; no; answers may vary.

5. EV = 1. After 20 games, you could expect to gain $20.

6. EV = -4.4; EV = -22; no.

7. The manufacturer is likely to earn money this year.

Chapter Review (p. 355)

1. **a)** $\frac{1}{8}$
   b) 0.125
   c) 12.5%

2. 20 pickerel

3. $\frac{12}{24\,000} = \frac{1}{2000}$

4. **a)** $\frac{25}{44}$ or 56.8% (assume y is a consonant)
   b) $\frac{2}{44} = \frac{1}{22}$ or 4.5% (rounded)
   c) $\frac{19}{44}$ or 43.2% (rounded)
   d) $\frac{11}{44} = \frac{1}{4}$ or 25%

5. **a)** $\frac{10}{134}$ or 7.5% (rounded)
   b) 100:34 or 50:17
   c) 90:44 or 45:22
   d) $\frac{34}{134}$ or 25.4% (rounded)

6. 1225 per week

7. $\frac{1}{100}$ or 1%

8. **a)** $\frac{1}{3}$
   b) $\frac{1}{5}$
   c) $\frac{99}{100}$
   d) $\frac{1}{2}$

9. a) 125:875 or 1:7
  b) 7:1
  c) 12 or 13 would go into overtime

10. a) Probability = $\frac{12}{36}$ or $\frac{1}{3}$; odds in favour = 1:2
  b) $\frac{30}{6}$ or 5:1
  c) 24:12 or 2:1

11. a) $\frac{2}{11}$
  b) 2:9
  c) $\frac{9}{11}$
  d) 9:2

12. 136 563 votes

13. 40 left-handers

14. −4.6; $2,300

15. a) $-1.85
  b) After 100 times, expect to lose $185.

16. EV = $4,000. Answers may vary.

17. a) Hospital B's raffle
  b) (EV)A = -$87.50; (EV)B = -$90
  c) (EV)A = -$175; with 2 tickets, the expected value is worse.
  d) Answers may vary.

18. $\frac{1}{2}$

Chapter 7

PERSONAL INCOME TAX

Exploration 1
Income Tax Rates
Notebook Assignment (p. 367)

1. 38.2%

2. 35.5%

3. She is incorrect. She will pay $942.50 more tax. She will still earn $1,557.50.

4. $957

5. Alberta

6. It increases.

7. Answers will vary.

8. Quebec and Newfoundland

9. $1,893.64

10. $4,570. Alberta. Yes, you can tell by looking at the tax rates for salaries of $100,000 or over.

Exploration 2
Completing an Income Tax Return
Notebook Assignment (p. 381)

1.
line 101:	6,160.00
line 104:	960.00
line 150:	7,120.00
line 236:	7,120.00
line 260:	7,120.00
line 482:	931.82
line 484:	931.82

Exploration 3
Tax Implications
Notebook Assignment (p. 385)

1. Net income of your spouse or common law partner and number of children.

2. Line 102

3. Yes. They are included under total income.

4. Lines 135–143

5. Line 212

6. Line 255

7. Line 219. Answers may vary.

8. Line 232 of Schedule 1 for federal tax; line 5856 for BC tax.

Extension

9. Answers may vary.

Chapter Review (p. 386)

1. Answers may vary.

2. Page 2 for total income; page 3 for net income.

3. In the *General Income Tax and Benefit Guide*.

4. Answers may vary.

5. One indicates that you owe money and the other indicates that you will receive money back.

6. Paul Mamelka:
   line 101:   20,540.00
   line 308:   732.38
   line 312:   462.15
   line 437:   1,905.00

   Ferne Cristall:
   line 101:   20,592.00
   line 308:   734.76
   line 312:   463.32
   line 437:   1,910.75
   line 349:   61.00

   Answers may vary. The main difference is that Ferne made a charitable donation that reduced her tax payable amount.

Chapter 8

PREPARING A BUSINESS PLAN

Exploration 1
What Is a Business Plan?
Notebook Assignment (p. 399)

1. Answers may vary.

2. Answers may vary.

3. A retail business sells goods to the general public. Examples may vary.

4. A service business provides services to its customers. Examples may vary.

5. A manufacturing business makes products. Examples may vary.

Extension

6. Answers may vary.

7. Answers may vary.

Exploration 2
Planning the Space for Your Business
Notebook Assignment (p. 403)

1. 300 ft^2

2. 55 m^2

3. $3,672

4. Monthly rent: $620; total cost of lease: $14,880.

5. Answers may vary.

6. Yearly leasing costs: $8,400; weekly leasing costs: $161.54 (rounded); daily leasing costs: $23.08 (rounded from daily figures) or $23.01 (rounded from yearly figures).

   Weekly sales (based on a 7–day week): $4,480; yearly sales: $232,960. Yes, its sales are greater than its lease costs.

7. $200/month

8. $2,500/month for lease cost; $3,854.17/month if all costs are considered.

Extension

9. The side street location is less expensive. Explanations may vary.

Exploration 3
Assessing Your Competitors
Notebook Assignment (p. 408)

1. Answers may vary.

2. Answers may vary.

3. Answers may vary.

4. First year sales: 109 200 kg; second year sales: 113 568 kg; third year sales: 118 110.72 kg.

Weekly sales: (Year 1) $14,700; (Year 2) $15,288; (Year 3) $15,899.52.

5. 250 students would become customers. The weekly sales would be $1,812.50, assuming the coffee shop is open during the school week. The weekly profit would be $1,250. Other answers may vary.

Extension

6. Answers may vary.

Exploration 4
Marketing Your Business
Notebook Assignment (p. 416)

1. Answers may vary.

2. Yes; explanations of effects may vary.

3. Premium Printers

4. Answers may vary.

5. $4,000, assuming a 30-day month.

6. Answers may vary.

Extension

7. Answers may vary.

8. $3,500 profit

Exploration 5
Staffing a Business
Notebook Assignment (p. 422)

1. $1,015

2. $3,927

3. $1,961

4. Schedules may vary; costs will be: Friday $620, Saturday $992, Sunday $620.

5. Answers may vary.

Extension

6. Answers may vary

Exploration 6
Financial Plan
Notebook Assignment (p. 432)

1. Estimated daily profit: $858

2. Weekly profit: $2,400

3. $9,600

4. $1,008.89

5. The store is not profitable. It loses $2,675.18.

6. The store loses $1,554.82 that month.

7. Answers may vary.

Extension

8. Answers may vary.

Chapter Review (p. 435)

1. Answers may vary.

2. $6,220

3. $540/month

4. Annual cost: $5,400; monthly cost: $450

5. Weekly cost: $850.00; annual cost: $44,200

6.

	Retail Price	Profit
Brand A	$9.00	$3.00
Brand B	$14.25	$4.75
Brand C	$18.00	$6.00

7. $468.67

8. **a)** $1,075

   b) $462.50

   c) $612.50

   d) $286.25/h

9. Answers may vary.

10. Answers may vary.

11. Answers may vary.

Glossary

adjacent: means beside; in geometry, it means the side adjacent to the angle is beside the angle.

administration fees: the fee a company charges for handling the paperwork of items purchased through an installment or buy-now, pay-later promotion.

amortization period: the number of months/years it will take to repay a loan.

arithmetic mean: the measure of central tendency found by adding the values in a set of data and then dividing by the number of values in the set. This is commonly called the mean.

at-fault claims: when you make an insurance claim for an accident that you caused.

automated teller machine (ATM): a self-service banking machine that lets you conduct routine banking transactions.

bank buying rate: the rate at which the bank buys foreign currency.

bank card: a plastic card with a magnetic strip that allows you access to bank services or to make a direct payment.

bank selling rate: the rate at which the bank sells foreign currency.

base price: the cost of a vehicle with standard equipment.

basic coverage: the minimum insurance required by law.

benefits: money or allowances such as life insurance, clothing allowance, dental coverage, or extended health care.

bias: inaccurate representation; if a sample is biased, it is an inaccurate representation of the population.

book value: a number of different books contain car prices; the black book lists vehicles made in the last five years; the red book lists older vehicles; the gold book lists exotic vehicles; the blue book lists older classic vehicles. The book value of a vehicle is the standard price given in these books for a particular vehicle. It may not be the same as the actual selling price.

budget: an estimate of the amount of money to be spent on a specific project or over a given time frame.

business: a company, corporation, or other commercial enterprise.

clinometer: a device used to determine the measure of an angle from the horizontal.

cluster: a place where values are grouped or clustered together.

collision insurance: this optional insurance covers damages to your vehicle due to a collision.

comprehensive (all-perils) insurance: this optional insurance covers all damages and mishaps (other than collision) that can happen to your vehicle, for example, vandalism, theft, or water damage.

cost of borrowing: the dollar amount of interest you will pay over the term of the loan.

credit application: a form to request credit.

credit rating: a rating used by financial institutions to indicate a person's ability to repay their credit debt.

data: a collection of numerical facts or information; may be a set of data gathered from a study.

deductible: when you make a claim on your collision or comprehensive insurance you must pay the deductible amount yourself; the insurance company pays the balance of the costs.

deferred payment: a plan whereby consumers do not pay for a purchase until a later date while enjoying their purchase immediately.

dependent variable: relies on the values given to another variable.

depreciation: a decrease in the value of something as it gets older.

depreciation rate: the percent rate by which something loses value.

diagnostic test: an inspection by a mechanic to evaluate a vehicle.

documentation fee: what you have to pay the dealership for doing the paperwork involved in purchasing a vehicle.

down payment: an amount paid in cash which goes toward paying for the vehicle; the amount borrowed for a loan is equal to the cost of the car minus the down payment.

exchange rate: the value of different currencies compared as a decimal or percent.

excise tax: a tax charged on non-essential goods produced and distributed within the country in which they were made.

experimental probability: the chance of an event happening based upon repeated testing or observation.

extrapolation: the process of inferring values beyond the existing data.

finance charge: 1. the amount of interest you pay for a loan; it is equal to the total payment minus the principal. 2. the difference between the installment price and the cash price of an item; also called carrying charges.

fixed rate: fixed interest rate for the term of the loan.

floor plan: a top-down view of a floor area that shows the placement of furniture or other structural features superimposed on the floor area.

freight charges: the cost of transporting a vehicle from the manufacturer to the dealership.

fuel economy: a vehicle that has good fuel economy burns less fuel and therefore costs less to operate than other vehicles. Fuel economy in the metric system is expressed as the number of litres of fuel required to travel 100 kilometres. The formula for fuel economy is:

$$\frac{\text{litres of fuel used} \times 100}{\text{km driven}}$$

full-serve transaction: when a teller performs a bank transaction.

gap: a large space between values.

gross pay: the total amount of money earned; also called gross earnings.

GST: Goods and Services Tax; a federal tax calculated on goods and services.

HST: Harmonized Sales Tax; combined federal and provincial tax applied in some provinces.

income: revenue earned by a business through the sale of products or services; for a person, it is money they earn or receive.

independent variable: a variable whose values may be freely chosen.

interpolation: the process of inferring intermediate values between existing data.

installment buying: making a down payment on an item and paying the remaining balance in equal payments.

installment price: the sum of the down payment plus all the installment payments.

Interac™: a computer network that gives people access to their money through banking machines and direct payment.

inventory: the items a business stocks for resale or as part of a product that they make.

irrational number: a number that cannot be expressed as a rational number.

isometric dot paper: used for technical and architectural drawings to illustrate three-dimensional perspectives where all distances between the dots are the same.

job-share: to split a job with another person; each person does part of the work and receives part of the salary.

labour cost: the amount paid for labour; is normally found by multiplying hours by the rate charged by the repair shop.

lease payment: the monthly payment for the lease; a taxable amount.

lease term: the time period of a lease in months; common terms are 2 years (24 months) and 3 years (36 months).

lien search: a search to see if there is a claim on a vehicle by another person to whom the owner owes money.

line of best fit: a straight line that best fits a set of data on a graph.

loan principal: the amount borrowed.

manufacture: to make a product, often in a factory setting.

market niche: a small, specialized segment of the total market.

market share: one company's proportion of the total sales of a particular product or service.

marketing campaign: a specific activity that is part of an overall marketing plan, such as a mailing campaign.

mean: the measure of central tendency sometimes referred to as the average or arithmetic mean; it is found by adding the numbers in a list and dividing by the number of entries.

measure of central tendency: a central measure that best represents a distribution of data.

median: the middle number when a series of numbers is arranged in either ascending or descending order.

micrometer: a gauge used to measure small distances or thicknesses to thousandths of a unit.

mission statement: a statement of a companiy's goals and operating principles.

mode: the most frequently occurring number in a list of numbers.

odds against: the ratio of unfavourable to favourable outcomes.

odds in favour: the ratio of favourable to unfavourable outcomes.

operating costs: the operating costs of a vehicle include the costs of fuel, regular maintenance, and repairs, as well as the registration and insurance costs; also refers to the cost of equipment, space, supplies, and other items needed to run a business.

optional equipment: extras that you can add on to a vehicle.

origin: the point where the x and y axes intersect; the coordinates of the origin are (0, 0).

outlier: a value that is widely separated from the rest of the data.

overdraw: to take out more money than is in your account.

overtime: 1. hours worked beyond the regular hours; 2. payment for this time.

payroll: the total costs to a company of its staff.

population: all members of the items or individuals being studied.

preferred equipment package: this is a set of optional equipment that can be bought as a "package" for a discounted price.

premium: the amount you pay for insurance.

prime lending rate: the lending interest rate set by the Bank of Canada.

probability: the likelihood of an event happening expressed on a scale from 0 to 1.

PST: Provincial Sales Tax; a provincial sales tax calculated on goods and services sold—different provinces or territories impose PST at different rates and on different items.

quotation: an estimate of the cost of something obtained in advance of making a purchase.

range: the difference between the smallest and largest values in the data.

rate: one quantity measured in relation to another quantity, for example, km/h.

reconcile: to make one account record consistent with another.

resale value: the value of something after it has depreciated.

residual value: the predicted value of a vehicle at the end of a lease.

residual value rate: the percent rate used to determine the residual value.

retail: sales of goods to the general public.

retail price: the price a retail store charges its customers.

rise: change in dependent variable.

run: change in independent variable.

safe driver discount: a discount you receive if you have a claim-free record over a given period of time.

salary: a fixed regular payment, usually calculated on an annual basis and paid monthly.

sample: 1. to sample means to select a number of items or individuals from a total population; 2. a sample is the group selected to represent a total population.

scale drawing: a drawing in which the dimensions are proportional to the actual object.

seasonal employment: work that occurs at specific times of the year, for example, a fishing guide.

sector of a circle: a section of the interior of a circle bounded by 2 radii and the arc between them.

security deposit: a refundable deposit used to pay for the repair of scratches or dents when you return a vehicle.

self-serve transaction: when you perform a bank transaction at an ATM, by telephone, or on the web.

semi-monthly: twice a month; twenty-four times a year.

service industry: businesses that provide services to customers rather than goods.

shop rate: This is the hourly rate charged by a garage to work on a vehicle.

similar triangles: triangles that have the same size of angles but whose sides are not necessarily the same size.

slope: the "steepness" of a line.

sticker price: the full asking price of a vehicle suggested by the manufacturer, including the base price plus options plus freight plus an air-conditioning tax if applicable; also called the manufacturer's suggested retail price.

take-home pay: often called net pay; refers to the money paid to an employee after deductions.

taxable income: the amount of income on which you pay tax.

term: 1. the period of a loan where the conditions remain unchanged; 2. may also refer to the number of years over which you pay off a loan.

theoretical probability: the chance of an event happening as determined by calculating the mathematical result that would occur.

total paid for a loan: the total amount you will have paid when you pay off a loan; it is equal to the monthly payment times the total number of months you make loan payments.

trade newspapers: newspapers of special interest to a particular type of business.

trade-in allowance: the amount that the dealership will give you for your old vehicle.

unit price: the cost of one unit of a product expressed as cost per unit.

utilities: heating and electricity for a building.

variable rate: a fluctuating interest rate that is a set amount above the prime-lending rate.

Vernier calipers: an instrument for making accurate linear measurments.

wage: payment made by an employer in exchange for work or services provided.

waive: in certain circumstances, a bank will not collect a service fee; in that case, the bank is said to waive the fee.

warranty: an agreement by the vehicle dealership to pay the costs for repairing a new vehicle if there is a mechanical fault within a specified period of time. Common warranties are three-year warranties and five-year warranties.

wholesale: sale of large quantities of goods to customers who will retail them to the general public.

wholesale price: the price a retail store pays to the supplier such as a manufacturer for items to sell.

Stein Valley Nlakapamux School
PO Bag 300, Lytton, BC, V0K 1Z0
Phone:(250) 455-2522 Fax:(250) 455-2512

Index

Credits

Credits and Acknowledgements

The publisher wishes to thank the following sources for photographs, illustrations, and other material in this book. Every effort has been made to determine and locate ownership sources of copyrighted material (text and photographs) used in the text. We will gladly receive information enabling us to rectify any errors or omissions in these credits

Photographs/Illustrations

Images in the text for which no page numbers are listed are copyright Pacific Educational Press.

Cover: orca: Lance Barrett-Lennard/Vancouver Aquarium and Marine Science Centre; Science World: Krista Mullally; 'Ksan longhouse: 'Ksan Village and Heritage Museum

Contents pages (in sequence): University of Northern BC; Linda Bily; Arlen Redekop/Province.

Chapter One: p. 12 VanCity Credit Union; p. 14 Dave Reede Photography; p. 17 Barbara Kuhne; p. 21 Laughlin McKenzie/Vancouver Community College; p. 22 Rick Loughran/Province; p. 23 Lee Kubica; p. 27 Brian Yamamura; p. 52 Peter Battistoni/Vancouver Sun.

Chapter Two: p. 81 Simon Fraser University; p. 87 Fred Lum/Globe & Mail; p. 100 University of Northern BC; p. 114 Jeff Vinnick/Vancouver Canucks; p. 118 Citizenship and Immigration Canada.

Chapter Three: p. 135 Selkirk College; p. 139 Brian Rettinger; p. 140 Nadine Lamoureux; p. 145 Brian Yamamura; p. 151 Laughlin McKenzie/Vancouver Community College; p. 158 General Motors, reprinted with permission of ICBC; p. 175 Laughlin McKenzie/Vancouver Community College; p. 177 Brian Yamamura; p. 183 David Edwards.

Chapter Four: p. 193 Laughlin McKenzie/ Vancouver Community College; p. 194 University of Northern BC; p. 198 Mark van Manen/Vancouver Sun; p. 200 Glenn Baglo/Vancouver Sun; p. 205 Al Harvey/The Slide Farm; p. 210 Aikens Lake Wilderness Lodge; p. 215 Brian Yamamura; p. 226 Lee Kubica; p. 229 Association of B.C. Professional Foresters (ABCPF); p. 234 Lee Kubica.

Chapter Five: p. 246 ABCPF; p. 252 Barbara Kuhne; pp. 253, 272 ABCPF; p. 281 Barbara Kuhne; p. 293 Linda Bily; p. 298 ABCPF; p. 301 Linda Bily; p. 304 Al Harvey/The Slide Farm; pp. 307, 317 ABCPF.

Chapter Six: p. 320 Barbara Kuhne; p. 323 Laughlin McKenzie/Vancouver Community College; p. 327 Dave Reede Photography; p. 340 Aikens Lake Wilderness Lodge; p. 342 Brian Yamamura; pp. 346, 352 Dave Reede Photography; p. 360 Barbara Kuhne.

Chapter Seven: p. 363 Stuart Davis/Vancouver Sun; p. 366 ABCPF; p. 368 Jon Murray/ Province; p. 379 Arlen Redekop/Province; p. 382 Jeff Vinnick/Vancouver Canucks; p. 383 ABCPF.

Chapter Eight: p. 393 Barbara Kuhne; p. 404 Debbie Gajdosik; p. 407 Wahl; p. 413 Ian McAllister/Raincoast Conservation Society; p. 416 David Gajdosik; p. 419 Barbara Kuhne; pp. 421, 423 ABCPF; p. 431 Catherine Edwards; p. 433 Aikens Lake Wilderness Lodge; p. 436 Lee Kubica.

Text Credits

p. 49, "Game of Kalah" is reproduced with permission from J. Gorman, "Strategy Games: Treasures from Ancient Times," Mathematics Teaching in the Middle School 3(2): 110-16. Copyright 1997 by National Council of Teachers of Mathematics. All rights reserved.

p. 85, "Twelve Top-Grossing Movies" is adapted from data at www.the-movie-times.com, January 2002.

p. 88, "Top 25 Albums Sold (2002)" is adapted from data at www.neosoul.com, January 2002.

pp. 105-108, "Criminal Code Offences" and the bar graphs "Criminal Code Offences per Year" are created from data from the Statistics Canada Website at http://www.statcan.ca/english/Pgdb/State/Justice/legal02.htm>. Statistics Canada information is used with the permission of the Minister of Industry, as Minister responsible for Statistics Canada.

p. 110, "World's Most Widely Spoken Languages" is reproduced from Russell Ash, *The Top Ten of Everything,* 2001, Dorling Kindersley, p. 100.

p. 111, "World's Richest People" is adapted from data at http://www.forbes.com/billionaires

p. 119, "Immigrants to Australia" is based on data from the Australia Department of Immigration and Multicultural Affairs. "Immigrants to Canada" is based on data from Citizenship and Immigration Canada.

pp. 120, 122 "Population per Province/Territory" is adapted with permission from the Statistics Canada Website at <htpp://www.statcan.ca/english/Pgdb/People/Population/demo31c.htm>

p. 124, "10 Most Expensive Paintings Ever Sold" is reproduced from Russell Ash, *The Top Ten of Everything,* 2001, Dorling Kindersley.

p. 128, "Table in # 10" is adapted with permission from the Statistics Canada Website at http://www.statcan.ca/

p. 129, "Table in # 11" is adapted with permission from the Statistics Canada Website <htpp://www.statcan.ca/english/Pgdb/People/Population/demo31c.htm>

pp. 170-171, "Traffic Impedance" is reproduced with permission from "Random Walks," *NCTM Student Math Notes,* 1985, National Council of Teachers of Mathematics. All rights reserved.

p. 276, "Checking Drainage in Metroburg" is reproduced with permission from *A Sourcebook of Applications of School Mathematics,* 1980, National Council of Teachers of Mathematics. All rights reserved.

p. 346, "Centennial Hockey League" is reproduced with permission from *A Sourcebook of Applications of School Mathematics,* 1980, National Council of Teachers of Mathematics. All rights reserved.